CRITICAL SOCIAL THEORY

SAGE was founded in 1965 by Sara Miller McCune to support the dissemination of usable knowledge by publishing innovative and high-quality research and teaching content. Today, we publish over 900 journals, including those of more than 400 learned societies, more than 800 new books per year, and a growing range of library products including archives, data, case studies, reports, and video. SAGE remains majority-owned by our founder, and after Sara's lifetime will become owned by a charitable trust that secures our continued independence.

Los Angeles | London | New Delhi | Singapore | Washington DC | Melbourne

CRITICAL SOCIAL THEORY

CRAIG BROWNE

Los Angeles | London | New Delhi
Singapore | Washington DC | Melbourne

Los Angeles | London | New Delhi
Singapore | Washington DC | Melbourne

SAGE Publications Ltd
1 Oliver's Yard
55 City Road
London EC1Y 1SP

SAGE Publications Inc.
2455 Teller Road
Thousand Oaks, California 91320

SAGE Publications India Pvt Ltd
B 1/I 1 Mohan Cooperative Industrial Area
Mathura Road
New Delhi 110 044

SAGE Publications Asia-Pacific Pte Ltd
3 Church Street
#10-04 Samsung Hub
Singapore 049483

Editor: Natalie Aguilera
Editorial assistant: Delayna Spencer
Production editor: Katherine Haw
Copyeditor: Catja Pafort
Proofreader: Jill Birch
Marketing manager: Sally Ransom
Cover design: Shaun Mercier
Typeset by: C&M Digitals (P) Ltd, Chennai, India
Printed in India by Replika Press Pvt Ltd

Library of Congress Control Number: 2016936388

British Library Cataloguing in Publication data

A catalogue record for this book is available from
the British Library

ISBN 978-1-4462-4692-4
ISBN 978-1-4462-4693-1 (pbk)

At SAGE we take sustainability seriously. Most of our products are printed in the UK using FSC papers and boards.
When we print overseas we ensure sustainable papers are used as measured by the PREPS grading system.
We undertake an annual audit to monitor our sustainability.

CONTENTS

ABOUT THE AUTHOR

Craig Browne is a Senior Lecturer in the Department of Sociology and Social Policy, University of Sydney. He is currently the Vice Chair of the European Sociological Association, Research Network on Social Theory, RN29, a member of the boards of the International Sociological Association, Research Committee on Sociological Theory, RC16, and the ISA Research Committee on Concepts and Terminological Analysis, RC35, and he was from 2013 to 2016 the co-convener of the The Australian Sociological Association Thematic Group on Social Theory, which he founded with Suzi Adams and Eduardo de la Fuente. His research interests include critique, praxis philosophy, social imaginaries, creative democracy, intersubjectivity and social change. He edited, with Justine McGill, *Violence in France and Australia: Disorder in the Post-Colonial Welfare State*, Sydney University Press, 2010. He guested edited a Special Issue of *Thesis Eleven* on the work of Luc Boltanski in 2014. His recent publications include 'Between Creative Democracy and Democratic Creativity', V. Karalis (ed.) *Castoriadis and Radical Democracy*, Brill, 2014, 'Critiques of Identity and the Permutations of the Capitalist Imaginary', *Social Imaginaries* 2016, 2(1) and 'From the Philosophy of Praxis to the Sociology of Practice', in M. Jonas et. al. (ed.) *Praxeological Political Analysis*, Routledge, 2017.

ACKNOWLEDGEMENTS

There are far too many friends and colleagues that I would like to thank for their support than I can mention here. I hope that this book reflects my long-term engagement with Critical Social Theory and I would like to acknowledge the contributions to my intellectual project of Maria Márkus, Johann P. Arnason, Richard Bernstein, William Outhwaite, Peter Murphy, Peter Beilharz, John Rundell, Paul Blokker, Colin Cremin, Suzi Adams, Jeremy Smith, Gilles Verpraet, Rob Stones, Nick Turnbull, Michael Pusey, Pauline Johnson, Nick Smith, Jean-Philippe Deranty, Eduardo de la Fuente and Yoshikazu Fujisawa. I would like to thank Luc Boltanski, Anthony Giddens, Hans Joas, and Peter Wagner for the research interviews that I conducted with them. I am most grateful for the work of everyone involved with this project at SAGE. In particular, I would like to thank Chris Rojek for his commitment to this book from the outset. I have developed some of the ideas in this work on the basis of my dialogues and collaborations with friends and colleagues. I would like to thank Simon Susen for our collaboration and the opportunity it provided to reflect on anti-austerity protests. I would like to thank José Maurício Domingues and Breno Bringel for the invitation to participate in the groundbreaking conference on Global Modernity and Social Contestation that they organised, as well as to contribute to the book that they edited on this theme. I owe an enormous debt to Jocelyn Pixley for her unfailing advice and solidarity. I would like to thank Phillip Mar for his comments on a draft of this work and for our research collaboration into the 2005 French riots, which informs some of the discussion of this topic in this work. The support of Daniela Heil has been invaluable and I would like to thank her very much for sharing my travails and bringing necessary critical understanding to them.

Earlier versions of Chapter 3 and Chapter 4 of the current book were previously published as:

Browne, C. (2015) 'Half-Positions and Social Contestation: On the Dynamics of Exclusionary Integration', in B. Bringel and J.M. Domingues (eds) *Global Modernity and Social Contestation*. London: Sage. pp. 185–202.

Browne, C. (2008) 'The End of Immanent Critique?', *European Journal of Social Theory*, 11(1): 5–24.

With permission from Sage.

INTRODUCTION

Introduction

The contemporary historical conjuncture appears to simultaneously justify the project of Critical Theory and contradict its basic preconditions. On the one hand, the material effects of the latest capitalist crisis would seem to be an extremely concrete expression of the connection between social injustice and the irrationality of the capitalist system. On the other hand, advanced liberal democratic societies are undergoing a protracted crisis of values (Castoriadis, 1991). Even though this crisis of values has generated a diversity of normative positions and it is possible to identify progressive tendencies, the values that appear the most practically effective, especially individualist definitions of self-interest, are those antithetical to Critical Theory. From a historical standpoint, Critical Theory has previously confronted equivalent dilemmas. The difficulty, even the tragedy, of such dialectical disjunctions was constitutive of the Frankfurt School's programme. Critical Theory was, in large measure, originally developed in exile, and the term itself reflected an awareness of the distortions of Marxism's emancipatory intentions, whether as a result of historical developments that Marx had not foreseen, the authoritarian and bureaucratic character of Marxist political parties, or the misinterpretation of the complexion of theory (Jay, 1973; 1984; Held, 1980; Dubiel, 1985; Wiggershaus, 1994). The possibility of radical change is nevertheless an irrevocable presupposition of Critical Theory. However, it is not prospective change in general that is presupposed, rather Critical Theory presumes that the potentials for the abolition or radical transformation of the conditions of oppression, suffering and injustice are immanent in the development of society.

It may appear paradoxical that the contemporary tendencies that seem to undermine Critical Theory's programme, such as the power of global markets, the comparative regression in social policies in many advanced nation states which undercut the rights of citizens and workers and the diminishing power of some progressive movements to mobilize, give rise to consequences that make Critical Theory necessary and justified. These consequences include growing material inequalities in advanced capitalist societies, the experience of vulnerability ensuing from the dismantling of welfare state protections, the erosion of social solidarity, ideological confusions that means that the contesting of subordination and alienation is open to irrational expression, and the decline in the horizon of expectations, to use Koselleck's term, that ensues from the disillusionment with the outcomes of former progressive initiatives (Koselleck, 1988). This situation only appears paradoxical because the contradictory character of capitalist society has been occluded or is forgotten.

There are many reasons for the occlusion of conflict and its sources in social relations of domination and the experiences of injustice. One reason is particularly consequential, because its appeal consists in disputing the negative assessment of the contemporary developments that were just enumerated. This is the view that the conflicts of earlier phases of capitalism have been superseded (see Boltanski and Chiapello, 2005). Now, while it is no doubt true that some of the parameters of addressing social injustice have changed, it is equally the case that preceding capitalist conflicts have been subject to *displacement* rather than overcome. What this means is that the major conflicts of capitalist society persist but that they are often manifested in new forms or in different domains, as well as undergoing periodic renewal at their source.

The two most influential critical sociological interpretations of *displacement* give a certain insight into how the notion of the superseding of the earlier conflicts of capitalist society could appear justified. Habermas argues that the dynamics of the capitalist economic system and the attendant conflicts of social class relations have been displaced through their mediation by other institutional mechanisms, especially by the state's intervention in the economy and the welfare state's consolidation of the social rights of citizenship (Habermas, 1976; 1987a). Boltanski and Chiapello (2005) argue that the displacement of conflict ensues from the establishment of a new legitimating regime of justification and the related processes of the re-categorizing of problems and the altering of interpretations of the instituted reality of capitalism more generally. In fact, Boltanski and Chiapello consider that the displacement that shaped the contemporary form of 'network' capitalism was conditioned by the social contestation over the regulated and organized capitalism that preceded it. Significantly, the model of organized capitalism had been the institutional basis of Habermas' interpretation of the displacement of the dynamics of liberal market capitalism and the modified expression of capitalist conflicts in crises of individual and social identity (Habermas, 1976; 1987a). Despite the evident semantic differences, in either case the modifications that underpin the displacement of conflict reflect progressive demands for reform and significant social struggles, whether for social protection, policy coordination, flexibility or participation.

The notions of displacement draw attention to how the persisting dynamics of capitalism, particularly the imperative of capital accumulation, limit and condition its modifications. Notions of displacement highlight the complications involved in comprehending these dynamics and the salience of ideological justification. In short, displacement serves to resituate and conceal antagonisms. It paradoxically introduces elements of uncertainty into critique while implying that capitalism incorporates supplementary justifications, such as that it is amenable to demands for fairness and autonomy. Claude Lefort's contention that ideology serves to fill 'the gap' that stems from the social order not being identical with itself discloses this purpose of supplementary justifications (Lefort, 1986). Lefort further argues that ideology seeks to contain the divisions that the social order constitutes through defining change in ways that reflexively articulates the principles of the existing social institution. In this case, displacement references capitalism's persistence and restitution, rather than the innovative character of changes that may point beyond it.

Given that these accounts of the respective phases of displacement are defined in terms of capitalism's historicity, it is important to underline that displacement is itself conditioned by struggles and gives expression to struggles. This means that institutional modifications are partly expressions of ongoing dialectics of control, including the empowerment of capitalism in recent decades with accelerated globalization. The concept of dialectics of control refers to conflictual relations of interdependency, such as Marx attributed to class relations and to how the dynamic of the reproduction of capitalism is contingent on the exploitation of wage labour (Marx, 1971; Giddens, 1979). Dialectics of control, however, apply to a broader range of social contexts and practices than those of class relations and wage labour.

The fact that the preceding conflicts of capitalist society have been reconfigured is only one of the reasons why Critical Theory is in need of revision. Critical Theory develops through reflection on the limitations of its extant formulations, particularly relative to its aspirations and the changes in the social-historical context. The recognition of the social and historical conditioning of knowledge originally distinguished Critical Theory from 'traditional' theory (Horkheimer, 1972). Critical Theory includes a series of demands that distinguish it from other approaches in social theory and philosophy (Calhoun, 1995). It aims to provide an explanation and analysis of present society that is able to apprehend the developmental possibilities it contains and to identify the potentials for emancipation immanent in the needs or moral experience of subjects. These needs are 'radical', Agnes Heller argues, because they could be satisfied only through an emancipatory social transformation (Heller, 1984a). Critical Theory does not juxtapose an ideal state against existing conditions of oppression and inequality; rather critique focuses on those existing trends and developments that prefigure an emancipated society. The normative standpoint of critique presupposes, Honneth argues, a sociological determination of a pre-theoretical interest in emancipation; such as he claims to find are present in demands for respect and the practices of mutual recognition (Honneth, 1994: 225).

In its original formulation, Critical Theory was distinguished by the ties it has to those socialized subjects that seek to bring about such a transformation and by its reflection upon the social-historical context of its emergence. Critical Theory subscribes neither to traditional philosophy's model of contemplative reflection, nor the disinterested standpoint of modern science (Habermas, 1974). The validity of critique depended on its initiating processes of enlightenment that facilitate the autonomy of subjects and the future emancipatory practices that transform oppressive social relations. Critical theory thus 'sees itself as a necessary catalytic moment within the social complex of life which it analyses' (Habermas, 1974: 2).

The relationship of theory and political practice may have been permanently under strain, but it remains one of the defining considerations of Critical Theory.

In part, this is because Critical Theory contends that theory always has practical implications and that these practical consequences are concealed by traditional theories in various ways. For instance, traditional theories may function as ideologies that veil, disguise and misrepresent injustice and oppression, traditional theories may not only reflect the hierarchical structure of the social division of labour but they may also perform an important role in social coordination and integration, and traditional theories confirm the distinction between theory and practice (Marcuse, 1968; Horkheimer, 1972; Habermas, 1974).

For these reasons, Critical Theory is the critique of alternative theories, as well as an approach that draws upon them where appropriate in order to constitute new theoretical syntheses. It is not, however, simply the critique of ideology and false representations, Critical Theory is the critique of the social reality that gives rise to false representations and ideological misunderstandings, such as in Marx's view of religious consolation in response to suffering that appeared unamenable to change or the never achievable notion of freedom as consumer sovereignty in a society founded on commodity production and exchange (Marx, 1971; 1977c). The leading contemporary representatives of Critical Theory have, however, more cautiously formulated its practical implications. This prudence is no doubt a consequence of a heightened reflexivity regarding the complications of theory's relationship to practice and a product of an acceptance of the fallible character of theory. Jürgen Habermas and Axel Honneth have been drawn to North American pragmatist philosophy because of its practical cast and appreciation of fallibility. Pragmatism's practical character is evident in the interconnections it establishes between intersubjective communication and democracy (Habermas, 1987a; Honneth, 1995a; Browne, 2009a; 2009b).

Phases, Generations, Paradigms

It has become commonplace to speak of phases and generations of the Frankfurt School tradition of Critical Theory. The initial 'interdisciplinary materialism' of the 1930s, that was consistent with Horkheimer's original vision as director of the Institute of Social Research, is regularly seen as giving way in the early 1940s to the period dominated by the 'critique of instrumental reason' (Habermas, 1984; Dubiel, 1985; Kellner, 1989; Wiggershaus, 1994). Similarly, the notion of a second generation of Critical Theory has been used to differentiate the work of Habermas and that of several philosophers and social scientists closely related to his programme, like Albrecht Wellmer, Klaus Eder and Claus Offe (Held, 1980; Kellner, 1989; Wiggerhaus, 1994). In my opinion, Habermas developed a significantly revised Critical Theory; one explicitly intended to be an alternative framework to that of the 'critique of instrumental reason'. In terms of the present, while the notion of a third generation of Critical Theory is not necessarily incorrect and possesses some utility, it is potentially misleading with respect to the continuities that Honneth's theory has with that of Habermas. Honneth's core notion of recognition may ultimately be considered an alternate elaboration of the intersubjective and communicative paradigm that Habermas initiated, rather than a movement beyond it (Deranty, 2009b). Be that as it may, the periodizing categories draw attention to how Critical Theory has undergone modifications in response to the changing social-historical circumstances and the advances in salient fields of knowledge, like the twentieth century 'linguistic turn' that emerged in otherwise quite different strands of philosophy and the social sciences (Rorty, 1967).

There is nothing unusual then about revising Critical Theory, but reorientations imply different trajectories of future development; and no doubt the continuity of current approaches with Critical Theory's original programme can be disputed. The original intention of Critical Theory was to give contemporary relevance, in some form, to the Marxian project of the radical transformation of society. It is therefore worthwhile briefly sketching some of those developments that put this project into question and the resulting innovations that were undertaken within Critical Theory. There are three factors in the present which bear acutely on Critical Theory's methodological preconditions: the longest standing stems from the demise of the proletariat as the historical agent of change, but the various actors Marxists have invoked as potential substitutes, like new social movements and struggles in developing nation states, have proven less than convincing alternatives. Likewise, the oppressive and bureaucratic character of state socialist societies has long cast a shadow over the project of a radical transformation of capitalist society. The dissolution of state socialist societies made the idea of a historical transition beyond capitalism appear utopian and at variance with the 'normal' pattern of social modernization. Last, production undoubtedly remains a central structure of modern society, despite whatever questions are posed by alterations in the distribution and organization of work, however anchoring a project of emancipatory change in production has itself become the subject of sustained critiques, especially by ecologists rejecting the 'productivist' value system of industrial society and contemporary analyses of the manifold sites of power. These critiques reflect a shift in definitions of emancipation and, somewhat paradoxically in light of the disrepute of notions of historical transition, an assessment of the intrinsic limitations to the implications of changes in the system of production. Above all, what makes these three factors outstanding amongst an array of problems is the fact that they represent second order difficulties consequent upon several original problems of Marxist critique.

In a sense, when measured against its aspirations, Marxism has been in perennial crisis, however, its contemporary predicament appears unprecedented (Arnason, 1980; 1984; Márkus, 1993). Of course, countervailing factors can always be cited in Marxism's defence and the richness of Marx's original statement means that it will continue to have adherents who consider it superior to later amendments. My analysis retrieves several important components of Marx's theory for Critical Theory; for example, the centrality of the notion of dialectics of control to my analysis restores social conflict to a prominent position in the explanation of injustice and the dynamics of social reproduction. In a similar vein, José Maurício Domingues has sought to renew Critical Theory through reactivating some the resources of Marxist theory (Domingues, 2012). Likewise, the recent economic recession and the entrenching of greater inequality have meant that discussions of neo-Marxist political economy have garnered interest outside their field. Nevertheless, the arguments for substantially revising Critical Theory appear incontrovertible in light of Marxism's problems. Honneth summarizes different strands of this predicament in commenting that:

> All in all, the suggestive potential of Marxist theory has clearly exhausted itself. Given that its scientific content has been refuted, its political claims historically relativized and its philosophical foundations subjected to critique, Marxism has become an object for the recollections of historians of theory. (Honneth, 1995b: 4)

Even if every aspect of this assessment is not taken to be definitive, Honneth's summation highlights why Habermas' rethinking and reformulation of the foundations of Critical Theory is significant. Habermas proposed that the paradigm of intersubjective communication and understanding is an alternative to the paradigm of production that derives from Marx. The paradigm change reflects a considerably different orientation to those previously taken within Critical Theory to the problems of Marxist social theory. The prior orientations can be loosely categorized as those of restoration and rectification. The first involved some attempt at restoring dimensions of Marx's propositions that had been subsequently obscured and distorted. The ensuing revisions were directed towards correcting the self-understanding, and misunderstandings, of the Marxist tradition, primarily through the presentation of a more sophisticated appreciation of Marx's thought and its philosophical sources. Indeed, the fact that some major texts of Marx only became available during the twentieth century, like the *Paris Manuscripts of 1844* and the *Grundrisse*, lent considerable justification to restorative approaches (Marx, 1977a; 1973). There can be little doubt that the restorative approach produced a greater understanding of the full range of Marx's theory. Whilst a restorative procedure could appear conservative, and no doubt this is the case in some instances, it more importantly often played a significant role in the renewal of Marxist perspectives opposed to the dominant strand of this tradition.

In any case, revisions of a restorative approach need not exclude the orientation of rectification, and they have clarified its basic prerequisites. Rectifying orientations seek to make good what appear to be omissions in Marx's theory; and, as such, the revisions which ensue result mainly from an extension of a Marxist perspective to new topics. Further revisions then emerge in response to problems that arise from so doing; within the tradition of Western Marxism the 'normal' response to compound difficulties was utilizing and integrating theoretical advances in related disciplines (see Habermas, 1979; Jay, 1984; Howard, 1988). The Frankfurt School belongs to the heterodox tradition of Western Marxism and its response to the confounding of aspects of Marx's prognosis was precisely to extend the Marxist critique of capitalist society to new domains. This is apparent in Habermas' claim that six themes dominated the work of the Frankfurt School 'Institute of Social Research' until the early 1940s:

> (a) the forms of integration in postliberal societies, (b) family socialization and ego development, (c) mass media and mass culture, (d) the social psychology behind the cessation of protest, (e) the theory of art, and (f) the critique of positivism and science. (Habermas, 1987a: 378–9)

It is worth noting that many of the Frankfurt School's extensions of the Marxist critique of capitalism were enabled by György Lukács' preceding conceptualization of reification. Lukács argued that the reification deriving from the prevalence in capitalist society of the commodity form conditioned the entire attitude of subjects to the world. Reification's expression of the dominance of objectivity over subjectivity therefore inflected bourgeois culture as a whole (Lukács, 1971). Under the influence of Lukács' synthesis of Marx's political economy and Weber's sociology of modernity, the Frankfurt School theorists would contend that the rationalization of production, as well as the rationalization of other institutions of capitalist society, intensified reification. In other words, rather than rationalization developing the forces of production that could underpin an emancipatory reorganization of society, it was consolidating social relations of domination and diminishing the potential of individuals to be autonomous (Horkheimer and Adorno, 1972).

The rectifying orientation towards Marx's theory of capitalist society produced, to be sure, significant innovations. The revisions deriving from it have certainly gone beyond those that would result from simply taking into account subsequent changes. However, over time rectifying procedures appeared less capable of convincingly addressing the full range of problems and dilemmas comprising the predicament of Critical Theory. In its turn, this circumstance brought the original deficiencies of this orientation to the fore; these deficiencies have been explored in reappraisals of Horkheimer's interdisciplinary conception of Critical Theory and the research conducted under his auspices during the 1930s. Even sympathetic critics argue that, in spite of the syntheses countenanced by the Frankfurt School's receptivity to other theories, the revisions actually proposed were limited by a reliance on the guiding framework of Marxist political economy (Habermas, 1974; Benhabib, 1986; Honneth, 1991; 1995b; Hohendahl, 1991). This 'latent orthodoxy' is apparent, for example, in a 'functional for capital' interpretation of the socializing role of the family and an underestimation of the freedoms guaranteed by the institutions of bourgeois democracy in the critique of ideology. But, above all, it reflected a conception of emancipation that was almost entirely conditioned by the Marxist philosophy of history and the Frankfurt School's adherence to the founding category of social labour. Habermas considered that the Frankfurt School Critical Theory reached a kind of theoretical and political impasse: its critique of instrumental reason and state regulated capitalism's totally administered society did not contain much prospect for emancipation (Habermas, 1984; 1987a).

Habermas' writings originally pursued the restoring and rectifying orientations, but, in the course of developing the revisions he saw necessary for Marxian theory, his critique underwent a process of increasing radicalization. Although it is certainly the case that these qualitative changes occurred in stages, they did culminate in a different orientation. Those problems Habermas identified in Marx's thought stimulated his construction of an alternative Critical Theory; especially determining this reorientation was Habermas' perception of the deleterious consequences that these problems had for Marxist theory and practice (Habermas, 1974). This lack of separation between Marx's thought and the failings of later Marxism contradicts a major tenet of restorative approaches. Despite his extended critique and presentation of an alternative communicative paradigm, Habermas claimed to have still retained in a revised form whatever remains of value in Marx's standpoint (Habermas, 1979; 1987b). Of course, the justification presented for this claim has changed substantially; it is based on conclusions drawn from orientations that are principally those of reconstruction and replacement.

Habermas' 'reconstruction of historical materialism' proved relatively unstable, because the core dimensions that would make up his alternative perspective, like communication, morality and rationality, informed his original critical analyses of Marx. Marx, he argued, had elided the difference between labour and social interaction; the latter is founded on the structure of communicative action and is oriented towards the achievement of mutual understanding, whereas labour is guided by an interest in the technical control of the material environment, and it is principally a type of instrumental action (Habermas, 1974; 1978a; 1978b). In retrospect, Habermas' 'reconstruction of historical materialism' appears to have only been a transitional work. Further refinements precipitated a much more far-reaching assertion: that is, that his theory of communicative action is an alternative and substitute for the original Marxist Critical Theory, instead of a component of the reconstruction of it. In other words, Habermas considers that his project displaces the Marxist original and should be considered, at least in some respect, a replacement for it (Habermas, 1979; 1984; 1987a; 1987b).

One of the major strengths of Habermas' alternate paradigm of understanding is its provision of normative grounds for critique. Habermas claims that the philosophy of consciousness, or the subject-centred reason, has exhausted its potential and that its irresolvable antinomies have been exposed, such as that it is perennially caught in the bind of converting subjectivity into an objectivity that the subject can reflect upon (1987b). Habermas' theory of communicative action sketched a different trajectory of rationalization in modernity, one originally initiated by the cultural transformation that derived from the rationalization of communication (Habermas, 1984). In short, Habermas argues that communicative rationalization initially shaped various spheres of society in the constitution of modernity, especially law and morality. Yet, the instrumental-functionalist rationalization of capitalism and the bureaucratic state would delimit and somewhat undermine the communicative infrastructure to which the identity of subjects remained attached. Nevertheless, Habermas argues that communicative action remains a source of potential emancipation and that legitimacy has increasingly come to depend on the satisfaction of the procedures of democratic discourses (Habermas, 1996a).

Habermas' theory's various revisions imply that the legal and constitutional institution of rights and democracy in bourgeois society could form the basis of future progressive transformations. In his opinion this is especially important, because the sphere of production no longer represents a domain of substantial emancipation and a source of general autonomy in other spheres of society. Habermas' thesis is more complex than this synopsis conveys. Still, its general implications are reflected in the fact that, following *The Theory of Communicative Action*, Habermas concentrated on developing his discourse theory of morality, justice and democracy, rather than extending and refining the social theoretical component of Critical Theory (Habermas, 1984; 1987a; 1990; 1996a). In short, discourse theory focused to a much greater extent on the concerns of normative political philosophy.

Normative Political Philosophy and Social Theory

After Habermas, it is hard to imagine that Critical Theory would revert to the paradigm of consciousness or the philosophy of the subject. Indeed, Honneth's theory of recognition has consolidated the intersubjective perspective in Critical Theory (Honneth, 1995a; 1995b). Nevertheless, Critical Theory does confront different lines of potential future development and, as will be explained in detail later, the normative and explanatory dimensions of Critical Theory have recently tended to diverge. The recent Critical Theory discussions have tended to be dominated by debates in normative political philosophy.

Given the substantial revival of normative political philosophy, especially under the influence of John Rawls' theory of justice, and the shift in Habermas' focus towards law and rights, there are good reasons why normative political philosophy has become so prominent (Rawls, 1971; Habermas, 1996a; 1998). This development is clearly related to Habermas' position on the emancipatory significance of the bourgeois constitutional heritage and the emphasis on democracy. For all the important and constructive discussions that have ensued, such as those on civil society and deliberative democracy, this predominance of normative political philosophy has some limitations from the perspective of a Critical Theory of Society. In particular, the dominance of the format of normative political philosophy has meant that the social theory component of Critical Theory has not received an equivalent elaboration. My book is, in large part, an attempt to rectify this deficit and to renew the social theory of contemporary society.

It would be misleading to claim that this assessment is exclusively my own. The very latest contributions of Axel Honneth, and Nancy Fraser, as well as those of other theorists, like Lois McNay, constitute a reaction to the predominantly political framing of contemporary discussions in Critical Theory (Honneth, 2014; Fraser 2009; McNay, 2014). Honneth identifies several problems that ensue from the independent development of the themes of normative political philosophy. In particular, normative political philosophy's method of formulating abstract principles and models contains the potentially irremediable problem that its conceptions of justice and freedom may have no actual connection to reality. In Honneth's opinion, there is no guarantee that the gap between claim and reality of these theoretically 'purified' conceptions can be bridged at all (Honneth, 2014: 63). Although this criticism does not entirely apply to the Critical Theory discussions, it illuminates some of the dilemmas that ensue from framing Critical Theory in the terms of normative political philosophy. Namely, it can lead to theoretical positions that are based on highly simplifying assumptions and to rather narrow conceptions of society. Honneth argues that there has recently been a tendency to conceive of all social relations as if they were legally constituted in order to make them consistent with the model of justice that is proposed. To some extent, a rather similar problem is present in extrapolating from Habermas' notion of democratic legitimacy depending on the fulfilment of formal procedures. It has to treat the substantive conditions of enacting justice and autonomy as either external additions or prerequisites that are presupposed in order to satisfy the procedure's basic criteria, like the participation of all concerned (Honneth, 2014).

There is much to be gained from engaging in normative political philosophy, although it is not difficult to perceive how its construction of principles and models often depends on a liberal and individualist conception of the subject (see Wagner, 2008). The more significant problem is the supplanting of the sociological standpoint that has defined Critical Theory. The original methodological intentions of Critical Theory ran counter to the notion of the independence of normative political philosophy. One of Critical Theory's defining features has been its interest in the sociological translation and practical realization of philosophical categories, like justice, reason and autonomy. In my opinion, it is important that this intention is retained, since it informs Critical Theory's heightened reflexivity and its method of immanent critique. Further, Critical Theory has always been defined as a programme of interdisciplinary research (Horkheimer, 1993). It presumes that knowledge drawn from different disciplines is necessary for comprehending the capitalist constellation. The recent relative lack of elaboration of the social theory component throws the whole interdisciplinary programme into doubt, because social theory provided the framework of this programme's integration and it established the historical perspective of Critical Theory's interpretation of emancipatory change.

The importance of synthesis to Critical Theory is evident in Fraser and Honneth's description of their respective ambitions 'to connect the usually discrete levels of moral philosophy, social theory, and political analysis in a critical theory of capitalist society'. This they claim is contrary to much of the work of those currently identifying with Critical Theory, who they claim assume a disciplinary division and are reluctant to theorize capitalist society as a 'totality' (Fraser and Honneth, 2003: 4). The original interdisciplinary synthesis of Critical Theory was broader than the three levels just described. Psychoanalysis, in particular, was a crucial dimension of the Frankfurt School's theory of capitalist society, since it revealed some of the sources of the integration of individuals into this social order and their attachment to it, as well as elements of the individual that were resistant to the social order and that may constitute demands for liberation (Marcuse, 1966; Fromm, 1971). In the case of Habermas, the interdisciplinary synthesis expanded to include a wider variety of theoretical perspectives, like linguistic theories, genetic psychology, and elements of sociological systems theory. Yet, this did pose the question of whether some of the perspectives that Habermas drew upon were compatible with the intentions of a critical theory of society. In my opinion, Habermas for the most part adapted frameworks in a way that overcame the potential inconsistencies with Critical Theory, but his drawing on strands of functionalism undercut his major critical diagnostic intention, that is, of presenting a critique of functionalist reason (Habermas, 1984; 1987a). One could argue that this antinomy is one of the major reasons for the subsequent subordinating of the social theory component of Critical Theory.

The dialectical approach of Critical Theory partly shaped its interdisciplinary syntheses. The dialectical approach has different connotations, but a commitment to it constitutes a distinctive methodological background to Critical Theory. In one sense, the very idea of critique bears witness to a commitment to the power of negation. For Critical Theory aims to disclose how existing reality is in contradiction with its rational potential and how this contradiction manifests itself in forms of suffering, oppression and pathologies. For instance, Habermas argued that the mechanisms of the material reproduction of capitalist society, exchange value and administrative power, have developed to a point where they undermine the rationality of communication. This erosion of communication has given rise, in turn, to contemporary social movements and protests over the conditions of living, such as resistance to urban developments, opposition to the unequal legal treatment of minorities and the welfare state policies that are based on prescriptive definitions of identity, such as in relation to gender and sexuality (Habermas, 1987a).

Habermas' paradigm of communication draws on the early sense of dialectics as dialogue. However, his theory came to downplay the more ontological connotations of dialectics, which Marx had foregrounded. That is, the dialectical sense of the historicity of social development and the process character of society (Adorno, 1989). In other words, Marx's dialectical approach concerns the unfolding dynamics rather than the static representation of society. Similarly, Honneth's development of Hegel's original idea of struggles for recognition implies that the expansion of moral understandings derives from opposition and conflict (Honneth, 1995a).

Critical Theory has consistently deployed the dialectical method in order to account for the conversion between the subjectivity of social actors and the objectivity of social institutions. The attempt to understand the interplay and mediations of this relationship necessitated the development of complex inter-disciplinary frameworks. Marx's labour theory of value naturally represented an interpretation of the conversion between the subjectivity of the worker and the objectivity of the capitalist institution (Marx, 1971). However, the tradition of Critical Theory sustains the dialectical intentions of value theory, but it treats it less as an economic proposition in the narrow sense. Rather, it considers that the theory of value is concerned with a more general social theory problem. Namely, the problem of the contradictions of social reproduction; the theory of value is concerned with the dialectical relationship between the potentials for autonomy and the actual institutionalized constraints upon it.

It is in this latter dialectical sense that value theory represents something of a guiding thread for my analysis of the conflicts and structural contradictions of the contemporary capitalist constellation. My analysis takes into account how Habermas' conceptualization of the interrelationship of the lifeworld and the social systems of the market economy and the state-administration was intended to revise Marx's theory of value (Habermas, 1987a). It accepts that the processes of conversion and interchange have become more complex and mediated, particularly owing to the intervention of the state in the economy and the current combination of the dynamics of subjective incorporation and social exclusion.

'Critical Theory' and 'Radical Thinkers'

Given that my book explores how Critical Theory can be developed through the critique and synthesis of insights drawn from other social theories of the present development of society, it is necessary to briefly contrast the Critical Theory perspective that traces its lineage to the Frankfurt School with the more elastic use of the term 'critical theory' in contemporary discourses in the humanities and the social sciences. The latter usage typically covers a broad range of theories that are critical of contemporary capitalism (see Keucheyan, 2013). It often includes post-Marxist or radical theorists like Alain Baidou, Slavoj Žižek, Jacques Rancière, Antonio Negri, Judith Butler, as well as some post-structuralist and post-colonial perspectives, feminist theorists, and others. Now, many of these theorists have affinities with the Frankfurt School version of Critical Theory and it is not entirely unreasonable to claim that a case could be made for the salience of their writings to revising conventional Critical Theory in a way that is relevant to contemporary circumstances. These writers have offered neo-Marxist critiques of capitalism, they are certainly concerned with the critique of domination, many of them are influenced by psychoanaly-sis (more so than some recent work in the main tradition of Critical Theory), and several of them continue the interest in aesthetics that was a distinctive feature of the Frankfurt School Critical Theory as well. Yet, for these theorists to be taken as continuous with the Frankfurt School tradition would require disavowing the internal development of Critical Theory, the previously outlined substantial considerations that led to its development and programmatic revisions. In particular, it would involve, to my mind, neglecting some of the core *problematiques* that have given Critical Theory its unique complexion.

It is certainly unfair to collapse a considerable diversity of 'radical' thinkers and critical approaches, but there are common divergences from the Frankfurt School tradition. In some respects, the key contrasts are the same as those that Habermas emphasized in his critique of postmodernism and post-structuralist approaches (Habermas, 1987b). Many of these radical theorists do not share Critical Theory's methodological orientation, with its commitment to the concept of rationality and its normative universalism. Similarly, Critical Theory's understanding of the dialogue between, and synthesis of, philosophy and the social sciences is not accepted by some of these radical theorists. The precise form and meaning of this relationship is contested within Critical Theory; however, it remains significant to the self-understanding of this tradition and it sets out some of the parameters for the justification of its critique.

Further, the political perspective of these 'radical theorists' regularly owes more to other strands of Marxism and it sometimes shades into the politics of orthodox or party Marxism. In the sense, that the approach that some 'radical theorists' have to politics is more instrumental and the other concerns or commitments of theory, like methodology, normative justification, or even rationality, are taken to be matters that are ultimately resolved politically or in combination with power. These are positions that tend to reflect the influence of Antonio Gramsci and Michel Foucault in fields like those of cultural studies and postcolonial studies. In fact, it is not the perception of the imbrication of theory and power that separates these approaches from Critical Theory, but the conclusions that are drawn from it. For instance, the fact that some radical thinkers, like Chantal Mouffe, have contributed to the renewal of interest in the politics of Carl Schmitt may be indicative of the divergence from Critical Theory, even though it is true that this interest has antecedents in Walter Benjamin's engagement with Schmitt in his 'critique of violence' (Benjamin 1978b[1955]; Mouffe, 1999). Schmitt's critique of liberalism and his conception of politics as based on a division between friend and foe are certainly contrary to the democratic and deliberative perspective of Habermas' Critical Theory (Schmitt, 2007[1932]; Habermas, 1998).

These heterogeneous strands of radical thought regularly dissent from Critical Theory's underlying adherence to the intentions of the 'project of modernity', or the modernist articulation of its vision of the autonomous constitution of society. In some respects, it is the aspect of dissent rather than affirmation which has led to many of them being labelled critical theories. In fact, there has actually been a proliferation of the category of critique or critiques, often with the intention of emphasizing the acceptance of disputation and the diversity, or fragmentation, of progressive social and political movements, such as feminist, environmental, and identity (see Boltanski and Chiapello, 2005). At the same time, the Frankfurt School tradition of Critical Theory may have come to be perceived as relatively less critical. This is probably because of its more affirmative relation to liberalism and rights, as well as the priority that Habermas' discourse theory accords to agreement in determining social justice and normative justification. But it may simply be due to the view that the founding problems of Critical Theory belong to an earlier period and that its 'institutionalization' simply makes its theses seem predictable (see Honneth, 2009: 19). There have always been, to be sure, radical critiques of capitalism that diverge from Critical Theory, and which are opposed to its basic standard of critique. Critical Theory bases its critique on the existing but unfulfilled rationality of society. Habermas claims that Critical Theory is 'critical of the reality of developed societies inasmuch as they do not make full use of the learning potential culturally available to them, but deliver themselves over to an uncontrolled growth of complexity' (Habermas, 1987a: 375). This dimension of critique equally applies to alternative theories, irrespective of whether they are traditional or radical.

The recent generalization of critique reflects an appreciation of the multiplicity of injustices and the delegitimizing of formerly uncritical positions. It is fair to claim that Critical Theory can learn from struggles for justice, yet its methodology and perspective differentiate it from many forms of these struggles. Ultimately, it serves as a critical standard for assessing perspectives. In this respect, it is worth recalling Critical Theory's standpoint in relation to the workers' movement and how the Frankfurt School sought to explain the proletariat's diversion from its emancipatory potential. From this starting point, Critical Theory was forced to commence a process of rethinking the prospects and meaning of a general interest in emancipation. Similarly, Habermas' theory of the colonization of the lifeworld sought to understand and explain the then new protest movements, like the ecological, peace and anti-consumerist movements, potentials and how new conflicts were connected to the strains on the welfare state from demands for services and legitimacy (Habermas, 1987a). In his opinion, the explanatory intention of his theory was that of enabling a better understanding of those sources of discontent that are not entirely clear to the movements, and, by this, to counteract indiscriminate rejections of modern rationality. The latter took the form of elaborating the more expansive and democratic conception of communicative rationality (Habermas, 1984; 1986).

One of the problems of this approach was that it appeared rather distant from the substantive concerns of these movements and it did not fully satisfy its own explanatory intentions. Even so, Habermas' basic assumption remains correct. Critical Theory should provide a revised account of the conflicts that underlie contemporary movements and protests. It should constitute, then, not just a normative clarification of social struggles' demands for justice, but also a sociological explanation of the prevailing forms of domination and suffering. This explanation may coincide with or enhance those understandings of progressive movements opposing injustices, but it may constitute a critique of movements' explanations and serve to initiate dialogical reflection. Of course, Critical Theory must be open to learning from movements and their capacity to reveal injustices.

There are other ways in which the commitment to rationality differentiates the Frankfurt School tradition of Critical Theory from many of the other post-Marxist and radical perspectives that are often labelled 'critical theory' today. One of them is the extent to which Critical Theory has been shaped by its reception of Max Weber's theory of rationality and Weber's ambivalent vision of modernity (Weber, 1930; 1958). For Weber, rationalization harbours constraining and destructive consequences; particularly those of bureaucratic domination and the dissolution of those meanings and values that could either limit 'purposive' rationalization or give it a purpose beyond itself. Despite these dangers and the negative dimensions of rationalization, Weber believed that rationalization in the form of efficiency, predictability, the application of means, technological expansion, the growth in expertise and the disenchantment of magic and spiritualist interpretations of reality is so effective in modernity that there is no realistic possibility of renouncing it. In fact, Weber claimed that even the major alternative to capitalist rationalization would not result in a rupture with the destructive aspects of rationality. Socialism, Weber argued, would consolidate bureaucratic control and domination (Weber, 1994). As noted already, the Frankfurt School's reception of Weber's theory of rationalization was anticipated and mediated by Lukács' theory of reification. Lukács argued that, although Weber's depiction of many of the tendencies of rationalization was correct, Weber's vision was affected by the reifying logic of capitalism and its tendency to make social processes appear to operate according to irresistible objective dynamics (Lukács, 1971). Without going into detail here, Lukács' conception of the transcendence of reification through proletarian revolution was implausible by the time of the formation of the Frankfurt School.

It is probably sufficient to demonstrate the degree to which Critical Theory has been shaped by Weber's theory of rationalization to note that it has pursued two almost contradictory positions in relationship to it. On the one hand, the Critical Theory of the Frankfurt School extended and generalized Weber's theory of rationalization. It detailed the penetration of rationalization into additional spheres of life, such as into leisure activities through the mass media, and sought to ascertain the deeper sources of instrumental rationalization, such as in the formation of human subjectivity and the mythical prehistory of Western civilization (Horkheimer and Adorno, 1972; Marcuse, 1966). On the other hand, Critical Theory has sought to contest the implications of Weber's theory of rationalization. In short, it has contested Weber's conception on the basis of visions of a more encompassing and fulfilling meaning of rationality, for instance, challenging the repressive character of the corresponding model of subjectivity or explicating aesthetic experiences that expose the internal limits of instrumental rationality (Marcuse, 1966; Adorno, 1985). Habermas' argument that communicative rationalization could enable a more balanced institutionalization of rationality similarly contests the conclusions that Weber drew about rationalization. Habermas envisages the possibility of a higher order democratic regulation of the currently dominant processes of the rationalisation of the capitalist market and bureaucratic state administration (Habermas, 1987a).

The Weberian *problematique* of rationalization in Critical Theory concerns the question of institutionalization. Rationality is considered a precondition for overcoming injustice and it underpins the interest in universal emancipation. Yet, rationalization not only extends organization and regulation, it expands domination. The dependency that rationalization creates upon its institution undermines prospective social alternatives.

Syntheses and *Problematiques*

In my opinion, the current interest in other strands of radical thought is partly a result of the deficiencies in the social theory component of recent Critical Theory. Still, it should be kept in mind that the limitations of much contemporary sociological theory and social scientific research have contributed to the distancing of Critical Theory from them. My analysis will later highlight how the implications of even relatively proximate sociological theories are somewhat inconsistent with the Critical Theory methodology of immanent critique. Moreover, Honneth is right to argue that several dominant strands of current sociology have become largely detached from the background of this discipline in practical philosophy (Honneth, 2012: 98). There are, of course, important exceptions to this thesis, such as the substantial works of Luc Boltanski, Laurent Thévenot, and Hans Joas, on social action, values, and morality (Boltanski and Thévenot, 2006; Joas 1993; 2000). Nevertheless, there are grounds for doubting the very possibility today of a synthesis of normative political philosophy and substantive social theory. However, such a synthesis is, in my opinion, a task that is necessary for the renewal of Critical Theory. For this reason, my analysis engages selectively and constructively with the arguments of contemporary critical sociologists, like Zygmunt Bauman, Ulrich Beck, Pierre Bourdieu, and Saskia Sassen, to clarify and expand its position on dimensions of capitalist modernity's new constellation, such as the contrast between the normative ideal of global cosmopolitanism and the actual experiences of injustices. In many ways, my conceptualization seeks to refine existing positions in Critical Theory. To this end, theories of the practical constitution and transformation of institutions, particularly those of Anthony Giddens and Luc Boltanski, are drawn upon to capture the dynamics of agency and the dialectics of control.

Similarly, Cornelius Castoriadis' notion of social imaginaries is relevant to the overall framing of my book, without this always being explicit. In some respects, Castoriadis' work developed from a confrontation with problems similar to those that shaped the Frankfurt School's Critical Theory. Castoriadis' engagement with Max Weber's theses is likewise pivotal to the development of his social theory. Weber's vision of the prevalence of bureaucratic rationality in modernity influences Castoriadis' interpretation of capitalist domination's hierarchical structure and this organizational form's contradictions, such as its dependence on the creative capacities of individuals that it is unable to generate, whereas Weber's theses about the cultural formation and long-term consequences of instrumental rationality are modified by Castoriadis in his conception of the modern imaginary of the project of the unlimited (pseudo-) rational domination and control of nature and society (Castoriadis, 1991; 1997a; 1997b). This conception has parallels with that of the Frankfurt School's critique of instrumental reason, particularly Horkheimer and Adorno's depiction of the dialectic of enlightenment, although the are differences in the respective historical genealogies (Horkheimer and Adorno, 1972; see Browne, 2016). In my opinion, the intentions of Castoriadis' critique of the contradictions of capitalism remains broadly correct, but this critique needs to be revised in order to take into account the changes in capitalist ideology and the partial rupture with the bureaucratic organizational form. These changes, I argue, are part of the contemporary redeployment of the capitalist imaginary. This redeployment has significantly altered the interpretative horizon of capitalist societies and projections of emancipatory transformation.

Although it is by no means fully developed in this work, my analysis implies that Critical Theory should pursue two apparently contradictory intentions in relation to capitalism. On the one hand, Critical Theory needs to develop its substantive political economy of capitalism. It might be argued that the revisions of Critical Theory, including the change to the communication paradigm, have contributed to stagnation in the area of political economy and a reliance on other accounts. In my opinion, this limits the critique of these other perspectives as well. If I have understood her correctly then the development of Critical Theory's substantive political economy would appear to be an intention that informs Nancy Fraser's recent work (Fraser, 2013a; 2013b). On the other hand, Critical Theory should question or deconstruct the entire notion of an economy and, to use Castoriadis' term, the social imaginary significations that enable the economy to appear as a coherent and self-contained social system. In this respect, the approaches of Castoriadis and Boltanski to institutions appear particularly suited to this task. In particular, they enable a more complete critical interrogation of the economy than Honneth's attempt to formulate a normative correction of the market so that it fulfils its potential as an institution of social freedom (Castoriadis, 1987; Boltanski, 2011; Honneth, 2014; Browne, 2014a; 2014b; 2016). To reiterate, even though there is a tension between these two demands and they appear methodologically opposed, it is important that both are pursued. In fact, Boltanski and Chiapello describe how a somewhat equivalent synthesis underpins their work on the new spirit of capitalism and its interpretation of a historical transition within this system of production (Boltanski and Chiapello, 2005).

The intentions of the Marxist adaptation of Weber's theses are salient to my analysis in another way. Critical Theory seeks to explain contemporary trends in a manner that delineates prospective transformations. It aims to provide a longer-term perspective on historical processes, bringing this historical perspective to bear on current developments (see Calhoun, 1995). I argue that this longer-term perspective has, to some extent, been absent from contemporary Critical Theory. My analysis does not, to be sure, fully rectify this omission, however, the historical standpoint of Critical Theory is a basic supposition of my approach. The diminution in Critical Theory's historical perspective is like-wise a reflection of its distancing from social theory and a product of the recent marginalizing of historical reasoning in sociology and other areas of the social sciences (see Inglis, 2013). My attempt to bring a historical perspective to bear on current social developments leads at various junctures to incorporating certain considerations drawn from the perspective of *multiple modernities* and the related, though different, approach of *global modernity*. These frameworks instructively combine historical sociology and social theory.

The multiple modernities perspective, that is particularly associated with Shmuel N. Eisenstadt and Johann P. Arnason, can be interpreted as building on Weber's comparative historical sociology, such as those of agrarian civilizations and world religion (Eisenstadt, 2000; Arnason, 2005a). Multiple modernities breaks with the former notions of historical convergence and emphasizes instead the diversity of the social-historical programmes of modernization and the various cultural backgrounds and *problematiques*, especially how the latter continues to impinge upon the former. The perspective of global modernity similarly involves an expanded perspective on historical change. It accentuates how intersecting developments in diverse temporal and spatial contexts gener-ate modifications in the forms of modernization and how change can be pre-cipitated by 'modernizing moves' that mobilize potentials for collective creativity, whether those of movements, institutions, and organizations (Domingues, 2012; Wagner, 2012). Of importance to the analysis of social conflict, the approaches of multiple modernities and global modernity have attempted to renew sociological conceptions of collective agency. Multiple modernities highlights how critique has been influenced by the antinomian strands of longer-standing cultural interpretations of the world. The perspec-tive of global modernity has, however, emphasized the significance of historical discontinuities, such as the ruptures that ensue from crises and the actions of collective agencies. According to the proponents of global modernity, this emphasis distinguishes its standpoint from the civilizational frameworks that are connected to the multiple modernities perspectives (Domingues, 2012; Wagner, 2012). The latter arguably prioritizes, to a greater extent, historical continuities and the 'commonality' of the beliefs, values and identities of col-lectives (Wagner, 2012: 68).

The considerations that shape the perspectives of multiple modernities and global modernity open the way for Critical Theory to engage with an expanded range of contexts and projects of transformation. It could be argued that such an extension was constrained, rather than precluded, by the approach to his-tory in Critical Theory. Multiple modernities and global modernity, however, enable a slightly different engagement with Weber's theory of rationalization. Like the theories of Castoriadis and Boltanski, they reopen the question of the contested institution of rationality while illuminating the reconfiguring of rationalization. Without expanding on this reconfiguration in detail here, there has been a departure from the equation of rationality with bureaucratic forms of organization and, to put it cryptically, an awareness that rationality needs to incorporate a greater sense of contingency (Wagner, 1994; 2001a; 2001b; Browne, 2010).

In some ways, these developments evidence the influence of Critical Theory's critique of instrumental rationality and the struggles that they inspired against the 'one-dimensional' society (Marcuse, 1964). The outcomes of these struggles have been significant in their undermining some of the former authoritarian forms of organizing social relations, such as in relation to the family and education. Yet, in other domains progressive changes have had perverse consequences. For instance, Boltanski and Chiapello (2005) detail how the meaning and referent of the values of the 'artistic critique of capitalism', like self-expression and self-actualization, were modified and rendered compatible with the market system. In a similar vein, it is possible to perceive how institutional changes that were inspired by progressive struggles have diverged from their original purpose; for example, the expanding of educational opportunities has coincided with the corporatizing of universities.

These kinds of processes undermining progressive social reforms are described by Honneth as instances of the contemporary 'hollowing out' of social freedom in various institutional spheres (Honneth, 2014). I argue that it is necessary to revise the notion of reification in order to explain the effects of contemporary institutions' contradictory imperatives and the disempowerment of subjects that ensues from the divergence of institutions from their intended purpose.

In short, my contention is that the original reform of institutions is shaped by conflicts anchored in dialectics of control, but that the changes tend to be of the order of the regulation and displacement of the injustice underlying the conflict, such as we saw at the outset in relation to the welfare state. The new form of reification results from the reflexive relationship that develops in relation to the altered constellation. For example, the welfare state did not just remain dependent on capitalist accumulation, but the implications of state actions became factored into processes of commodification in markets. Further, this results in second order processes that intervene in the original context of interaction and that qualify the capacities of institutions, so that the trade in currencies comes to affect the action of national states. Naturally, second order processes have always been part of social interaction and the exchange of commodities and the commodification of money have a long historical development under capitalism. What differs in the contemporary period is the scale and intensity of second order abstractions; this derives partly from increasing complexity, altered temporal horizons, appreciations of contingency, and globalization's dynamics, especially deregulation and 'financialization'.

In this context, it might be argued that the recent Critical Theory of Honneth and Fraser are much less concerned with the problem of rationality and that they are more concerned with the questions of justice and freedom. It is certainly true that Honneth has questioned the continued relevance of the former Critical Theory conception of the structural constraints on rationality and capitalist rationalization, such as the constraint implied by Habermas' notion of the limits set by the communicative reproduction of the lifeworld (Habermas, 1987a; Honneth, 2012). Indeed, Honneth argues that formerly critical 'normative principles' have become, in somewhat inverted forms, elements of system reproduction and legitimations of capitalist expansion (Honneth, 2012). Given this development, Honneth proposed a programme of Critical Theory that investigated the paradoxical contradictions of capitalist modernization and the attendant injustices in various spheres of social relations, like the family, work, law, and politics. 'A contradiction is paradoxical', Honneth and Hartmann argue, 'when, precisely through the attempt to realize such an intention, the probability of realising it is decreased' (Honneth and Hartmann, 2012: 178).

My analysis consolidates this critical conception of contemporary developments, but proposes that they should be explained in terms of the social dynamics of dialectics of control. Similarly, I contend that this critique of the paradoxes of capitalist modernization in the advanced nation states should be supplemented by the analysis of global modernity (Domingues, 2012; Bringel and Domingues, 2015). One important implication of this supplementation is that it results in a qualifying of the assumed transcendence of the conflicts and contradictions of the earlier phases of capitalist modernization, rather it opens the way to a better understanding of their current forms of articulation and displacement. Indeed, it is a central thesis of globalization theories that developments are regularly contingent on processes in a different context. Nevertheless, Critical Theory still aims to perceive potentials for emancipatory change in rationalization. It is probably worthwhile at this point briefly restating some of the intentions and presuppositions of Critical Theory that have been sketched. These intentions and suppositions give Critical Theory its distinctive orientation and they have been highlighted in the introduction because they demarcate the Frankfurt School tradition from the more elastic contemporary use of the term 'critical theory'. In addition, they clarify elements of the framework elaborated in this text and its justification.

First, from the outset, Critical Theory has always involved a synthesis of different perspectives. Second, Critical Theory has applied some version of a dialectical method. Third, the synthetic orientation and dialectical method are salient to the interest of Critical Theory in clarifying and transforming the relationship between the subjectivity of social actors and the objectivity of social institutions. Fourth, the problem of rationality has been central to Critical Theory; rationality has been a basic justification of critique and a determinant of progressive change, yet the predominant versions of rationality in capitalist society have been an object of critique. Fifth, after Marx's turn to social practice, Critical Theory has sought to determine the practical function of philosophical ideal and endeavoured to explicate the sociological translation of philosophical categories. Like the notions of reason and rationality, philosophical notions are criticized as ideological legitimations of domination and simultaneously understood to be normative aspirations to be practically realized. Sixth, the sociological framework of Critical Theory has been shaped by theses about capitalism's historical evolution and the diversion from Marx's predictions. In this regard, the assessments of the class compromise of post-liberal capitalism and the Weber-inspired view of the extension of bureaucratic administration in modernity were particularly significant.

Contradictions and Social Conflicts

It is undoubtedly the case that the current historical phase of capitalism contains new dimensions that Critical Theory needs to take into account, whilst contemporary capitalism preserves many of the features that have been the object of earlier critique. In fact, the commodity form and instrumental rationality remain integral to the capitalist system as a whole and what is really novel is the modes of their ideological concealment, including the explicit equating of formerly antithetical values like aesthetic experience with them. Taking these changes into account, this work makes a substantive contribution to the development of the social theory component of Critical Theory. In the first three chapters, it presents an analysis of the structural contradictions of contemporary capitalist modernity. These contradictions, I argue, involve differing dialectics of control and they are found to involve different forms of conflict. It may be said that these structural contradictions involve different institutions and dynamics of domination and injustice. To reiterate, I take the labour theory of value as something of a guide, but treat it not so much as an economic proposition. Rather, it is taken to be concerned with the transaction or interchange between the subjectivity of actors and the objectivity of institutions. The concern with this interchange, which Habermas, for instance, sought to explicate in terms of the transference between lifeworld and system, is not simply an analytical consideration, such as with regard to the effectiveness of social coordination (Habermas, 1987a). For Critical Theory, the processes of emancipatory change presuppose the formation of a new subjectivity and not just an alteration of the 'objective' institutional structures.

There are three contradictions that are explored in these chapters: first, that of collective self-determination in relation to the tension between globalization and democracy, second, that of the alienation intrinsic to the compelled, but thwarted participation in the interchange between social action and social institutions, and, third, that of the exclusionary integration that is connected to the contemporary misalignments of social integration and system integration. Of course, these are by no means the only forms of social contradictions that give rise to injustice and oppression in capitalist societies. However, these contradictions are considered relevant to other conflicts and, to some extent, they have a mediating role in relationship to them. For example, Nancy Fraser's account of the 'fortunes of feminism' highlights intersections between gender subordination and capitalism which are analogous, if not equivalent, to the mediation that is disclosed in my analysis of these three contradictions and dialectics of control (Fraser, 2013b). In short, Fraser shows how the adaptation of capitalism complicated and limited the project of the emancipation of women.

There are equally relations between each of the contradictions, with one being in some respects a subset of the other. This is especially the case for the way in which the contradiction between globalization and democracy, partly expressed through the crisis of the welfare state, then become manifested in the displaced form of the exclusionary integration of half-positions, such as that of workers without citizenship. The latter forms of exclusionary integration have a longer history; the purpose of my analysis is to highlight how their contemporary expression is connected to unfolding tendencies and conflicts involving dialectics of control. In particular, I analytically contrast the reification that is manifested in such instances of social disintegration and exclusion with the alienation of the compelled, but thwarted, participation of subjects in institutions. There are overlaps and complex entanglements between the three contradictions in substantive or empirical contexts. These interconnections reflect the institutional displacement of conflicts in capitalist societies and how the structuration of social contradictions is more complex and layered than logical contradictions. In other words, the dialectic of control in each domain of conflict affects the others, although there are substantial differences in the degrees and formats of the respective conditioning of one another. The sense of contestation that ensues from the social contradiction of an 'incompatibility among the elements or parts of a system' is conveyed by Alberto Melucci's claim that:

> In diachronic terms, any remedial action to keep a system within its compatibility limits tends to produce contradictions. These contradictions, furthermore, generate a form of collective action which, depending on the area one is referring to, will fall under one of the various categories analysed above. Incompatibilities among the inner elements of a specific system (for example, with a political system or an organization) and incompatibilities between different systems are factors which activate social movements and other forms of collective action. (Melucci, 1996: 52–3)

There is, moreover, always a type of hermeneutic contradiction present in conflicts involving dialectics of control. That is, hermeneutic contradictions in the general sense of the meanings attached to antagonisms and in the more specific sense Luc Boltanski proposes: where there is a tension between the pragmatic enunciation and the semantic, which is stabilized by institutions (Boltanski, 2011; see Browne, 2014a; 2014b). For this reason, hermeneutic contradictions point to the elements of indeterminacy and reflexivity that pervade conflicts. These can make it difficult to define the exact parameters of conflicts, because the linkage between conflicts and contradiction presupposes some framing of the relationship between the semantic 'reality' and, what Boltanski terms, the 'world' that goes beyond it (Boltanski, 2011). In a similar vein, Castoriadis' contention that in heteronomous societies the creation of coherence depends on concealing the tension between the instituted social imaginary and the instituting imaginary draws attention to the horizons of meaning that are mobilized in conflicts and delimited in the identification of contradictions

(Castoriadis, 1987; 1997a; 1997b). What this means is that the constitution of institutions is at stake in dialectics of control, even though this is generally veiled and concealed by the reliance on instituted realities, including the mundane modes of signification in language and the distributing of value through money.

At the same time, each of the three contradictions represents potentials for normative progress and they are each connected to demands that link justice and autonomy. This is particularly important, because Critical Theory seeks to overcome the division between normative and empirical modes of analysis. It likewise seeks to disclose immanent potentials for emancipation and democracy, which contradict the instituted actuality of domination and injustice. The fourth chapter explores the contemporary dilemmas of the distinctive Critical Theory methodology of immanent critique. It sketches, on the one hand, how Habermas responded to the Frankfurt School's diagnosis of the decline and diminution of immanent potentials for transformation through the change to the paradigm of communication, which opened the way to an alternate conception of rationality and democracy. At the same time, Habermas' primary interest in the normative grounding of critique would result in a distancing of Critical Theory from the sociological analysis of the historical development of contemporary society. In some respects, this outcome was inconsistent with Habermas' intentions, but the ensuing deficiencies in Critical Theory warrant a consideration of the potential syntheses and selective incorporation of conceptions drawn from the seemingly most relevant theories of the present. However, it is found that the approaches of postmodernism, the risk society perspective and the implications of significant theories of globalization may intensify the conundrums of immanent critique and that they each represent deficient perspectives. This analysis equally shows that Critical Theory remains the critique of the limitations of other theories of society and that it bases this critique on its claim to greater reflexivity concerning conditions of theorizing in the present.

There have been two distinctive, though related, responses to the current conundrums of critique. In some respects, both reflect the turn to democracy as the basic orienting signification and intention of critique. One response has been partly conditioned by the crisis of the welfare state and the loss of confidence in the possibility of a transition from capitalism. In this case, critique has turned to 'utopian' modes of justification and to the category of 'hope' (Browne, 2005). This is because these notions seem to combine a temporal orientation to the future with normative principles. The affective and emotional complexion of hope and utopian imaginaries is a major source of their appeal, but this reveals some of the limitations of such an approach to the renewal of critique. The other response is that of reworking the synthesis of positive liberty and social justice that has been a general formulation of the emancipatory intentions of Critical Theory. Although there are considerable overlaps between these two responses, the latter is more strongly grounded in the specification of an immanent potential for social progress, whereas the recourse to hope and utopia are reactions to the questioning of social progress. It is the synthesis of positive liberty and social justice that is explored across the latter chapters of this work.

Habermas' discourse ethic and Honneth's theory of the struggle for recognition are suggestive of the synthesis of positive liberty and social justice, although it is Honneth's later conception of social freedom that is found to most approximate to the intentions of this synthesis. Fraser's notion of participatory parity is shown to be another attempted formulation in recent Critical Theory of the intended synthesis of positive liberty and social justice. Her conception, arguably, does not have as fully developed a notion of social constitution. Fraser's critical presentation of the respective justice claims of recognition and redistribution serves to highlight the revisions of Honneth's theory of social freedom, particularly its emphasis on institutions. In many respects, my analysis agrees with the intentions of the notion of social freedom, but considers that Honneth's formulation is seriously flawed in its actual elaboration. In this respect, I argue that Honneth's important notion of social freedom cannot deal with the dynamics of the three contradictions that are outlined in the earlier chapters. It neither fully encompasses the corresponding sense of emancipation, nor does it adequately explain the conditions of domination, oppression and injustice that limit social freedom. I propose that incorporating a stronger sense of dialectics of control would lead to a better understanding of social freedom. Further, I claim that an effective transformation of social relations of domination would involve the sense of collective, as well as individual, agency that is alluded to in the aspired nexus of positive liberty and social justice. The connection of Critical Theory to social practice is preserved in the radical democratic implications of this nexus.

In the tradition of Critical Theory, the explanation of historical processes has coincided with the theoretical elaboration of concepts and categories. This work seeks to explain the relevance of many of Critical Theory's key categories, like alienation, critique, injustice and domination. Naturally, even simply restating conceptions in this manner necessitates revisions and redefinition. This is one way in which this work deploys the reflexive and synthetic approach of Critical Theory. Despite its some times abstract formulations, including proposing new conceptions, this work accepts the methodological requirement of grounding its conceptions in the practical experience of subjects and their potentials for emancipation. It seeks to disclose and clarify potentials for autonomy and justice through theoretical reflection, as well as illuminating the social structures that impede them. At the same time, it is worth noting that this work does not deal with certain themes that were integral to the original Frankfurt School programme of Critical Theory. Notably, it does not deal with aesthetics and the mass media; similarly, its discussion of psychoanalysis and later psychological perspectives is limited to a few cursory remarks. The proposals advanced in this work still have, in my opinion, a certain relevance to these themes. Finally, this work does not circumvent the vicissitudes of critical theory; it nevertheless hopes to demonstrate the open-ended dialectical imagination of Critical Theory. The dialectical imagination is contrary to so much of contemporary reality that conspires against it.

1

A NEW NEXUS OF SOCIAL CHANGE

Introduction: Collective Self-Determination and Critical Social Theory

Critical Theory considers that the structure of capitalism limits the potential for collective self-determination and that this is a major source of injustice and domination. Of course, the possibility of collective self-determination presupposes that it already exists as a norm (Habermas, 2001a; Taylor, 2004; Wagner, 2012). Democratic political orders have typically sought to present themselves as embodying, to varying degrees, a principle of collective self-determination, such as in the form of popular sovereignty or public opinion. On the one hand, this is one reason why there is a considerable tension between capitalism and democracy. Capitalism is an economic system founded on private appropriation and an asymmetrical distribution of wealth and power. On the other hand, it is by no means the case that the existing institution of democracy satisfies the conditions of collective self-determination (Browne, 2006; Blokker, 2014). Critical Theory seeks to discern the conditions that would enable society to autonomously act upon itself. It considers, for this reason, that collective self-determination depends on broad social conditions and not just formally democratic political institutions. These social conditions include effective participation and social solidarity (Habermas, 1996a; Honneth, 2014). Moreover, Critical Theory equally considers that the existing norm of collective self-determination has been open to regressive ideological expression, and hence its distorted institution is an object of critique.

The aspiration of collective self-determination existed prior to the nation state system. It is part of what Castoriadis (1991) describes as the modern social imaginary of the project of individual and collective autonomy. Castoriadis considers that this project originated with the Ancient Greek institution of democracy and then reemerged around the twelfth century with the creation of self-governing city-states in Europe. This connection to the social imaginary of autonomy draws attention to how collective self-determination is open to different articulations (Domingues, 1995; 2006; Eisenstadt, 1999a). Marx believed that collective self-determination presupposed the transcendence of capitalism and the structuring of society according to radically different principles, including those of the abolition of class and the distribution of resources according to need (Marx, 1977b; Marx and Engels, 1977). Yet, the perspective of Critical Theory has developed through an apprehension of how Marx elided different dimensions of the problem of collective self-determination. Marx seemed to alternate between conceptions of socialism as defined by the free association of producers and that of the rational administration of things by the state. Marx once proposed a historical sequence in which the institution of the latter preceded and enabled the former (Marx, 1977b). In any event, Marx arguably lacked an adequate appreciation of the potential tension between these two conceptions of a self-determining collective and twentieth century developments would reveal the conflicts between them.

Contemporary Critical Theory has sought to systematically rethink two assumptions of Marx's proposition concerning collective self-determination. It argues that collective self-determination should not be juxtaposed to individual autonomy and that it is important then to make explicit the institutional means of facilitating the integrity of individual and collective autonomy (Honneth, 2012; 2014). Critical Theory has sought to democratize the idea of collective self-determination through emphasizing its dependence on practices like public participation and democratic deliberation (Habermas, 1996a; Fraser, 2003a; 2003b). Indeed, Habermas (1998; 2009) considers that his model of deliberative democracy is an alternative to Republican notions of collective self-determination. Critical Theory contends that individual autonomy requires the autonomy of other individuals. In other words, it rejects the view of individual autonomy as something that can be achieved either at the expense of other individuals or by becoming independent of them (Anderson and Honneth, 2005; Browne, 2010).

For Critical Theory, the notion of collective self-determination is a historical category. It is a normative-political concept that has been reformulated and reinterpreted, and an explanatory-diagnostic notion that reveals the institutional limitations to social autonomy. Of particular significance, notions of collective self-determination presume social agency (Domingues, 1995; Eisenstadt, 2000; Wagner, 2012). The original Marxian vision equated social agency with the dialectic of class relations, hence this agency may itself represent a potential that is subordinated and oppressed. The Frankfurt School and Habermas argued that this class dialectic had been modified and consequently that class relations tended to be increasingly expressed in mediated forms (Marcuse, 1964; Horkheimer and Adorno, 1972; Habermas, 1976; 1984; 1987a; 1987b). For the Frankfurt School circle, these modifications were primarily due to the expansion of technological and instrumental rationality, the development of administrative systems of domination, and the intrusion of the commodity form into spheres beyond that of wage labour, such as through the mass media and consumerism, with the concomitant tendencies for reification and the eroding of the subjective capacity for agency.

By contrast, the Critical Theory of Habermas and Honneth highlights how the potential for collective self-determination expanded in capitalist societies with the extension of democratic rights to wider categories of persons and the institution of the welfare state (Habermas, 1987a; 1987b; 1996a; Honneth, 1995a; 2014). These social reforms equally demonstrate the extent to which the idea of collective self-determination became assimilated to the nation state formation. The welfare state reduced some of the injustices of capitalism that limit the potential for collective self-determination. However, Critical Theory has never considered the welfare state to be an institution capable of giving full-expression to the idea of collective self-determination (Habermas, 1976; 1987a). The resurgence of market capitalism reinforces this awareness of the welfare state's limitations and deficiencies in terms of collective self-determination, whilst enabling a renewed appreciation of its measures to reduce injustice and to underpin equal liberty.

In this chapter, I examine arguments about how the structural contradictions of capitalist modernity that limit collective self-determination have been reconfigured. The new nexus of social change is often depicted as deriving from the conflict between globalization and democracy. My analysis sketches some of the significant dimensions of this conflict and outlines aspects of influential interpretations of its central dynamics, including some of the relevant commentaries on the recent global financial crisis and austerity regimes. I find that changes associated with the contemporary phase of capitalist development precipitate revisions in Critical Theory and its conception of collective self-determination. In the 'Excursus' following the chapter, I draw attention to the political self-understanding of the broadly conceived alter-globalization (or global justice) movement. I suggest that two dimensions of this movement's interpretation of its practices are particularly salient to the interest of Critical Theory in democratization and emancipatory social transformation.

Globalization and Democracy

A distinctive feature of recent versions of critical sociology is the assumption that the nexus between globalization and democracy supersedes the earlier class conflict between labour and capital. It is regularly suggested that the amelioration of class inequalities through the social rights of citizens is itself bound to national governance. Globalization threatens this dimension of the democratization of capitalist society, because the authoritative power of the state is anchored in its sovereign control over territory. Ulrich Beck presents a version of this argument in commenting that

> globalization means one thing above all else: denationalization – that is, erosion of the national state, but also its possible transformation into a transnational state. (Beck, 2000a: 14)

Beck's definition points to the democratic parameters of 'first' modernity; it is often the self-organizing capacity of civil society that is the point of reference for accounts of democracy in contemporary modernity. It is equally possible to

contend that the earlier class conflict still underpins the tension between globalization and democracy, particularly by way of reference to the increasing
inequality in the distribution of wealth in advanced capitalist societies and the
neoliberal reforms of labour markets over the past decades (Harvey, 2005;
Therborn, 2011; Piketty, 2014). Globalization is popularly considered the primary cause of the regeneration of class relations and its dynamic of anti-
capitalist struggle, with highly visible landmark moments like the Seattle protests, the World Social Forum, and the Occupy movements contesting global
capitalism and its legitimations (Browne and Susen, 2014; see Excursus below).

Nevertheless, the same structural changes inform the arguments for the
resurgence of class antagonism and the assertion of a new dynamic associated
with the polarity of globalization and democracy. Specifically, they each refer
to the system integration of the capitalist economy having reached a critical
threshold. This change compounds what Habermas (1976; 1987a) and Claus
Offe (1984) described as the structural limitations of the welfare state, that is,
the dependence of the state upon capital accumulation to obtain sufficient
taxation revenue to fund compensatory and redistributive measures. In an
attempted critical updating of Offe and Habermas' thesis, Wolfgang Streeck
(2011: 5) argues that over the past forty years the 'basic underlying tension in
the political-economic configuration of advanced capitalist societies' has manifested itself in various institutional forms. Streeck defines this basic underlying
tension as that between *market determination* in accordance with the supposed
principle of marginal productivity and *social rights* that are largely contingent
on the state and allocated according to need or the social justice criteria of
equity. The 'migration' of this structural conflict's manifestations is due to the
transference that results in each case from addressing its specific institutional
appearance and the perpetuation then of the tension's basic dynamic (Streeck,
2011). Its full detrimental social effects were basically delayed, Streeck claims,
through 'buying time', that is, the deleterious effects were deferred and partly
concealed through public and private borrowing (Streeck, 2014).

Streeck argues that after the decades of the post-Second World War consolidation of 'democratic capitalism', which included major developments like
expanding the welfare state, enacting rights to collective bargaining, guarantees
of full employment and neo-Keynesian policies, the distributional conflict of
labour and capital came to manifest itself in the late 1960s and 70s in the
monetary form of inflation. Public expenditure initially moderated inflation's
deleterious consequences; however, as Duménil and Lévy (2004; 2011) similarly argue, inflation's depreciation of the value of existing capital and the
perception promoted by neo-classical economics that public debt diminished
private investment resulted in the neo-liberal reaction. Neoliberal responses
typically included reductions in certain areas of public expenditure, prioritizing
the limiting of inflation over commitments to full employment, and the undermining of labour market conditions and associated social protections, as well
as restricting or reducing the social rights of citizenship that expanded with the
institution of the welfare state (see Chapter 3). In many respects, the changes

associated with the resurgence of market capitalism can be seen as mediated expressions of dialectics of control and the resistance of capital to the regulatory and redistributive 'social contract' of the welfare state (Duménil and Lévy, 2004; Streeck, 2014). Streeck believes that Habermas' and Offe's model of the strains and tensions of late-capitalism did not foresee the changes that would actually come to pass because it treated capital 'as an apparatus rather than an agency, as means of production rather than a class' (Streeck, 2014: 13; see Habermas, 2015: 85).

The neo-liberal programmes brought the basic conflict of democratic capitalism to the surface again, but this struggle did not conform to prior expectations concerning capitalist crises. It had previously been presumed that mass 'unemployment would undermine support, not just for the government of the day but also for democratic capitalism itself' (Streeck (2011: 14). Like Streeck, Craig Calhoun (2011: 26) highlights the paradoxical outcome of the negative implications of public austerity being responded to by increasing private debt. In many advanced capitalist societies, citizens used private debt to sustain, and in some cases increase, consumption patterns and to meet needs that had previously been met as a social entitlement, such as to health care or education (Crouch, 2009). Indeed, the financial liberalization of the last decades of the twentieth century promoted increasing private indebtedness. Although this is not a full explanation of the causes of the recent financial crisis and recession, the increasing provision of need through private debt proved to be a precipitating condition. Democratic capitalism's structural tension became increasingly internationalized during this period and the financial crisis revealed some of the consequences of economic globalization. In many advanced nation states, public debt substantially increased as a result of the initial system preserving measures of refinancing banks and failing corporations and the subsequent increased social expenditure in response to the economic contraction and the simultaneous decline in taxation revenues (Calhoun, 2011; Schafer and Streeck, 2013). Streeck details the changing and perverse character of the ensuing struggles:

> In the three years since 2008, distributional conflict under democratic capitalism has turned into a complicated tug-of-war between global financial investors and sovereign nation-states. Where in the past workers struggled with employers, citizens with finance ministers, and private debtors with private banks, it is now financial institutions wrestling with the very states that they had only recently blackmailed into saving them. (Streeck, 2011: 22)

The sequence of displacements of capitalism's 'basic conflict' modifies some of the dynamics of the relationship of the welfare state to market capitalism. The general tendency of this historical sequence is one that Peter Wagner rightly considers consists in 'a relative decoupling of capitalist practices from their national institutional embedding, and, thus, an escape from the reach of

democratically voiced demands' (Wagner, 2012: 98). The transnational policies of neo-liberal economic coordination and the development of a myriad of
complex economic instruments, like leveraging and derivatives, not only transfigure the former distributional conflicts but also appear to increase the
autonomy of capital. This is the case even though the economic coordination
of the global system involves agreements between sovereign nation states, like
the North American Free Trade Agreement, and nation states are the financi-
ers, albeit unequally, of international agencies, like the International Monetary
Fund. However, it is, a new kind of global economy, according to Colin
Crouch (2005) and Saskia Sassen (2011),

> one centred in global firms using national governments to make global
> space for them, rather than a global economy centred in international
> trade and capital flows governed in good part by states, no matter their
> unequal power to do so. (Sassen, 2011: 22)

In particular, transnational finance's empowerment appears to qualify the
state's capacity to underpin social rights, given that even minor increases in
borrowing costs through rising interest rates have substantial implications for
indebted nation states (Streeck, 2011; Duménil and Lévy, 2011; Lapavitsas
et al., 2012). There can be little doubt that this restraint extends to the capacity
of labour to organize and mobilize in struggles over distribution, although
globalization has involved more direct changes to the conditions of labour,
including the relocating of production and the institutionalizing of the legal, as
well as illegal, remuneration of migrant labour below those of national economic standards (Sassen, 2011; 2014).

The earlier dynamics of modern capitalist societies, particularly those of the
dialectic of class relations and the structural tension between market determination and social rights underpinned by the state, have not so much been
superseded as radically transformed. On the one hand, the processes of globalization have, to varying degrees, altered the dynamics of inequality and social
conflict. On the other hand, the nexus between democracy and globalization
increasingly modulates the dynamic of class conflict. These changes are consistent with Boltanski and Chiapello's (2005) depiction of the new spirit of capitalism's displacement, rather than resolution, of the conflict between labour and
capital. In Boltanski and Chiapello's opinion, displacement was originally a
response to the industrial contestation of the period of the consolidation of
welfare state capitalism. Focusing on the transformation of industrial and
managerial practices and their justifications, Boltanski and Chiapello (2005)
argue that the model of hierarchical authority was displaced by another sense
of control, that is, of control as self-control and coordination through self-
organization rather than managerial direction. However, new capitalism's claim
to have dissolved the alienating and authoritarian dimensions of the conflict
between labour and capital was contradicted by the industrial reforms that it
enacted. These produced greater insecurity and new versions of managerial

authority, yet the paradigm change in capitalist managerial practices and the corresponding discourses served to fracture the class-based modes of collective solidarity (Boltanski and Chiapello, 2005; Boltanski, 2011; Browne, 2014b).

Rather than adjudicating between a cosmopolitan and a national paradigm of critical sociology, I want to argue that the nexus between globalization and democracy should be understood as part of the process of the contested constitution of the social. It is a contestation that can give rise to different institutional configurations and the conflicts of the earlier phases of modernity can be perceived as implicated in those of its latest phase. Although the multiple modernities perspective has been subjected to significant criticisms (Bhambra, 2007; Domingues, 2012; Wagner, 2012), it illuminates important dimensions of this contested constitution of the social and the problem of collective self-determination (Arnason, 1991b; 2002; Eisenstadt, 1999a; 2000).

Multiple modernities highlights how collective self-determination is connected to the distinctively modernist understanding of the social order as something that is constructed through social action and amenable to transformation. This ontological standpoint informs a variety of cultural and political programmes, but the multiple modernities perspective has equally emphasized the degree to which these projects were shaped by historically long-term cultural understandings and the forms of political authority of different world-religions and civilizations. In other words, it emphasized the tensions that produced different institutionalized outcomes and how variations in modernity ensue from the intersection of various conflicts, like the competition between political centres and peripheries, the cleavages in the world economic system at different historical conjunctures, as well as the contrast between particularistic and universalistic collective identities which can appear within, as well as between, political or religious groups.

From the standpoint of Critical Social Theory, many of the movements that the multiple modernities perspective considers agencies of modernization and sources of its variation, such as authoritarian nationalist or communal religious movements, are not themselves committed to versions of collective self-determination that represent social progress and that are consistent with the implications of the social imaginary of the project of autonomy. Rather, many of these movements distort the emancipatory sense of collective self-determination through equating it with a vision of the social order that is contrary to its democratic implications, such as that of the ethnically homogeneous nation or even forced economic development. Indeed, the analyses of multiple modernities have shown, for example, how the background of Russian imperial domination influenced the Soviet model of socialist modernization and how politicized religious movements in different parts of the world became mobilized in response to other movements, like the feminist movement in the West and the perceived failures of Arab nationalism in the Middle East (Arnason, 1993; Eisenstadt, 1999a). For Critical Theory, these contemporary forms of the contested constitution of the social represents a normative and an analytical problem.

Without detailing the qualifications and various attenuated conceptions of collective self-determination that have been proposed in Critical Theory, the potentials that it discerns for collective self-determination are post-traditional and democratic in character. Critical Theory questions substantive representations of collective self-determination, such as those equating popular sovereignty with the nation. It accordingly seeks to delineate social practices that represent an immanent potential for extending autonomy and justice, like those of mutual recognition, discursive deliberation, and justification (Honneth, 1995a; Habermas, 1996a; Benhabib, 1996b; Fraser, 2003a; Forst, 2011). These practices should generate a more democratic sense of the collective and transform the subjectivity of social actors. Nonetheless, the capacity of these practices to contest capitalism's power to determine subjects' living conditions is open to question. This is not just because the practices' normative dimension has to be translated into institutional processes or given expression by social movements, but it is also due to the tensions and contradictions of globalization's restructuring of social relations. This has led to attempts to reimagine an autonomous society in cosmopolitan terms (Benhabib, 2006; Delanty, 2009).

It is worthwhile looking further then at some of the reasons why critical sociology needs to address the processes of globalization and what seems to be at issue in globalization. The basic questions arising from globalization are relatively well known. In fact, social theorists, like Habermas (2001a) and Giddens (1994a; 1994b), have offered accurate and at time acute descriptions of the detrimental effects of globalization. They have discussed the new forms of inequality and social exclusion, the democratic deficits of supranational institutions and non-government organizations, the recent xenophobic and fundamentalist reactions to cultural interchanges and immigration patterns. Both Habermas and Giddens have highlighted the limited vision of neo-liberalism and its effects on state policy, with the consequent insecurity over work and problems of taxation revenue that arise from increasing 'locational competition' (Habermas, 2001a). Now, these depictions of various tendencies associated with globalization should not in themselves be taken to imply that globalization is a wholly negative phenomenon, neither in general, nor from the perspective of either Habermas or Giddens. In contemporary sociology, Pierre Bourdieu (1998b; 2001) and Zygmunt Bauman (1998) have more critical views of globalization.

In Bourdieu's opinion, globalization signifies the tyranny of the market and an attack on the institution of a civilized way of life. Globalization represents the dominant ideology in its contemporary form, since it depicted a series of changes for which there is supposedly no alternative (Boltanski, 2011). Unlike visions of globalization as an anonymous sequence of processes, Bourdieu considered it to be the product of elite social actors' actions. Under these conditions, the representation of globalization as due to anonymous processes that are detached from the *habitus* of social groups is a version of symbolic violence (see Calhoun, 2007). In a similar vein, Bauman (1998) argues that globalization amounts to a 'space war'. However, unlike the earlier class struggle's basis in a relation of interdependence, globalization produces an increasing disconnection between a mobile social elite and the immobile population that is tied to particular locations. In a sense, this is the personal equivalent of the tendency towards displacement that altered the relation of the state to capital. Bauman emphasizes the enormous difference in the power of the globally mobile to control their life situations compared to that of the immobile.

According to Bauman (1998: 8, 9), the 'relentless wrenching of decision-making centres' from the constraints of locality has gone together with an 'unprecedented' disconnection of power from obligations, whether to employees, the young, the weak, the unborn, or simply to the reproduction of community. Despite the overlaps between Bourdieu and Bauman's critical analyses, there is a tension that impinges on the potentials that they perceive for transforming globalization. Bourdieu (1998b) argues that a new international solidarity is necessary to resist globalization and preserve institutions limiting inequality. Bauman concurs with the intent of this proposition; however, he considers that the contemporary period is one of liquid modernity (Bauman, 2000). The current embracing of flexible modes of association and individualization significantly qualify the possibility for rejuvenating solidarity.

The tendencies that have been highlighted suggest the magnitude of the changes that cannot be ignored and the significant implications that they hold for the problem of collective self-determination. In my opinion, the challenges these changes pose for the distinctive perspective of Critical Theory are of a different order to the analytical depiction of problems. Namely, globalization challenges the theoretical framework of critical sociology. The list of detrimental effects implies, but does not specify, that the proper analysis of globalization is one that accepts that it is not a singular developmental process. In other words, globalization does not always conform to a linear sequence of modernization. This is the sense in which globalization generates multiple modernities, rather than a uniform logic of modernization and change. On the basis of this perspective, it is possible to consider globalization to be a vehicle of democratization and, at the same time, a challenge to democracy.

Although neither has developed an elaborated conception of multiple modernities, this dialectical interpretation of the nexus between globalization and democracy is that of Habermas and Giddens. On balance, Giddens tends towards the position that globalization is a vehicle of democratization, whereas Habermas' theory entails a more detailed appreciation of the threats to democracy. Even so, this contrast is more apparent in the differences in detail rather than intent, since both Habermas and Giddens contend that far-reaching democratization can offset globalization's detrimental consequences. They consider that democratization involves higher levels of social participation and they respectively seek to develop the claim that any just redistribution of material goods is conditional on increasing autonomy. Despite the significance of these considerations, it will be argued that Habermas and Giddens each develop elaborate theoretical and practical proposals that simultaneously extend and significantly limit democratization.

Globalization alters the perimeters and parameters of democracy (Browne, 2006). A fundamental problem for Critical Theory at the beginning of the twenty-first century is the expansion of social forms beyond the nation state (see Urry, 2000). In this sense, the notion of the *social* needs to be rethought and the ideas of socially structured interconnections and cultural interchanges are central to this rethinking. Structural interconnections tend to be associated with the extension of social systems and institutional networks, hence the importance of technological changes, like the diffusion of information technology and mass media of communication to globalization (see Castells, 1996; Sassen, 2008). In the contemporary context, the idea of cultural interchange refers not simply to cultural exchange but processes of continuous assimilation and transformation. If the latter idea of cultural interchange is accurate, globalization tends toward the constitution of 'hybridity' and hybrid identities, as the concept of interchange accentuates the plasticity of culture. Namely, interchange points to the propensity of 'post-traditional cultures' for reshaping and rearranging constituents on the basis of an immanent reflexivity (Giddens, 1994b; Pieterse, 1995). In critical sociology, Touraine (2000) has a more negative view of this development. He argues that there is a fragmenting of the culture that underpinned democracy at the same time as systemic institutions gain greater autonomy. Modern nation states institutionalized universalistic norms as part of a project of attempting to shape the direction of historical change, however, this project's combination of culture and institutions is fracturing and the result is increasing 'dissociation' (Touraine, 2000).

As the references to the media of communication and information technology indicate, the structural and cultural dimensions of globalization are substantially intertwined. For this reason alone, it seems to me that a reversal of globalization's major formative features is unlikely and probably undesirable, given increasing interconnections that are created, not just through trade and manufacture, but also through the cultural ties influenced by immigration patterns and the mass media. There may even be an immanent potential for the creation of a progressive cosmopolitan outlook in response to globalization (Delanty, 2009: 250). Yet, cosmopolitanism remains more fully developed as a normative political theory of global institutions and transnational justice than as a social theory of the transformation of the global order (see Domingues, 2012). In any event, if we accept the conclusions of Wallerstein (1996) and Elias (1978), it appears the case that what happens in semi-autarkic national societies still tends to be determined by the global system. The historical record suggests that in the longer term the isolation of an individual state will be reversed. Framed in this way, the issue is on what terms do social formations participate in the global system and what dimensions of globalization are under consideration. In fact, the costs of national 'closure' are liable to produce such undesirable reactions as xenophobia and insularity, rather than initiating a re-imagining of globalization. Seyla Benhabib sketches some of the implications of the danger of closure itself originating in forms of solidarity generated in reaction, if not resistance, to globalization.

> The challenge to contemporary social and political thought in the new
> global constellation is the following: can there be coherent accounts of
> individual and collective identity which do not fall into xenophobia, intoler-
> ance, paranoia and aggression toward others? Can we establish justice and
> solidarity at home without turning in upon ourselves, without closing our
> borders to the needs and cries of others? What will democratic collective
> identities look like in the century of globalization? (Benhabib, 1998: 98)

Although the normative perspective of Critical Theory needs to be somewhat
revised, it is probably the conception of social formation that informs its
understanding of change that is more in need of revision. This is because globalization is the product of the intersection between different developmental
currents and can produce potentially conflicting tendencies. At the same time,
there are undoubtedly some dominant processes associated with globalization,
like the extension of capitalist markets and the reorienting of time and space
that is associated with the globalization of the media of communication and
finance (Rosa, 2005; 2013). There are diverse subordinate trends to do with
specific contextual manifestations of these predominant globalizing changes,
such as the variations in the conflicts between types of fundamentalism and the
culture of consumer capitalism (Eisenstadt, 1999a; 1999b; Barber, 2001).

The existing debates over whether globalization implies homogenization or
diversification, fragmentation or unification, is conditioned by how different
components are situated and combined. Beck's distinction between the *globalism*
of a 'world market that eliminates or supplants political action', and the *globality*
of a world society, where 'the notion of closed spaces is illusory' and 'nothing
which happens on our planet is only a limited local event', offers a way of
approaching the juxtaposition and combination of globalizing processes (Beck,
2000a: 9–11). Nancy Fraser (2009) similarly emphasizes the significance of *scale*
and the corresponding need to revise the 'frame' that is applied to problems of
justice. According to Fraser, the former frame derived from the imaginary
of national sovereignty and it has been unsettled by a range of interpenetrating
processes, like the flows of trade, migration, and information, that cross boundaries and generate a need to rethink public space and definitions of political
membership of a community. The disparities in participation which Fraser draws
attention to constitute a major dimension of the structural conflicts over
citizenship and work in contemporary capitalist modernity.

Global Modernities and the Movements of Critique

Despite its sometimes highly Eurocentric outlook and what Domingues (2012)
describes as a general disinterest in developing societies, Critical Theory has
always held a cosmopolitan or internationalist perspective. For this reason,
Critical Theory is interested in the constitution of another form of globalization, rather than a total rejection of globalization. The distinctive approach
of Critical Theory is no less relevant to this context, though complicated

by the demands of a polycentric theoretical framework and the multiplicity of identities created by more constant cultural interchanges. Even so, a discriminating analysis of the immanent trends and the needs of actors that point to the democratic transformation of globalization are basic requirements of Critical Theory today. It justifies an interest in the self-interpretation of the struggles and protests over globalization. The background structural conditions of these struggles are not difficult to discern, but Critical Theory is distinctively interested in clarifying and appraising the orientation towards change of these movements.

A feature of the multiple modernities of globalization is the emergence of both progressive and regressive versions of resistance, as well as occasionally unusual alliances between them. It could be argued that these kinds of alliances are a prominent feature of the recent struggles against the regimes of authoritarian nation states, such as in the case of the Arab Spring involving otherwise ideologically heterogeneous participants, like liberal democrats, Islamists, and socialists. The contestation that is more specifically focused on globalization or global capitalism will be examined later, but it would certainly be a mistake in terms of the dynamic of contemporary conflicts and historical potentialities to deny that the perceived loss of national sovereignty has provoked regressive national populist and national authoritarian movements, from support for the National Front in France, anti-immigration parties in the Netherlands, to New Dawn in Greece, to mention only some prominent European examples.

The recent tendencies toward globalization in the advanced western nation states have coincided with the dominance of neo-liberal politics and market determination of increasing dimensions of social life. In particular, this has meant the transference of market considerations into formerly bureaucratic realms of social organization, like state services relating to health and the determination of employment relations. The expansion of market considerations is especially connected to the increase in the commodification of services and leisure. At this structural level, globalization is the product of the liberalizing of trade regimes and the effacing of what Karl Polanyi termed social protection (Polanyi, 1957[1944]; Schwartz, 1998; Habermas, 2001a).

This particular trend has a number of definitely negative consequences, but I will focus on a few that have already promoted widespread interest in the 'possibility of another form of globalization'. First, the capitalist market reinforces social inequalities and processes of social exclusion. These inequalities may not conform to the class structured type of industrial capitalism. Nevertheless, the 'destructuration' of earlier class solidarity in the context of declining social protection suggests that the new inequalities are liable to become entrenched. This 'individualization' of inequality is especially due to how the expansion and structural transformation of advanced capitalist economies interconnect with traditionally less organized sectors, like employment in the secondary labour market and non-unionized groups such as casual employees in the service sector. The decline in class solidarity, and the experiences of socially excluded groups which are discrepant with the contemporary

cultural ethos of individualization, mean that these contemporary manifestations of inequality are also characterized by a psychological demoralization
(Cox, 1997; Faux and Mishel, 2001). In this context, the comparative mobility
of capital compared to labour and the economic significance of finance capital
are highly consequential.

Likewise, the extension of the 'new' international division of labour is connected to processes of the redistribution of work and employment. Or, as Beck
(2000b) suggests, the distribution of 'unemployment' or lack of work becomes
a type of organizing principle of the late-modern societies. Globalization of this
neo-liberal type exacerbates not only socio-economic inequalities but also
experiences of alienation and detachment from politically consequential processes. On the one hand, this detachment has a certain justification, given the
alleged limitation of a national state to determine economic policies and the
apparent need to conform to demands of international capital under the conditions of 'locational competition' (Habermas, 2001a). One of the reasons for the
revived interest in Karl Polanyi's arguments about the nineteenth century
'disembedding' of the market and the subsequent movement of society against
the market's autonomy is its highlighting these dimensions of the problem of
collective self-determination (Polanyi, 1957). On the other hand, Hirst and
Thompson (1996) describe the alleged loss of national sovereignty as primarily
a 'necessary illusion' (see also Weiss, 1997). Likewise, irrespective of whether
they are relatively weak and less consequential compared to capital, supranational bodies have been both a focus of discontent and seen as sources of
democratic potential. Even so, the disregard for processes of the democratic
formation of mass opinion by national and supranational political institutions
and systems of governance is equally a source of detachment or indifference to
politics. These contrasting possibilities have to some extent been played out in
relation to the European Union. Habermas' perspective on the type of social
solidarity that would enable the democratization of the European Union will
be returned to later.

The analysis of the nexus between globalization and democracy cannot
neglect the substantial divisions in wealth and power within the world capitalist system and between nation states. Globalization has hardly overturned the
distinction between core and peripheral states in the capitalist system, but the
intersections of its mechanisms and institutions with the division in the world
system have contributed to significant changes. There remain indisputable differences in development and massive global inequalities that constrain potentials for collective self-determination. Even so, globalization is related to some
important modifications in transnational relations and by definition it emphasizes the effects of interconnections. Those trends that have already been highlighted, like the international division of labour and the liberalizing of trade,
need to be supplemented by consideration of the implications of specific
regional modernization, such as that of East Asia, China and Latin America
(Bringel and Domingues, 2015). Yet, in no sense do these instances of modernization dissolve the tension between globalization and democracy. Rather, they

represent different articulations of this tension, because the nexus between globalization and democracy intermeshes with conflicts over national systems of political authority that are, at best, limited institutions of political democracy and citizenship rights. Nevertheless, these regional modernizing developments have come to underpin mass consumption in the advanced capitalist nation states. At the same time, the movement in global manufacturing has coincided with the relative marginalizing of the former working class in advanced capitalist nation states, with the decline in manufacturing occupations in many advanced capitalist nation states producing very high rates of regional and generational unemployment. In addition, the related reductions in trade union membership as a proportion of overall employment has undermined the workers' movements' economic and political capacity to mobilize, as well as affecting the general collective consciousness of these nation states (Therborn, 1995; Streeck, 2014).

The period in which globalization emerged as a dominant social scientific discourse overlapped that of the application of 'structural adjustment' regimes in many parts of the developing world, such as in Latin American states. Structural adjustment typically involved a set of austerity measures that were intended to enable a market solution to crises of national indebtedness. These measures included the reduction of state services that depend on public finance, from housing, health-care, pensions, utilities, and the depreciating of wages and employment conditions, especially the work conditions of state employees. Structural adjustment generally included the liberalizing of the standards of international investment in a national economy and the privatization of state industries. The fact that structural adjustment was largely administered by the institutions of the global economic system, such as the International Monetary Fund, and embodied the neo-liberal philosophy of the so-called Washington Consensus, constitute major sources of the view of globalization as antithetical to democracy. Indeed, the more recent European austerity programmes mirror some of the structural adjustment measures and movements resisting austerity explicitly pose the question of collective self-determination. The alter-globalization movement developed from an appreciation of the need to address the transnational dimensions of injustice, opposition to neo-liberal reforms of trade and labour, the struggles against programmes of structural adjustment, and attempts to regulate the power, as well as limit the unpredictability, of global financial capital (Pleyers, 2010).

The alter-globalization movement is a coalition of a variety of groups and movements. Southern or periphery oppositions to structural adjustments and the market integration that was enacted by trade agreements and transnational institutions were important to the emergence of alter-globalization. Similarly, social theory interpretations of the present as a third phase of modernity, that is, after the original liberal modernity of nineteenth and early twentieth century market capitalism and the more state regulated capitalism of the subsequent period of 'organized modernity' that came under strain in the last decades of the twentieth century, have highlighted the extent to which emancipatory energies and novel democratizing initiatives have developed in the global South or capitalist periphery, such as in the original location of the World Social Forum and the Brazilian democratic experiments with participatory budgeting (de Sousa Santos, 2005; Wagner, 2012; Domingues, 2012;). It would be a Eurocentric bias for Critical Theory to ignore these initiatives and movements. However, the normative and analytic considerations that Critical Theory brings to the problem of collective self-determination apply to these movements. The normative-political evaluation is relatively straightforward, but the empirical-analytical perspective that should be brought to bear upon these movements' struggles is more complicated. It depends on the position that is taken on the diversity of modernizing trajectories and the extent to which the welfare state model of citizenship is regarded as the critical counterbalance to the insecurities of contemporary capitalism.

From Organized Modernity to the Postnational Constellation

Contemporary Critical Theory cannot simply reformulate or reconstruct the perspective of Frankfurt School theorists, nor can Habermas' extant account of the relationship between the system and the lifeworld simply be transferred to the plain of globalization. In both, the context of analysis is an 'organized system of capitalism', although Habermas' theoretical framework was tailored to the critical problems of the welfare state and the fracturing of the political consensus that had underpinned it. Globalization would intensify and exacerbate these critical problems and Habermas (2001a) subsequently amended his position in *The Postnational Constellation*. Globalization promotes a new balance in the relationship between the state and the capitalist economic system. Despite the centrality of the problem of the interchange between system and lifeworld, Habermas had focused on the internal constitution of society (Habermas, 1984; 1987a). He paid less attention to external boundaries and intersocietal connections and interconnections. This could be due to his relative lack of concern with the dynamics of capitalist economy and his lesser concern with the internal dynamics of the structuration of the capitalist system results, in turn, from his interest in the normative problem of distribution, rather than processes of production. Habermas believed that class conflict had been transformed and offset by the welfare state, and that the destructive price of this intervention and class compromise would be pathologies of the lifeworld, with Weber's diagnoses of a loss of meaning and a loss of freedom in modernity providing the prototype for contemporary reification (Habermas, 1984; 1987a; 1987b).

In the third chapter, this critical diagnosis will be reformulated and consideration will be given to how the real abstraction of globalizing processes reinforces the dynamic of social disintegration. In one sense, Habermas' colonization of the lifeworld argument seemed to reflect the capacity of the state to intervene and influence economic development (Habermas, 1984; 1987a). But globalization suggests a different trajectory of economic restructuring and development; it points to the disembedding rather than just the differentiation of social relations and, in Arnason's terms, 'modernity as a field of tension' (Arnason, 1991b). Polanyi (1957) considered 'disembedding' to be the process by which the market system became autonomous and appeared to be self-regulating in its operation. Giddens likewise emphasizes the temporal and spatial 'lifting out' of social relations, but he considers 'disembedding' to be a broader tendency (Giddens, 1991; 1994b). It is promoted by media like communication technologies and the circulation of expertise, as well as by money and markets. In Giddens' opinion, this conception of disembedding breaks with the functionalist assumptions that are typically present in notions of social differentiation. Differentiation often suggests that change is a matter of adaptation and culminates in a new degree of institutional cohesion, that more complex social structures are superior to less complex, and that a self-contained societal entity undergoes a diversification of functions (Giddens, 1991). It would be extremely difficult to convincingly reconcile these functionalist assumptions with the processes of globalization and the social conflicts that they appear to generate and reinforce, although it is certainly the case that differentiation in the specific sense of *decoupling* is a primary feature of global capitalism and a major reason for the apparent limits to the democratic constitution of the social (see Domingues, 2006).

Given the changes reviewed, the Frankfurt School theorists' interpretations of capitalist modernity appear to have little to offer concerning the specifics of contemporary globalization. Yet portions of their analyses of capitalist modernity remain relevant and applicable, specifically, those relating to the commodity form and the critique of technological rationality. But the broad direction of their theory of capitalist modernity was traced out against a background that no longer applies. In this respect, their work cannot provide an orientation for constructive political change, and, in this sense, they forfeit the distinctive claims of a Critical Theory. The Frankfurt School circle wrote in the context of what Peter Wagner (1994) describes as 'organized modernity' and their critiques remain bound to this social-historical context. In the case of Adorno, this resulted in a highly sophisticated protest that is far from having exhausted its capacity for illumination. However, the more social structural groundings of his arguments are both the least original and the most dated. The key features of organized modernity were a series of conventions and corresponding practices that were generally intended to have a universal application and that were largely based on the rationality of administrative planning (Wagner, 1994). These characteristics of organized modernity can be seen in the twentieth century transformation from liberal to managed capitalism, the consolidation of the welfare state and social policy, and the standardization of mass consumption. For Wagner, organized modernity developed in response to the crisis of liberal market capitalism and in relation to socialism, it presumed the nation as the basic unit of state regulation and coordination (Wagner, 1994: 75).

Now, there is one feature of the Frankfurt School perspective that does remain relevant and that is the fact that many interpretations of globalization replicate the problems of the Marxist theory that the Frankfurt School rejected. That is, many interpretations of globalization are economically reductionist and technologically determinist. This applies even to the excellent work of Castells (1996) and authors influenced by the perspective of world systems theory (Wallerstein, 1974). Even during the phase of the 'critique of instrumental reason' and the 'dialectic of enlightenment', the Frankfurt School circle attempted to apply the method of immanent critique to discern progressive trends and development in a manner that was neither determinist nor reductionist. In my opinion, significant methodological questions are posed precisely to this facet of Critical Theory by the new types of 'disembedded' and 'distantiated' social relations that shape globalizing processes, and especially, if Beck (1994) is correct, by the predominance of side-effects in reflexive modernization. Whether these processes could mean the definitive end of immanent critique will be the topic of a later chapter, but Critical Theory's central concept of reification can be readily reworked. The concept of reification discloses a major impediment to collective self-determination and, indeed, to the recognition of the possibility of collective self-determination, by revealing the subjective experience of the forms of objectivity in capitalist society and the apparent domination of the subject by impersonal social processes (Lukács, 1971; Adorno, 1991).

There are significant globalizing developments that involve a specific type of reification due to their second order abstraction. In other words, disembedding processes, especially global financial exchange and the environmental crisis, can appear either resistant to the possibility of collective self-determination, or they seem to problematize the agency of collective self-determination by generating unanticipated outcomes and side-effects in reaction to intervening actions. This tendency for global processes to have cascading consequences is partly due to their temporal and spatial extension, but it is also a result of what Fraser describes as the problem of 'abnormal justice', which ensues from multiple confrontations generated by the same globalizing phenomena, such as disputes over variations in labour conditions, the outsourcing of production, the classification of the political rights of citizens (Fraser, 2009). What Fraser's notion of 'abnormal justice' refers to are not really new problems of justice; rather it is the dynamic of disputation that has changed. Globalization, Fraser argues, has generated uncertainties about the scope of those affected, the institutional sources of legitimate authority, and the rights of citizens, as well as workers.

These are second order abstractions that transform subjects' practices and creations into phenomena that are seemingly determined by their own logic and that now condition the objective context of the 'first order' social practices. First order abstractions result particularly from the processes of the commodification of labour and the diffusion of the instrumental attitude of commodity exchange. Because many of the same mechanisms are involved in second order abstractions, the distinction between first and second order abstractions is mainly analytical. However, second order abstractions involve a kind of reflexivity or doubling. The *mechanisms* of abstraction have increasingly become an *object* as well as the means of abstraction, such as in the case of money not only enabling the abstraction involved in exchange value and an indifference to qualitative differences between things and people that is basic to quantification. In fact, it is these processes of abstraction that become themselves objects of monetary exchange, especially after the end of the Bretton Woods agreement and the massive growth in the trade in currencies. The development of complex economic instruments, like credit default swaps, objectify the operation of first order financial mechanisms and, importantly, become the point of reference, so to speak, of their functioning. For instance, the trading in debt can directly and indirectly affect the level of indebtedness, through influencing the valuation of currencies and the rates of interest repayments (Amato and Fantacci, 2012).

These processes are undoubtedly continuous with capitalism's tendency, in Wallerstein's words, of the 'commodification of everything', yet their implication is to change some of the parameters of social action and its perceived implications (Wallerstein, 1983). First, second order abstractions are related to the growth of specific sectors of the capitalist economy, especially the expansion of finance. Second, the sense of reification that these types of abstractions generate affects not only the perspective of subjects in relation to their own action but also that of the mediating agency of the state. In fact, reification could be described as connected to the agency of the state being conditional on mechanisms that tend to diminish its effective agency, although there are elements of the dialectic of control connected to this situation and considerable variations, of course, between nations. Third, there is a certain distortion of the value system of first order commodity exchange, for instance the 'securitizing of debt' increases liquidity and becomes an intervening element in the expansion of consumption. Yet, securitization is based on distributing and diffusing risk according to principles that are quite different from those that had formerly determined the allocation of consumer credit, like the capacity to pay and the long-term calculus of mortgage repayments (Amato and Fantacci, 2012). The perverse consequence of these parallel developments is not just the paradox of the means intended to reduce the effects of risk producing an increase in risk, but also the undermining of the means of determining value and assessing outcomes. It is not by chance that commentators like Streeck state that it is 'difficult for even experts to know where their interest lies in relation to finance' and Susan George to admit that some aspects of 'credit default swaps' are difficult for her to explain and, on my reading, her comment suggests that it is difficult to determine whether what is presented as reality is actually the case in practice (Streeck, 2011; George, 2010).

The Frankfurt School's critique of the domination intrinsic to instrumental rationality and bureaucratic-administrative practices equally applied to organized modernity's models of democracy. Democracy amounted to the electoral competition of mass political parties, which were organized in a manner consistent with the same 'modernizing' principles and involved leadership by elites and experts. In this way, organized modernity's model of democracy limited the scope for participation and gave a restrictive meaning to the idea of collective self-determination. Habermas' argument that demands for greater public participation in decision-making would become a source of legitimation problems for the political-administrative system of capitalist mass democracies proved broadly correct (Habermas, 1976). However, the demand for public participation and democratization was not the only response to the crisis of legitimation in advanced capitalist societies. It was not so much the technocratic mode of suppressing normative considerations that was to alter the problems of legitimation. Habermas had envisaged that technocratic solutions were the most likely means of reducing public participation. This vision of state regulated technocratic planning amounted to an extrapolation from the principles of organized modernity. Instead, legitimation problems were somewhat reconfigured by the transfer of many state responsibilities and provisions to the market and the subjecting of the state to constraints set by the market. It modified the institutional positioning and justificatory reasoning that technical expertise and instrumental rationality applied (Pusey, 1991; Boltanski and Thévenot, 2006).

According to Streeck, the critical theory model of legitimation crisis was unprepared for the renewal of 'self-regulating market capitalism' and the actions of

> a state which, to rid itself of social expectations it could no longer satisfy, deregulated and liberalized the capitalism it was supposed to place in the service of society; and for a capitalism which found its politically organized freedom from crises too constrictive. (Streeck, 2014: 20)

As we have seen, the tendencies towards displacement of structural conflicts converged with the consolidation of globalization; and this, too, altered the conditions of legitimation. The implications of the increasing transnational flows of capital was that of enabling the market to be a greater arbiter of legitimation, whether through financial transactions or the more indirect processes of shaping expectations, such as over labour market reform and public policies. The reification of the institution of the state is evident in its apparent inability to do anything other than conform to market expectations and, in many cases, to even seek to replicate them, such as through 'outsourcing', 'downsizing', and introducing 'price-signals'. There is nothing inevitable about the fetishizing of the market and the state's veiling of its agency in conforming to the alleged expectations of the market. At the same time, demands for democratization have persisted and the models of democracy have somewhat changed and expanded, with the emergence of such models as those of deliberative democracy and associative democracy (see Browne, 2006). These recent models of democracy point to potentials for collective self-determination that have not been fully incorporated into the liberal democratic model. In short, they challenge liberal democracy's prioritizing the protection of negative liberty over the abolition of injustices that limit

substantive freedoms and they reject the instrumentalist conception of politics as mainly about citizens' choice and preferences.

Democratization and Transnational Solidarity

The contemporary modifications in the theory and practice of democracy then
inform the contention that the polarity of globalization and democracy is
superseding the preceding class dynamic as the major nexus of social change.
The work of Habermas and Giddens probably represent the most influential
attempts to explicate the implications of this new nexus of change and to
rethink the project of social democracy. Giddens' theory of modernity, as it
developed out of his deconstructive critique of historical materialism, and the
basic categories of the theory of structuration, were initially far more tailored
to the processes of globalization than Habermas' social theory. Habermas has
acknowledged that the focus of his theory of communicative action upon
developments internal to the nation state is a major limitation (Habermas,
2000). Although Habermas' theory is superior in its depiction of the cultural
suppositions of a cosmopolitan global consciousness and the cultural underpinning of democracy in modernity, Giddens' theory originally offered a better
account of the dynamics promoting globalization and the processes of their
institutionalization.

Giddens' conception of power is more fluid and complex; power is fundamental to his entire theoretical proposition. Likewise, the temporal and spatial
constitution of society is a central concern of the theory of structuration and
considered a basic feature of the elaboration of power. For Giddens, the discontinuity of capitalist modernity is specifically connected to the shifting alignment
of the relationship of social integration, that is, relations anchored in presence,
and the more abstract mediation of system integration. The latter enables
increasing 'time-space distanciation' – the interconnecting of formerly disconnected social relations and the forming of extended interdependencies. For
instance, historically the invention of writing is a major means of distanciation
compared to the oral preservation of myth, but a major historical change in
distanciation is the commodification of property (Giddens, 1981; 1990). The
latter is of decisive importance to the formation of capitalist modernity. Giddens
contends that formerly the fixed character of property in land constituted an
impediment to distanciation, whereas the commodification of property as capital enabled extended chains of exchange and the mobility of value characteristic
of monetary systems. In this sense, globalization is a species of time-space
distanciation. In the case of Giddens' (1981; 1985) theory, the notion of distanciation informs a polycentric view of societal change and analytical accounts of
social forms as involving the concentrating of developments, such as in the
expansion of social power that occurs with cities and then nation states. Rather
than presuming a central social location that subsequently undergoes internal
differentiation, the implication of this theoretical framework is that there is a
permanent tension over the boundaries of the social.

The intent of Giddens' theoretical approach is clear, though it is not always compellingly elaborated. It represents a perspective on globalization that stresses the conjunction of intersocietal processes and intersecting developments. Giddens argues that modernity is constituted by several institutional clusters: capitalism, industrialism, surveillance, and violence, although these institutional dimensions can really be related to the twin overarching changes of capitalism and the nation state (Giddens, 1981; 1985; Harrison, 2001). Leaving aside whether it is justified assertion or a simplification, Giddens further claims that the classical sociological theorists tended to focus on one dominant trend, which they regarded as constitutive of modernity. Finally, distinctive to Giddens' approach is the emphasis upon processes and dynamics of modernity; this leads to various metaphors of modernity as a 'juggernaut' and the 'runaway world' (Giddens, 1990; 1999). Despite these metaphors being descriptive rather than critical and normative in the manner of Marxist conceptions of reification, this emphasis entails certain important explanatory requirements, such as the rejection of all functionalist and teleological arguments, including particularly those of evolutionary theory. It also leads to an innovative interest in the connection of the intentional and extensional dimensions of societal change. For instance, these categories point to a connection between the intensification of the labour process and extension of the capitalist market. Yet, Giddens' (1990; 1991) later writings on modernity partly undercut this innovation of his theory of structuration and the first two volumes of the critique of historical materialism by reinterpreting the notion of intentional in strictly individualistic and personal terms; its suggestiveness is nevertheless evident from Wagner's depiction of high intensity democratization processes in former authoritarian nation states, especially Brazil (Wagner, 2012).

The point that I wish to make here is that Giddens' theory of structuration originally contained some valuable conceptions that are relevant to the problem Critical Theory has to address. That is, the problem of developing a methodological perspective appropriate to understanding the globalizing processes' transformation of the social. Giddens' later writings on globalization do not always apply these concepts to their best advantage and there is a discernible shift away from the problems of domination. It may be for these reasons that Giddens' 'the Third Way' political position appears to accept much of the parameters established by the neo-liberal interpretation of globalization, especially in terms of policy requirements. Despite its avowed aim of contesting neo-liberalism, critics argue that his version of third way politics presses the dilemmas of the welfare state in much the same ideological direction (see Giddens, 2000). Significantly, in attempting to derive a cosmopolitan model of democracy from globalization's immanent processes, David Held and his collaborators systematically apply the social distinction that Giddens drew between 'extensity' and 'intensity' (Held et al., 1999). They conclude that a 'double democratization' is the most appealing and appropriate response to the dilemmas of the establishment of global interconnections and the emergence of modes of power beyond the nation state. Double democratization is, on the one hand, the processes of the 'deepening' of democracy within a national community, through its introduction into realms outside of formal political authority, and, on the other hand,

> the extension of democratic forms and processes across territorial borders. Democracy for the new millennium must allow cosmopolitan citizens to gain access to, mediate between and render accountable the social, economic and political processes and flows that cut across and transform their traditional community boundaries. (Held et al., 1999: 450)

Double democratization is undoubtedly desirable, but the analysis of Held and his collaborators presumes that there should be a convergence between 'extensity' and 'intensity'. A parallel argument is the neo-liberal belief that market extension produces efficiency. Now, leaving aside the empirical objections that have been marshalled against free trade regimes, the extensity and intensity of democratization is logically different from that of the market. But this logical difference implies that the two types of democratization are liable to contradict one another and that the alignment between them cannot be taken for granted. The multiple modernities perspective points to how democracy can mobilize prior cultural orientations, political authority and long-standing social identities, and thereby promote contradictions between layers and domains of democracy. In fact, this explains why many democratizing transitions, like those recently in Egypt or two decades earlier in Russia, are not just fragile but subjected to processes of delimitation and reversal. Similarly, modernizing movements, including sometimes those for democracy, have been countered by opposed movements that may not have been previously as effectively mobilized, such as in the case of the decolonizing Arab nationalism being subsequently challenged by politicized Islam (Eisenstadt, 1999a; Kepel, 2006). These contradictory developments do not constitute grounds for opposing double democratization, but they are suggestive of how it depends on social preconditions that go beyond formal political institutions and how reactions to other dimensions of globalization may precipitate democratic, as well as undemocratic, challenges to democracy. Despite the further qualifications suggested by Albrow's (1996) conception of world society as 'multiplicity without unity', the combination of these two dimensions of democratization would be a nascent global civil society.

It is at the level of theorizing a postnational civil society that Habermas' writings make possibly their most important contributions to the task of analytically and normatively coming to terms with the polarity of globalization and democracy. Habermas argues that there is a line of development for the constitution of national identity that corresponds to the abstract principles of democratic citizenship. Namely, the version of citizenship that conforms to universalistic principles, and for which then, the application of basic rights implies the equal treatment of all. He believes that this universalistic perspective is the basis for 'the inclusion of the other', or the two-fold expansion of the rights of citizenship (Habermas, 1996a; 1998). First, the extension of citizenship rights to groups that were formerly excluded from full participation and the application of formal equality. Second, the expansion of the areas of social relations that receive rights and guarantees. Indeed, these developments are central, for him, to the development of the welfare state and this expansion of rights is connected to the democratic principle of enabling the participation of citizens in the authorship of the laws that they are also the addressees of (Habermas, 1996a). In this participatory democratic sense, the ideal of an autonomous citizenry needs to address factual inequality. Of course, what distinguishes Habermas' approach is his grounding of all of these notions of rights, citizenship, and popular sovereignty in communicative action and its translation into a concept of deliberative politics. Moreover, this approach provides a framework for explaining processes of democratization and evaluating the extent of these processes.

Habermas' general model of modernity is tied to the idea of coordination between money, power and solidarity, as three means of integration (Habermas, 1996a). In Habermas' opinion, it is clear that globalization has unfolded primarily through the extension of the market; and hence, to a large extent, the problem of democratization is precisely whether democratic structures and democratic procedures of will-formation will follow the same process of extension as that of the market. At times, Habermas seems to think that there is the potential for such an extension in the European community. In other words, he argues that just as the economic integration of Europe has proceeded, it is necessary to institutionalize a postnational or cosmopolitan version of democracy. The legitimating conditions of democracy, however, imply that this initiative should emanate from social solidarity. Postnational solidarity encounters the discrepancy of the modern nation state applying universal standards internally to its citizenry and the nationalist consciousness that regularly accepts the state's disregarding of these principles in relation to external communities. Habermas' rethinking of collective self-determination then confronts what Fraser has described as the 'metapolitical' question of defining 'who' is the subject of justice or rights, and the way in which this cosmopolitan position may stand in tension with other sources of collective identification (Fraser, 2009).

In *The Postnational Constellation*, Habermas (2001a) points to the contrasting phases of the structural and cultural opening and closure of European societies in arguing for a new regime of economic regulation. His concern with social forms beyond the nation state centred originally on the relationship of national communities to supranational institutions and non-government organizations. In effect, he addressed the prospects of postnational identity and postnational citizenship. Habermas' analysis of these fit his general historical model of the development of moral consciousness and social identity. The chief achievement of national consciousness was the establishment of a 'solidarity amongst strangers' (Habermas, 1998: 111). He believes that national identity is a form of social integration, which involves a higher level of abstraction than that of the premodern and early modern modes of integration. In this sense, he sees national identity as a functional solution to the dissolution of early modern forms of integration. It was not so much popular sovereignty and human rights, but the

> modern idea of the nation, which first inspired in the inhabitants of state territories an awareness of the new, legally and politically mediated form of community. (Habermas, 1998: 113)

This analysis leads Habermas to consider how a postnational identity would be a further application of the same logic of abstraction. In other words, it is another mode of the mediation of the universal and the particular. However, this conception also requires his underlining two features of his broader theoretical perspective. The first is his arguments concerning the emergence of a transnational public sphere. He perceives an immanent trend towards an enlargement of the public sphere beyond the framework of singular nation state. Habermas' analysis of nationalism draws on his own model of the public sphere, as well as Benedict Anderson's (1983) account of an 'imagined community' constituted partly through the media of the press, and consequently similar types of developments at a transnational level constitute another form of the public sphere. Of course, Habermas is aware of the limitations of this process and the extent to which this type of public sphere would probably be driven by the imperatives of commercial media. The criticism that under present conditions transnational communication would be just another version of the integration of the market fits entirely with Habermas' own critique of the actually existing public sphere (Habermas, 1989b; 1992b).

The barest outline of a transnational or possibly global public sphere indicates that Habermas' basic intuition of the intersubjective communicative constitution of a social identity cannot apply to it in quite the same way that does in the case of more direct and less mediated interaction. The foundation of identity in the practice of communicative action persists, but globalizing processes raise complexity to a new level. This complex mediation of identities, through largely privately owned technological apparatuses of communication, inevitably influences the framing of cultural interchange in the transnational public sphere. This is where the second broad theoretical component of Habermas' argument becomes significant. Habermas' (1996a) conception of the intrinsic connection between the rule of law and democracy becomes a critical feature of postnational modes of social integration. He argues that from the outset of a democratic institutionalizing of a modern territorially based state, the rule of law provided a significant translation between identity and citizenship. In part, this argument is the distinctive component of his understanding of nationalism and postnational citizenship, because it is the grounds of his notion of 'constitutional patriotism'. Habermas contrasts this constitutional and legislative definition of a national community with the more ascriptive ethno-nationalist versions. The latter accentuate features of the pre-political community, believing these to be the ultimate basis of solidarity. From this contrast, it is evident that unlike constitutional patriotism, this ascriptive version of nationalism is not, on Habermas' analysis, logically or intrinsically democratic. In fact, he wants to suggest that the Janus-faced character of nationalism goes back to this version of nationalism; that is, the conception of the nation as a community of shared history and destiny. The alternate 'constitutional patriotism' exhibited in a liberal political culture

> heightens an awareness of both the diversity and the integrity of different forms of life coexisting in a multicultural society. In a future Federal Republic of European States, the same legal principles would also have to be interpreted from the perspectives of different national traditions and histories. (Habermas, 1996b: 500)

The limitations of Habermas' notions of constitutional patriotism and cosmopolitan democracy lie less in their normative content and more in the empirical wedding of them to a version of a linear modernization. His approach does not change to the perspective of multiple modernities that is relevant to a globalizing context. Still, Habermas does not make the mistake of presuming that democratization is intrinsic to the process of globalization. Unlike some critical sociology, his critique does not participate in the same discursive space as the neo-liberalism it contests. Touraine (2000) argues that this space is itself the problem, because it legitimates too many dimensions of the 'desocializing' tendencies of globalization. In my opinion, there is no immanent dialectic to the nexus between globalization and democracy. This lack could represent a substantial problem for twenty-first century Critical Theory, because the interdependent quality of social relations has provided a guide for locating the trajectory of social change. Globalization can be seen to both create and destroy social interdependence. Yet, because it does so in multiple, rather than singular, fashion, globalization introduces another degree of indeterminacy about the parameters of a democratic society.

Conclusion

The contradiction between globalization and democracy is not the kind of contradiction that is examined in the next chapter's reconceptualization of alienation. That chapter is concerned with a specific form of the contradictory relationship of social action and social institutions. The contradiction between globalization and democracy is less one of direct interdependency, partly because it is concerned with conditions relating to the constitution of interdependency and the negation of it. For this reason, the nexus of globalization and democracy involves a complicated and multi-faceted dialectic of control. It is not really a contradiction in the Hegelian sense that Marx intended in his interpretation of capitalist class relations, that is, a contradiction in which the unfolding of one process generates another that negates it. In this sense, the argument of much critical sociology that the conflict of globalization and democracy supersedes class conflict is somewhat misleading. Rather, the dialectical relationship of globalization and democracy is a contradiction in the sense of the antinomy of opposing social imaginaries. All the same, there is a version of globalization that already involves, or could involve, the extension of democracy, since it could lead to the institution of a cosmopolitan form of democracy against its limited national definition (see Browne, 2006; Beck, 2005; 2006; Benhabib, 2006; Fine, 2007; Delanty, 2009). Indeed, as recent social theory discussions of the European Union appear to demonstrate, the more globalization unfolds, the more limited is the national institution of democracy. And consequently, the greater is the necessity of democratizing the transnational order and its major institutions.

Similarly, the alter-globalization, or global justice, movement perceives globalization as creating opportunities for democratization from 'below' (Eschle, 2001; Brecher et al., 2002; della Porta et al., 2006). This points to the contradiction between the potentiality and the actuality of globalization. Alter-globalization opposes existing globalization and argues for 'another world'. It thereby alludes to the deep-seated conflict between two contradictory social imaginaries, which amount to different ways of constituting the 'world' or understandings of reality (Castoriadis, 1987; Karagiannis and Wagner, 2007). One is based on processes that equate social progress with capitalist development and whose global extension limits democratic control. These processes of globalization are continuous with, what Castoriadis described as, the capitalist imaginary of the unlimited rational domination and control of nature and society (Castoriadis, 1991; Browne, 2005). Streeck (2014: 46) rightly points out that market capitalism's limiting democratic control and regulation of its operations is not the same as capitalism being free from its dependence on 'governance'. Governance is still necessary for coordination and the protection of interests through the exercise of power. For this reason, there is the possibility that the effects of globalizing processes and 'second order abstractions' are the 'hollowing out' of political democracy or, in Crouch's terms, 'post-democracy' (Crouch, 2005).

The preceding analysis drew attention to some elements of the capitalist imaginary's contemporary reconfiguration. It proposed that these changes were connected to the dynamic of the dialectic of control, the new systematic form of reification, and the complicated redefinitions of the relationship that the capitalist system has to political orders. In reviewing social theory discussions of the conflict between globalization and democracy, Habermas and Giddens were shown to offer broadly social democratic responses to the new nexus of change and they each discerned varying potentials for democratization. It could be argued that Habermas and Giddens have redefined the way in which society acts upon itself, such as in terms of the model of deliberative democracy and cosmopolitan law, and that this is a constructive response to the problem of collective self-determination. Nevertheless, there is still something highly counterfactual about these proposals. It is not even clear that the outcomes of realizing such proposals would be superior to the welfare state compromise. By contrast, some strands of the alter-globalization movement have sought to far more radically mobilize parts of modernity's other major social imaginary: the project of autonomy. From the perspective of Critical Theory, it is worth noting how the alter-globalization movement seeks to prefigure a different future on this basis. The Excursus that follows discusses how these strands of alter-globalization engage in practices that they believe may enable the creation and diffusion of another set of values.

Excursus: Alter-Globalization and Anti-Austerity Protests

The problems of collective self-determination have been somewhat reconfig-ured. It is not just that accelerated globalization has altered the relationship of capitalism to democracy; the prospects for collective self-determination have been modified by dissatisfaction with liberal democratic institutions. This dissatisfaction has given impetus to various attempts to instantiate par-ticipatory democratic forms of politics. Globalization not only challenges the sovereignty of the nation state as a result of worldwide economic processes, transnational political integration and the impact of distant events on the national and local. It changes some of the conditions of the constitution of the social, and thereby problematizes the framing of the sense of collective that is the point of reference for the notion of collective self-determination. I have argued that globalization's dynamics are incorporated into the contested constitution of the social, although the diversity and unevenness of contexts means that globalization does not have uniform consequences. It has been noted that there are enormous differences between the capitalist core and the periphery's capacities for collective self-determination, although one of the significant modifications of the past decades has been the development of, what Peter Wagner (2012) terms, 'high intensity' democratization in nation states outside of the capitalist core, especially notable is the Brazilian demo-cratic innovations. José Maurício Domingues (2015) contrasts this with the retraction of elements of democracy in core nation states during the period of accelerated globalization or the third phase of capitalist modernization (Wagner, 1994).

Likewise, the power to mobilize of movements committed to different politi-cal ideologies and religious beliefs has been seen to be important to the genesis of multiple modernities. Although the alter-globalization movement is a het-erogeneous coalition of struggles, there is a broadly shared set of oppositions that unites these movements. There are two features of strands of alter-globali-zation and anti-austerity protests that are salient to the Critical Theory prob-lem of discerning potentials for immanent-transcendence. The first is a rejection of aspects of the capitalist imaginary, and the second is how the practices of these protests and movements incorporate elements of democratic creativity. The latter involves the extending and deepening of democracy through democratizing practices and innovations. In particular, it seeks to make democracy a 'way of life' through the communicative experiences of collective problem solving and to transform the unjust and heteronomous relationships that social institutions have to the practices of their social instituting (see Browne, 2014c).

The typical themes of alter-globalization are not difficult to identify and the contesting of these dimensions of globalization are generally compatible with different types of politics. There is the opposition to the neo-liberal developments that have facilitated the globalizing of capitalism and the privileging of the world market. In other words, there is the opposition to trade liberalization, the increase in foreign direct investment, and the expansion of the power of transnational corporations. These developments are considered to have resulted in an exacerbating of the injustices of the global capitalist system, such as through enabling the exploitation of labour in both developed and developing nation states. More specifically, there is the opposition to the various transnational agencies and economic agreements that facilitate and enforce the global market system, like the International Monetary Fund, and the General Agreement of Trade and Tariffs. The most high profile protests of the alter-globalization movement have often been those directed at the meetings and summits of global economic coordination, such as the Seattle protests and the initiation of the World Social Forum as an alternative to the World Economic Forum.

For the most part, the alter-globalization movement considers that the agencies of the global economic system impose unjust conditions and that they have usurped the power of communities to control their life situations. In this way, alter-globalization addresses the problem of collective self-determination, because it challenges the legitimacy of global economic forums, meetings, and agreements to formulate and implement policies that will affect states, groups and individuals, that did not participate in their formulation and whose situations, as well as opinions, they believe are disregarded. In this, the alter-globalization movement challenges some of the distinctive contemporary transnational institutional forms of the capitalist imaginary and their power to define the future.

The opposition to the elite coordination of globalization can nevertheless take diverse forms. It has already been noted how many national populist responses to globalizing processes differ from alter-globalization. Indeed, the change from 'anti-globalization' to alter-globalization as the prevailing definition of the movement demonstrates this quite different orientation. Unlike nationalist oppositions to globalization, alter-globalization is a movement that is, in principle, constituted by its commitment to transnational justice. Of course, transnational or global justice can be formulated as an abstract normative goal and it is certainly the case that segments of the alter-globalization movement do not hold a cosmopolitan outlook in defining the institutional means of achieving it. Breno Bringel, however, considers that the evolution of the alter-globalization movement points to a shift from expressions of transnational solidarity with particular national projects for justice and autonomy 'towards a growing solidarity with a cause, movement and/or experience'. He suggests that one can even speak of '*a progressive de-nationalization of contemporary internationalism*' (Bringel, 2015: 123; emphasis in the original).

Despite the difficulties and the different ways of defining transnational justice, what is important in the present context is the contrasting conceptions of the immanent potentials for transformation that are found in the practices of the alter-globalization movement. In fact, it is not very difficult to discern parallels here with earlier political struggles and divisions, like those between reform and revolution, or spontaneous action versus party political organization. Geoffrey Pleyers makes a useful ideal-typical distinction between two strands of alter-globalization: the 'way of reason' which seeks to promote a superior economic and political rationality to that of existing globalization, and the 'way of experience' which prioritizes the experience of another reality to that of global capitalism (Pleyers, 2010). In my opinion, the normative-political orientation of Critical Theory is one that should aspire to reconcile and overcome the underlying binary between these two 'ways' of alter-globalization. This synthetic aspiration was one of the senses in which Critical Theory was distinguished from more orthodox strands of Marxism, since Critical Theory argued that radical social transformation entails both objective and subjective change, which are interrelated but non-identical.

The radical questioning of the capitalist imaginary and elements of democratic creativity can be found in the two strands of alter-globalization. My focus here will be slightly more on the practices of the 'way of experience' and the recent anti-austerity mobilizations, particularly those of the Occupy protests and the Spanish *Indignados*. Broadly, the political orientation and proposals for transformation of alter-globalization's way of reason often overlap those of Habermas and, to a lesser extent, Giddens. Giddens' third way politics is undoubtedly based on a more positive view of market capitalism and a more optimistic assessment of liberal democratic institutions and their potentials (Giddens, 1998). However, the way of reason shares the broad social democratic interest of these two theorists in the consolidation of institutional regulations that limit the social inequalities resulting from the intensification of globalization and the market's disorganizing of other mechanisms of social coordination. For instance, the Attac organization, which is Pleyers' main exemplar of the way of reason, originated as a supporter of the proposed Tobin tax on financial transactions and Attac has sought to mobilize on the basis of citizenship.

Similarly, it is not difficult to appreciate why non-government organizations and other representations of interests, like trade unions and diverse rights groups, seek to achieve change through processes that are grounded in rationality. These organizations define their objectives in terms of altering institutions and their policies, for instance, through the promotion of international agreements on climate change or the reduction of poverty. It is equally important to point out that the distinction between the way of reason and the way of experience should not be taken as one that is invariant. How this distinction is actually drawn would change according to different global contexts and in relation to different political cultures. It should be understood as representing broad general tendencies. Indeed, seen in these terms, the distinction between the ways of 'reason' and 'experience' is not just conditioned by the practical orientation of struggling actors. It is influenced by the configuration of institutions, especially those of the political order, and the variations in the historical accretions of the social imaginary of autonomy. Pleyers' distinction between the ways of reason and experience is nevertheless important in clarifying different general orientations and the contrasting positions on questions enfolded within the practices of alter-globalization, like those of the import of expertise and intellectuals, the meaning of democracy, the conception of social change, and basic political concerns like the relationship between means and ends (Pleyers, 2010).

Sections of the alter-globalization movement and protests against austerity programmes can be considered to have gone beyond the social democratic objective of regulating global capitalist markets. These strands of the movements seek to enact practices that constitute a rupture with the meanings and orientations of capitalism. Of course, the extent to which these movements are actually able to accomplish this rupture beyond the more sporadic and delimited instances of actual protests is an open question. It would be reasonable to conclude that it is probably quite limited, especially if the overall range of participants is taken into account and the actual dynamics of contestation are carefully scrutinized (Calhoun, 2013). Even so, the notion of a rupture with capitalist ideologies is important to the self-interpretation of these sections of the alter-globalization movement and the protests against austerity, like those of the *Indignados* in Spain and the Occupy movement that originated in the USA (Browne and Susen, 2014). These movements against austerity have sought to enact radical democratic modes of association in attempts to prefigure a type of collective self-determination that is not a capitalist form of power (Graeber, 2012). There is another sense in which these movements are anti-power in a way that contrasts with the more social democratic aim of regulating and reorienting globalization. These strands of the alter-globalization seek to resist the notion of collective self-determination being channelled through the state. Pleyers sketches these experiments in alternative modes of association and organization in the following terms:

> The organizations of the movement constitute other *spaces of experi-ence* which must allow individuals to realize themselves and experiment concretely with practical alternatives. The way of organizing the movement thus assumes a crucial importance, 'because it also projects what could be another society'. It must consequently reflect the alternative values of the way of subjectivity: horizontal organization, strong

> participation, limited delegation, rotation of tasks, respect for diversity, etc. (Pleyers, 2010: 43; emphasis in the original)

Like segments of the broader alter-globalization movement, the *Indignados* and the Occupy protests accentuate the capacities for self-organization and adhere to a radical democratic conception of autonomy. Although the alter-globalization movement, in the broad sense, overlaps many existing political parties, trade unions and other associations, the radical democratic strands of the movement are in principle opposed to existing organizations assuming a directing position. Indeed, this represents a significant source of tension within the alter-globalization movement and there is a considerable dispute over whether institutionalization undermines the potential to constitute an alternative to the capitalist order. Now, this critical distancing from existing forms of political practice is simultaneously apparent in the original construction of large-scale events, like the World Social Forum, and it is sometimes undermined by the organization of these events, such as through the participation of select national leaders or the seeming lack of accountability of the event organizers. The original charter of the World Social Forum explicitly sought to avoid the dominance of party political organizations (Gautney, 2012). Over time this intention has arguably come into conflict with the significant role of non-government organizations, as well as the involvement at times of state representation, in the Forums. Despite the risk that institutionalization may undermine its utopian potential, the World Social Forum's radical democratic principles constitute an alternative to capitalist societies' dominant mode of political organization. Boaventura de Sousa Santos argues that it is the utopian design of the World Social Forum that enabled cohesion and mutual dialogue.

> It helps to maximize what unites and minimize what divides, it celebrates communication rather than disputes over power, and it emphasizes a strong presence rather than a strong agenda. (de Sousa Santos, 2008: 254)

Similarly, strands of the anti-austerity protests sought to instantiate the principles of radical democracy through breaking with the typical structures of delegation and representation that prevail in liberal democracies and party political organizations. The Occupy protests sought instead to promote full participation through giving all those present opportunities to voice their opinions in the public assemblies and to directly participate in the decision-making (Castells, 2012). In a similar vein, there were no official spokespersons for the Occupy movements who were delegated with the authority to represent other participants' opinions. In addition to the long established participatory democratic critiques of political delegation and representation, sociological analyses have highlighted the salience of experience to these alter-globalization movements'

practices (McDonald, 2006; Pleyers, 2010). The experience of alternative possibilities is considered to depend on actual participation and that the experience of
participation enables the self-transformation of subjectivity, as well as the opposition to the institutional reality of global capitalism. In this understanding of
experience, there is something of a melding of the Romantic ideas of the creative
imagination and authentic subjective self-expression with the more contemporary view of the creative capacity of self-organizing networks and autopoetic
systems (Boltanski and Chiapello, 2005; Roberts, 2012).

These anti-austerity movements sought to challenge notions of hierarchical
authority and the mechanisms that separate participants from authority. By
rejecting vertical structures, the movements attempted to organize themselves
horizontally. Horizontal organization presupposes that equality and autonomy
are reconciled and mutually reinforcing. There can be no genuine direct democracy without participants who are autonomous and equal. Naturally, even
where there is general agreement regarding the principles of autonomy and
equality, horizontal organization is difficult to realize in practice. It entails not
just the renunciation of a hierarchy of positions, but also the presumption that
hierarchical authority accrues to expertise and experience. Given the national
form of the historical institutionalization of citizenship, it is sometimes
assumed that intense participation and an acceptance of the equality of participants requires a very strong sense of communal bonds and shared values.
Manuel Castells (2011; 2012) suggests that the horizontal organization of
these anti-austerity movements drew instead on different orientations. That is,
the potential for discovering commonality through the process of participating
in the movement's practices. A sense of meaningful 'togetherness', Castells
argues, emerged from the horizontal 'multimodal' networks of the Internet and
urban public space.

> The horizontality of networks supports cooperation and solidarity while
> undermining the need for formal leadership. (Castells, 2012: 225;
> emphasis in the original)

In these ways, the anti-austerity movements' practices sought to realize a key
intention of John Dewey's original conception of creative democracy, that is,
that democratic ends require democratic means (Dewey, 1993; see Browne,
2009a; 2009b; 2014c).

The anti-austerity movements deployed the ideal of reappropriation. That is,
they sought to initiate a re-invention of social relations in ways that break with
the capitalist logic of private appropriation and expropriation. Specifically, it
is through the practices of direct democracy and public participation that they
seek to transform subjective experiences and collective understandings (Browne
and Susen, 2014). There is a strong connection between the aspiration of reappropriation and collective self-determination, because reappropriation contests
the tendencies of displacement and disembedding that are so significant to

global capitalism. Although the regulation of global markets may be important to achieving reappropriation, reappropriation requires a strong sense of meaningful control and active engagement in the constitution of global process. One of the contradictions of austerity regimes is that they deploy the same market rationality that generated the crisis and recession to achieve their resolution. This contradiction is itself indicative of the power of the instituted capitalist imaginary and the reification of 'second order abstractions', particularly those associated with 'finacialization'.

The broad alter-globalization movement and the protests against austerity programmes have importantly sought to contest the capitalist imaginary's definition of reality and they have, through their respective reflections on the nexus of theory and practice, inspired experiments in participatory democratic forms of organization. One important feature of this movement's self-understanding is the acknowledgement that the most progressive current initiatives for radical democratization originate in diverse global contexts, rather than being founded on developments in the most highly modernized nation states. The alter-globalization movement is particularly significant in another respect. It has to some extent explicitly confronted the problem of collective self-determination and the potential need to redefine the relevant 'collective', particularly beyond what Fraser has termed the national frame (Fraser, 2009). Alter-globalization is a significant constituent of a nascent transnational public sphere and it has broached some of the conundrums of a cosmopolitan mode of collective self-determination, particularly with respect to the need to transcend the injustices of the global capitalist order (Kurasawa, 2014).

In this Excursus, I have highlighted the positive potentials of the alter-globalization movement, whilst noting some of the dilemmas that it has confronted and the innovative responses that have ensued from this confrontation. At the same time, the questions explored in the subsequent chapters could form the basis for a more complete assessment of the alter-globalization movement. Notably, it is clear that the participatory democratic practices of the alter-globalization movement have sought to address the problem of alienation. However, if the problem of alienation is to be fully addressed then it is necessary to take further into account the complications of institutionalization. Similarly, even though alter-globalization may prefigure a progressive transformation of capitalist social relations, the processes of social disintegration that ensue from accelerated globalization have led to displaced reactions and political forms of contestation that diverge from the normative expectations of a cosmopolitan public sphere. The dialectics of control that are present in these two dimensions of the structural contradictions of contemporary capitalist modernity will be explored in the next chapters.

Moreover, while the alter-globalization movement can serve to illuminate the distinctive Critical Theory intention of synthesizing normative and substantive critical analyses of the present phases of capitalist development, the ensuing synthesis can be applied to the movement and utilized in the assessment of its potentials. In a similar vein, these movements' practices point towards a synthesis of positive liberty and social justice, but the characteristics of this synthesis demands further justification. In particular, it is necessary to demonstrate how such a synthesis can be broadly grounded in the processes of the constitution of society. Nevertheless, the alter-globalization movement and anti-austerity protests interface with the utopian component of Critical Theory through positing alternatives to the capitalist imaginary and engaging in practices that contain elements of democratic creativity. In short, the alter-globalization movements are implicated in the dynamics of dialectics of control and they have disclosed contradictions that risked being obscured by the closure of the world enacted by the capitalist imaginary.

2

FROM THE CRITIQUE OF OBJECTIFICATION TO THE RECONCEPTUALIZATION OF ALIENATION

Introduction

There are few categories that were as affected by the twentieth century's political and intellectual vicissitudes as that of the concept of alienation. The prominence that the concept of alienation had during the 1960s and 70s would be followed by its virtual disappearance from Critical Theory. However, there has recently been an international revival of interest in alienation and the critical potential of this category (Haber, 2007; Jaeggi, 2014[2007]; Rosa, 2010). The renewed interest is primarily a response to two interconnected factors. The first is some dissatisfaction with the predominance in Critical Theory of normative concepts derived from liberal political philosophy, like social justice, rights and even democracy (see Renault, 2007). These concepts are perceived to be limited in their capacity to articulate experiences of subordination and unable to account for structural transformations in society. In these Critical Theory discussions, the concept of alienation serves either as a way to rethink the normative categories derived from liberal political philosophy or as an alternative to them. The second factor precipitating this conceptual renewal is, then, the restructuring of contemporary capitalism and the need to apprehend the paradoxical consequences of these changes in social relations and work organization. There is already a considerable literature on how contemporary capitalism generates discordant relationships to oneself, others and the world (Deranty, 2008; 2009a; Dejours, 2012; Sennett, 1998; 2006; Hochschild, 1983). Of course, the term 'alienation' never disappeared from popular discourses, yet even here it appears increasingly apposite to interpreting recent disaffection and social conflict, as in the case of the United Kingdom's 2011 riots (Bauman, 2012; McDonald, 2012).

Now, in my opinion, these considerations justify the reconceptualization of alienation and they specify some of its key requirements: the concept of alienation has to be explanatory as well as normative, it has to elucidate features of contemporary capitalism and forms of social organization from the perspective of participants, and it should extend on the pre-theoretical everyday usage of the term through a more precise specification of the social processes of alienation and their reproduction. If these stipulates can be satisfied, then the concept of alienation would remain central to Critical Theory, particularly because it signifies a condition that social agents resist and struggle to transform. The persistence of alienation is damaging or destructive of subjectivity, yet it endures through the contribution that alienated practices make to the reproduction of social structure.

Although the conception of alienation that I propose highlights its convergence with other dimensions of subordination, alienation is not adequately captured in categories like inequality and injustice. Rather, the concept of alienation should be formulated in terms of a social ontology, as it refers to practices that are foundational 'for our existence' and that generate social institutions (Honneth, 2008: 21; see also Giddens, 1979; 1984; Stones, 2005). This means that the reconceptualization of alienation should be consistent with the broad intentions of Marx's notion of objectification (Marx, 1977a). Significantly, it was through its connection to objectification that the concept of alienation obtained widespread application and could exemplify an account of social constitution that focused on the interplay of social action and social structure. Nevertheless, any reconceptualization of alienation has to take into account the substantial criticisms of the notion of objectification and their sequels.

Of the manifold criticisms of Marx's original philosophical anthropology of labour as objectifying activity, the most consequential were those concerning its deficiencies with respect to symbolic meanings and the cultural construction of identity. These critiques would, on the one hand, shape endeavours in Critical Theory to develop conceptual equivalents for the concept of alienation based on new theoretical syntheses, drawing particularly on linguistics, psychoanalysis and phenomenology. On the other hand, these critiques spoke to demands for categories that are relevant to different, though related, experiences of suffering and subordination, like those of dehumanization, subjection, and exclusion. This array of concepts enhances the complexity and precision of critical analysis, yet the significant methodological and practical differences that many of these categories have with the concept of alienation warrants clarification. The second section's exploration of these conceptual equivalents' theoretical suppositions and social-political implications enables a clearer delineation of the concept of alienation and explains how its reconceptualization is informed by debates over social action in contemporary social theory.

The notion of alienation that I develop is intended to be relevant to a broad range of institutional contexts, although the capitalist work organization remains exemplary and practices pioneered there tend to be reiterated in other domains. In this respect, my intention is similar to that which Cornelius Castoriadis (1987) pursued in extending the task of elucidating alienation to the entire range of contexts in which *instituted* society appears independent of the practices of its social *instituting*. At the same time, how I define alienation has strong continuities with Castoriadis' earlier interpretation of capitalism's basic contradiction and Boltanski and Chiapello's (2005) account of how new capitalism reformulated this contradiction. Castoriadis (1974a; 1987) argued that capitalist production is dependent on the creativity of individuals while excluding them from actual control over their activity. I argue that alienation involves the thwarted participation of individuals and experiences that are destructive of subjectivity. Individuals' experiences and interpretations of compelled, but limited, action expose the contradiction between institutions' normative representations and the structural conditions of their reproduction. Institutions have an appropriative relationship to action, because they are, to use Boltanski's (2011) term, incomplete and therefore dependent. I suggest that the concept of alienation should clarify the deformations that ensue from these contradictory forms of interdependence. In particular, I claim that alienation manifests itself in social conflicts and the discrepancies between the life-projects of individuals and the orientation of institutions. It is one of the paradoxes of contemporary capitalist modernization that institutions claim to facilitate the realization of individual life-projects but are actually organized in ways that undermine these projects (Honneth and Hartmann, 2012).

Objectification and its Critique

The social ontological significance of objectification is a general underlying assumption of Marx's theory, since the capacity of labour to create and transform the world through objectifying itself in products is central to Marx's conception of the paradigmatic character of production (Marx, 1977a; Márkus, 1986a). It is through production, Marx argued, that human needs are satisfied and the reproduction of society depends on objectification (Heller, 1976; 1982; Márkus, 1986a). For Marx, the objectifying activity of labour was the basis of the self-constitution of the subject and he criticized Hegel for mistakenly equating objectification and alienation (Marx, 1977a). In Marx's opinion, alienation was the outcome of a historically distorted form of objectification and this distortion manifests itself in the inversions inherent in capitalist production. Marx argued that under capitalism the object dominates the subject, or, in different terms, that the product becomes independent of the producer and the means of the worker's social subordination. Marx explained alienation in terms of the capitalist division of labour's dispossession and appropriation of direct producers' objectification. However, following Hegel, Marx's concept of alienation was influenced by the Romantic Movement's expressivist interpretation of creation (Taylor, 1975; 1989). Marx contended that the objectified product was an externalization of the subjectivity of the labourer and he claimed in the *1844 Manuscripts* that the alienated relationship that the labouring subject has to its own activity possesses a certain genetic primacy (Marx, 1977a; Márkus, 1982). In effect, Marx argued that the process of alienated labour gave rise to private property, but that capitalism's cyclical inversion subsequently meant that private property conditioned alienated labour.

The notion of objectification enabled Marx's concept of alienation to be simultaneously normative and explanatory. Marx's critique of alienation implied a counter-image of objectification that incorporated aspects of the Romantic Movement's idea that self-actualization depends on creative modes of self-expression and the Aristotelian sense of praxis as those types of action that find their ends within themselves (Habermas, 1987b). Of course, Marx considered that such self-determining and creative actions presupposed the transcendence of capitalism, however, this did not mean that they had to be posited as normative ideals that were external to historical development. Marx's notion of objectification delineated the potential for social progress, because it disclosed the historical basis of alienation in the antagonism between the actual social reality of capitalism and the unrealized potential that it contains.

Although the conflict between the capitalist form of ownership and the strictly technical-industrial potential of the forces of production is a dimension of this antagonism, Marx's conception of alienation 'brings into focus', as György Márkus explains, the process of 'involuntary socialisation' (Márkus, 1982: 146). Marx argued that the increasingly interdependent and social character of capitalist production is not the outcome of the actions of a self-determining collective and the free association of individuals. Rather, just as individuals experience their labouring activity as belonging to capital and the appropriated products of their objectifying activity as independent of them, individuals misinterpret the actual social and cooperative character of production as an attribute of capital and subjects experience themselves as alienated from one another in their social relations.

The young Marx additionally distinguished the potential from the actual in terms of the alienation of individuals from their essential humanity or species-being [*Gattungswesen*]. According to Marx, production should be the mode by which individuals participate in the universality of humanity and it should enable the realization of the distinctive potential of the species. Marx's claim that the abolition of alienation enabled the reconciliation with species-being and the overcoming of philosophically deep-seated divisions, like that between essence and appearance, was somewhat metaphysical. Even so, Marx's critique of alienation gave a social meaning to the concept of autonomy that Critical Theory has either sought to develop or find equivalents for it. Marx suggested that the self-determination and self-actualization of the subject through objectification was conditional on production being organized for the collective good, rather than the private and particular interests of capital. Similarly, the explanatory-analytical format of Marx's concept of alienation distinguishes it from other categories. Marx could describe the foundation of society on itself through the notion of objectification and clarify then how social action constitutes social institutions. Objectification highlights the problem of social reproduction and the conversion between subject and object that is accomplished through social action. Despite the experience of alienation being that of the subject's divorce and separation from its creations, alienation pertains to the circular process of objectification. That is, capitalist property relations condition objectification – without completely determining it, owing to objectification's connection to the producer's subjectivity – and the objectifying activity's products or outcomes contribute, in turn, to the reproduction of capitalist social relations. In effect, alienation concerns the 'duality', rather than simply the experienced dualism, of action and structure (Giddens, 1979; 1984).

The general dissatisfaction with the concept of alienation was not always connected to systematic critiques of objectification. The concept of alienation arguably lost some of its illuminating power due to its familiarity and its excessive usage exacerbated a certain conceptual imprecision. On the one hand, these deficiencies partly ensue from the connection that alienation has with subjects' everyday pre-theoretical experiences, but the concept was undoubtedly weakened by its arbitrary application and its equation with subjective states of consciousness. On the other hand, empirical sociological studies of alienation tended to involve a dilution of the concept's broader philosophical background and mainly detailed mundane and degrading forms of work. The more specific theoretical rejections of the concept of alienation tended to be informed by the development of new social scientific perspectives. The extension of structuralist methods from linguistics gave rise to critiques that questioned the nexus between objectification and alienation, since this nexus seemed to typify the modernist privileging of the subject. Indeed, Louis Althusser (1969) argued that the focus on alienation was a mistake and that there was an epistemological rupture in Marx's thought with humanist notions of subjectivity. Similarly, Michel Foucault's critique of the futility of the modern episteme's 'doubling' of the subject could be applied to Marx's notion of objectification as an externalization of the subject and the attendant need to overcome the self-alienation of the subject from its creations (Foucault, 1970). The substantial impact of these Neo-Structuralist critiques of alienation owed a good deal to their convergence with the general dissatisfaction with the concept, since their underlying structuralist assumptions are open to significant counter-questions, such as whether their methodology is descriptive rather than explanatory and conditioned by its discontinuity with individuals' experiences and interpretations of their actions.

Neo-Structuralist critiques depend on two things. First, a shift from a concern with the constituting subject to that of investigating the subject as constituted. The second is a challenging of the normative notion of the liberation of the subject through its own actions. In fact, these two desiderata would be addressed through the category of *subjection*; and this category's differences from that of alienation will be explored in the next section. There are other critiques of objectification that are more consistent with the normative and explanatory intentions of Marx's conception of alienation. Those of Jürgen Habermas and Cornelius Castoriadis are particularly relevant, because they gave rise to significant reformulations. Habermas developed a variety of criticisms, but central to his reconstruction of Critical Theory is the thesis that objectification is limited to the categorical framework of the relationship of subject and object. Marx, he claimed, elided the difference between the objectifying activity of labour and the inter-subjective character of social interaction (Habermas, 1978a).

In Habermas' opinion, the objectifying activity of labour is oriented by an interest in technical control, whereas social interaction is based on the achievement of mutual understanding. The communication between subjects, which is basic to the cooperative organization of work, is constitutive of norms and morality. Habermas argues that the potential reorganization of labour is limited by the universal human interest in technical-instrumental rationality. In his opinion, Marx came to recognize that the development of capitalist production made unrealistic the normative aspiration of the expressivist idea of objectification, that is, of labour as the free and creative externalization of the subjectivity of the producer and the subject's reconciliation with the objectified product. According to Habermas, Marx then modified the normative standard of critique and instead critically opposed the capitalist exploitation of labour in terms of its distortion of the principle of fair exchange, which derives from the natural law tradition (Habermas, 1982; 1987b). In addition, Habermas pointed to empirical sociological tendencies in advanced capitalist societies that undermine the significance of work in determining social structure and the increasing predominance of social conflicts that are concerned with lifestyles and identities (Habermas, 1971; 1982; 1987b).

It has often been pointed out that Habermas' conception of labour is less complex than Marx's notion of objectification and that his objections neglect Marx's interpretation of intersubjective cooperation (Arnason, 1979; 1982; Honneth, 1995b). The various criticisms led to refinements in Habermas' theory, but the basic demarcation between instrumental and communicative action orientations remained. It is not surprising, then, that Habermas opposed the Budapest School's developing the notion of objectification through applying it to broader social contexts (Heller, 1984b; Tormey, 2001; Grumley, 2005). Like other strands of the philosophy of praxis, the Budapest School utilized the concept of alienation to critique capitalism and to suggest that State Socialism failed to substantively realize Marx's notion of autonomy. That is, autonomy presupposed practical forms of self-determination and self-actualization, whereas State Socialism enacted a merely formal, or legal-political, change in property relations. The concept of alienation highlighted how emancipation entailed a combination of both objective and subjective transformation. Now, to this end, Agnes Heller sought to clarify the connection between the 'expressivist' dimension of objectification and the attributes of the fully realized human personality. Heller argued that, as a human creation, the entirety of everyday life is an objectification, although she also defined production as a sphere of 'objectivation in itself' (Heller, 1984b). In a related, though different, manner, György Márkus (1986a) argued that language and production are each forms of objectification. According to Márkus, Marx's conception of the paradigmatic character of production was conditioned by an appreciation of human finitude and how social reproduction is contingent on the satisfaction of human needs (Márkus, 1986a). The centrality of the category of needs to the Budapest School's theorizing is indicative of how this circle developed the humanist implications of Marx's notion of objectification and sought to clarify, as well as deploy, the philosophical anthropology that underpins the Marxist critique of alienation (Márkus, 1978).

The Budapest School's reworking of the notion of objectification drew attention to the creative aspects of human practices and its constitution of human life forms. In a survey of several strands of praxis philosophy, Johann Arnason (1991a: 77) notes how this tradition included conceptions of creation that were not limited to the predominant Marxist understanding of creation as the fabrication of the '"artificial environment" (Labriola)'. Karel Kosik's *The Dialectics of the Concrete*, Arnason comments, contains a notion of creation as 'the ontological originality of structures brought into being through human action' (Arnason, 1991a: 77; Kosik, 1976). In expanding on the implications of objectification and explicating the broad significance of human creativity, the Budapest School and other strands of the philosophy of praxis developed approaches that have certain affinities with Castoriadis' elucidation of the social imaginary and Castoriadis' critique of the subordination of individuals to the instituted society that is their own collective social-historical creation. Even so, like Habermas, Castoriadis' emphasis on meaning and signification substantially determines his critique of Marx's paradigm of production. Society, Castoriadis contends, is the social-historical creation of a world of meaning; it should not be equated with the young Marx's model of the externalization of the subject. Rather, the instituted imaginary is the work of society as an anonymous collective. For Castoriadis (1988), the category of objectification cannot capture social imaginary significations' complex associations of meaning. Rather, objectification is part of the broad process of social instituting or 'making-doing', but production is always oriented and organized by the social imaginary.

Despite this rejection of the Marxian paradigm of production, the problem of self-alienation is at the core of Castoriadis' theory. Castoriadis argues that heteronomous societies veil their own social creation and consequently that the 'instituted society' appears to subsist independently of its social instituting. According to Castoriadis, this occlusion of the 'self-creation of society' generally derives from the provision of some extra-social explanations of the social order, such as religious accounts of divine providence or secular interpretations of scientific rationality. In his opinion, Marx succumbed to the latter extra-social interpretation. Marx undermined his original insight into society's practical creation and developed a theory of production's universal significance. The result was a theory that displaced the question of social instituting. In Castoriadis' opinion, Marx's theory's continuities with the capitalist imaginary and its representation of rationality had significant theoretical and political implications. In terms of political organization, it facilitated the development of hierarchical structures and bureaucratic organizations that were precisely contrary to the concept of alienation's critique of the division between the control and the practical execution of activities (Castoriadis, 1974a; 1987; 1974b).

These debates over objectification and alienation were strongly connected to the political contexts and interpretations of capitalism's contemporary phase. Like other strands of praxis philosophy, The Budapest School's critiques of alienation were related to State Socialism's potential for internal reform. Marx's categories could be deployed against the existing socialist order whilst there was a residual commitment to Marxist ideology and there appeared, albeit briefly, the possibility of internal reform. In this sense, the critique of alienation was blunted by the reaction against the initiatives for socialist humanism in Eastern Europe. In the Western European context, the disputes over the concept of alienation likewise had political ramifications. Although it was grounded philologically and appealed to the value of science, Althusser's critique of humanism could be read as justifying the authority of Communist Party orthodoxy and as a reaction against the progressive struggles that were occurring outside of its authority, such as the student movement's employment of the category of alienation in its critique of education systems (Althusser, 1969).

From different standpoints, Habermas and Castoriadis' respective critiques of the notion of objectification reflect their assessments of the limitations of Marx's theory with regard to advanced capitalism. Like Castoriadis' critique of Marx's implicit acceptance of the capitalist imaginary's instituted representation of the world and its equation of human purpose with the rational domination and control of nature and society, Habermas contended that 'Marx's latent positivism' impeded the critique of the 'technocratic ideology of late-capitalism.' In short, Habermas argued that the concept of objectification does not demarcate the moral from the technical in a way that is necessary for the critique of contemporary technocratic capitalism (Habermas, 1978a; 1978b; 1984; 1987a; 1987b).

Habermas' and Castoriadis' respective critiques of the paradigm of objectification were similarly related to the critiques of the commodity form in domains beyond that of alienated labour. Of course, this contestation was anticipated by the Frankfurt School's critique of reification and works like Herbert Marcuse's *One-Dimensional Man* had a direct influence on the struggles contesting alienation in the 1960s and 1970s (Marcuse, 1964). Specifically, the Frankfurt School explicated how the dominance of the commodity form was consolidated by the culture industry and sought to explain the deleterious effects of the dominance of instrumental rationality on institutions like the family. Although the critique of the alienating character of late-capitalist everyday life, consumption and mass media was originally considered to be consistent with the objectification framework's critique of alienated labour and an extension of it, the increasing importance that was attributed to symbolic forms, like 'spectacle' (Debord, 1995) and 'sign value' (Baudrillard, 1975; 1998), as well as to the informality and diffuse experiences of late-capitalist everyday life and the urban environment (Lefebvre, 2008) eventually resulted in positions that reinterpreted the problem of alienation in cultural and semiological terms. In other words, disclosures of the depth and diversity of late-capitalist alienation eventually challenged the objectification model and the paradigmatic character of production.

Despite the inevitable intersections and overlaps, I consider that many of these critiques of consumption, the mass media, and everyday life to be more extensions of the critique of reification than reinterpretations of alienation. These experiences of social relations as structured in the same way as the objective world of things that can be exchanged and treated instrumentally do not necessarily entail the forms of thwarted participation and institutional appropriation that I consider intrinsic to alienation. This is one of the reasons why I consider contemporary practices like sex tourism to be exemplars of reification rather than alienation, because they involve the colonizing of consciousness in a way that neutralizes subjectivity and the reification of the instituted reality that enables these practices. Of course, the global dynamics that such practices depend upon condition the alienation of sex workers, but which the sex tourist accepts as preconditions of their own practices (Jeffreys, 2009). Be that as it may, the appreciation of the significance of experiences of alienation or reification beyond the sphere of production influenced in some cases the theoretical supplementation of the objectification perspective and the growing resonance of various categories intended to disclose equivalent forms of injustice and suffering. In the next section, I investigate these supplements, syntheses and synonyms in order to clarify some of the implications of the critical categories that came to overshadow that of alienation and to derive from this analysis a clearer delineation of the requirements for reconceptualizing alienation.

Before turning to these supplements, syntheses and synonyms, I want to briefly comment on the notion of institution that underpins my subsequent reconceptualization of alienation. The notion of institution takes into account some of the implications of the critique of objectification whilst still developing the concern of the category of objectification with social constitution and creative action. Institutions have material form, but the conception of institution that is being proposed here equally emphasizes their symbolic constitution (see Browne, 2014a). It is particularly intended to incorporate the sense of instituting that was originally proposed by Maurice Merleau-Ponty (1973; 2010) and that has been subsequently extended by Castoriadis (1987) in his elucidation of the relationship between instituting society and instituted society. Merleau-Ponty highlighted the generative sense of forms of human doing that are conditioned by particular orientations to the world (Merleau-Ponty, 1964). Of course, the implication of these conceptions of institution is to undermine the ontological sense of institution as a fixed objectivity and to enable an exploration of the processes by which this appearance is created or constituted. Institutions are, as Boltanski (2011) puts it, implicated in the constitution of the 'whatness' of the 'what is'. In other words, they are *reality* defining and the power of the institution is to equate itself with reality or assimilate reality to it (Browne, 2014a). Boltanski's notion of institution appears to contrast with that of Castoriadis in one important respect, it tends to presume a plurality of institutions. Whereas Castoriadis considers the plurality to be a second-order product of instituting or, as he puts it, the deployment of the social-historical (Castoradis, 1987; 2007).

Castoriadis' conception is concerned initially with the institution of society and this has led to criticisms of it representing an over-integrated image of society (Klooger, 2012). Nevertheless, one important implication of this sense of imaginary institution of society is that it seeks to develop a conception that moves beyond a framework that is focused on 'institutions' as discrete and self-contained entities. Since this characteristic of institutions is something that is itself established or instituted, it should neither be presumed as a given nor should the legal-political form of delineating institutions be taken as the primary or predominant conception. In some ways this notion of discrete and self-contained entities is how the diversity of institutions in the plural is thought about and this reflects aspects of the ontology of determination that Castoriadis seeks to contest. Institutions depend on the background horizon of the social imaginary and this means that there is always some blurring, blending or interpenetration of the general imaginary institution and the secondary institutions, like the labour market, or organizations. The reason for emphasizing this is because formally constituted institutions derive some of their 'reality' and legitimacy from the background and the social imaginary shapes their orientation. It is important in the context of alienation because this involves some process of appropriation and it is relevant to why marginal reforms that appear to address the manifestations of alienation do not necessarily dissolve it. Likewise, the recent forms of alienation appear much more symbolic in their texture. In any event, this conception enables an appreciation of alienation in contexts other than that of the capitalist work organization, whilst showing that these other instances can be simultaneously different and related. One further point is worth noting; the contemporary concern with the 'institution' has to some extent been developed in economics but it has also been particularly relevant to the discussion of art, since art has simultaneously confronted the fact of its institution in institutions (Weichman, 2006).

Supplements, Syntheses and Synonyms

The critiques of objectification often served to justify new theoretical syntheses and the elaboration of conceptual equivalents for the concept of alienation. The characterization of distorted experiences reflected the basic concern of the supplement or alternative to the paradigm of production. Phenomenology identifies alienation with misperception and experiences of inauthentic relationships, linguistics focuses on misunderstanding and the implicit manipulation of communicative exchanges, and psychoanalysis discloses the disabling consequences of psychic imbalances and the disturbances of the misdirection of desire and inappropriate repression. It could be argued that these three fields' reframing of alienation recapitulate some of the concerns of what Schacht (1971) describes as the major pre-Marxian conceptions of alienation: theology, health and political economy. The concept of alienation has also been somewhat displaced by notions that are tailored to different aspects of experiences of subordination, particularly those of the suppression and marginalizing of identity. The contrast between these critical diagnostic formats is instructive for alienation's reconceptualization. I delineate these differences in relation to interpretations of postcolonial estrangement, the notion of subjection and Honneth's reinterpretation of the category of reification (Honneth, 2008).

Phenomenology has often been drawn upon to clarify the nexus between objectification and alienation, since its investigations highlight important dimensions of subjects' experience, especially perception and temporality. In a sense, the question of alienation is a basic concern of phenomenology, as its approach seeks to disclose the connection and potential discrepancy between subjectivity and objectivity. Phenomenology has been a methodological supplement to notions of objectification, however, it lacks a notion of the social division of labour and this notion differentiates the Marxian conception of alienation. The specifically phenomenological interpretations of alienation are concerned with the duplicity of experience and the questions of authenticity that are its corollary. That is, phenomenology emphasizes how reality is constituted as a world of meaning through experience, but it considers that the subject relates to its experience as simultaneously mine and not mine. This negative dimension of experience poses the problem of authenticity, as it is possible for the subject to exist in a manner that is alienated from its authentic self, or the subject (or *Dasein* in the case of Heidegger) can lapse into a state in which the inauthentic excludes the potential for authentic being.

There are different interpretations of the inauthentic and its source. Existential phenomenology arguably contributed to the indiscriminate employment of the concept of alienation, because it is concerned with existence in general. Even so, my reconceptualization of alienation utilizes the phenomenological notion of project. Projects frame experience and shape its interpretation through incorporating an anticipated future into the present. I suggest that it is partly in relation to individuals' life-projects that alienation is disclosed and that life-projects are relevant to assessing how the relation of social action to social structure is institutionalized (Schutz, 1967). Similarly, as Arnason's (1991a) assessment of Kosik's conception of ontological creation indicates, the phenomenological Marxist synthesis expanded the sense of constituting practices beyond a more narrow materialist interpretation of objectification and traces of this approach – in conjunction with other theoretical developments – inform the notion of *institution* that is applied in my reconceptualization of alienation.

Psychoanalysis originally served as a supplement to the Marxian notion of objectification in order to explain the complications of subordination and the tolerance of oppression. Its initial contribution to Critical Theory corresponded to a sociological division of institutional spheres and psychoanalysis was taken to give insights into the dynamics of the family. Whilst this enabled an appreciating of how the effects of alienation were transferred onto family relations, psychoanalysis equally pointed in the other direction and implied that the family and repression facilitate the acceptance of alienation in the sphere of work. Yet, as Schacht (1971) notes, mental disorder has long been perceived as a major manifestation of alienation and psychoanalysis's subsequent impact on theorizing alienation has been more extensive, diverse and even subliminal. Psychoanalysis expanded the instances of the subject's being divided and how one can be opposed to oneself, extended the categories for equivalent experiences, and theorized that individuals can paradoxically desire their own alienation. Freud's theory of the dynamic unconscious presents a challenge to notions of authenticity but certain psychoanalytic interpretations come close to making alienation a permanent condition, suggesting that distortions owe to the civilizing processes' repressive character or the unconscious perpetually compensating for lack and disappointment. Despite these limitations, psychoanalytic appreciations of ambivalence, loss and fantasy have powerfully resonated with post-colonial suffering, as well as certain feminist positions. There can be no denying psychoanalysis's relevance to comprehending alienation, but my reconceptualization takes into account the fact that psychoanalysis was not constituted as an action theory. The objectification framework contended that alienation is instantiated primarily through the interchange between action and structure, whereas psychoanalysis is directed more towards elucidating the psychological and normative preconditions and consequences of action.

Many of the critiques of objectification argued that this notion does not adequately capture the signifying and intersubjective characteristics of communication. It could be suggested that the notion of ideology supplemented and complemented the category of alienation, and that ideology is explicitly concerned with symbolic and cultural practices. Nevertheless, the notion of ideology need not convey the social ontological complexion of communication. In Castoriadis' opinion,

> I cannot call my relation to language a form of alienation. [...] Alienation appears *in* this relation, but it *is* not this relation – just as error or delirium are possible only *in* language but *are* not language. (Castoriadis, 1987: 114; emphasis in the original)

Linguistic reinterpretations of alienation have to then explain double meanings and to offer precise analyses of how understanding can be simultaneously misunderstanding. In different ways, Habermas and Bourdieu explained linguistic alienation in terms of the contradictory instantiation of the invisible rules that enable communication. Habermas argued that systematically distorted communication is analogous to pathology, because it generates misunderstandings that contradict the purpose of communication. Linguistic disturbances are like symptoms; they manifest the effects of social domination upon communication. Under the conditions of social domination, Habermas (1970a; 1978a) claimed, understanding is disingenuous, since it derives from communication that conceals aspects of the social context and disguises its own strategic-manipulative intentions. Like Freud's conception of the unconscious, the repressed meanings can only be indirectly expressed and this systematic distortion damages the intersubjective construction of identity through communication.

Habermas' later theory of the internal colonization of the lifeworld is less an account of the self-alienation of communication and more an interpretation of the dysfunctions ensuing from the displacement, subordination and reorientation of communication (Habermas, 1984; 1987a). The social pathological consequences of this dysfunction are due to the instrumental orientation of exchange value and administrative power replacing the orientation to understanding of communicative action in domains where it is necessary, like the family, law and culture. Bourdieu's reinterpretation of linguistic alienation does not rely upon the distinctions that Habermas drew to demonstrate distorted communication's external conditioning; rather Bourdieu sought to explain the economic dynamics of the symbolic, that is, symbolic power's distribution and accumulation. In part, this difference between these frameworks results from Habermas' theorizing non-class specific distortions to communication, whereas Bourdieu investigated how communication expresses class differences and contributes to class reproduction (Bourdieu, 1990; see Susen, 2007). Similarly, Bourdieu's anthropological studies suggested that the activity and product of objectification were subject to the symbolic determination of value, but that these processes of symbolic expression and interpretation involve a kind of alienation. Social agreements over meanings and values can entail subordinate groups and individuals' enactment of *symbolic violence* towards themselves. Bourdieu defined symbolic violence in various ways; its primary signification concerns how subjects' expressions and actions reinforce their subordinate position. Symbolic violence is meant to explicate a particular experience of alienation, one that is conveyed through subjects' dispositions, cognitive schemas and bodily practices.

> Symbolic violence is the coercion which is set up only through the consent that the dominated cannot fail to give to the dominator (and therefore to the domination) when their understanding of the situation and relation can only use instruments of knowledge that they have in common with the dominator. (Bourdieu, 2000: 170)

Bourdieu's notion of symbolic violence rephrases two features of the objectification perspective on alienation. First, symbolic violence discloses an implicit compulsion in the process of enabling action, for instance, the education system facilitates learning but the mode of communication and education's substantive themes are asymmetrically related to the prior experiences of different classes. Second, symbolic violence sustains social reproduction and inverts the logic of social struggles, that is, it leads subordinate groups to view their own practices as less valid and those practices of the dominant social group as legitimate. For Bourdieu, the recognition of legitimacy is central to symbolic power, but it actually derives from misrecognition, for example, subordinate groups may assume that there is equivalence when there is not, or that outcomes simply reflect achievement rather than the weight of social background. Drawing on phenomenological and psychoanalytic perspectives, Bourdieu's notion of *habitus* explicates how social practices manifest the continuities and tensions between the individual's body and consciousness. The practical dispositions that are instilled in the body through socialization processes constitute some of the unrecognized grounds for the submission to symbolic violence. This second nature quality of the *habitus* is one reason why challenging symbolic power is difficult and may entail a different order of alienation from oneself. Despite Bourdieu's demonstrating linguistic alienation in a variety of social fields, his analyses' potential limitation is related to the question of whether the struggles they detail actually represent dialectics of control. This question is a variation of the criticism that Bourdieu's theory ultimately emphasizes the determining effects of social structure over action and that his conception of practices is primarily strategic and instrumental, rather than equally moral and normative (Honneth, 1995b).

To the extent that symbolic violence reveals that it is part of oneself (or one's habitus, like speech patterns, taste structure, deportment) that reinforces one's own subordination, it has decided parallels with the concept of subjection. Subjection entails an even stronger sense of the entanglement of the subject in its own domination, because theorists like Foucault and Butler contend that subjection is implicated in the constitution of the subject and the very demand for autonomy. For instance, Butler argues that a

> redescription of the domain of psychic subjection is needed to make clear how social power produces modes of reflexivity at the same time as it limits forms of sociality. (Butler, 1997: 29)

It is not coincidental that the concept of subjection gained prominence during the period in which that of alienation declined. Subjection implies that the normative expectations of authenticity and autonomy led to the self-imposition of domination. Foucault's histories showed the subjection involved in the making of modern subjects; they highlight the power-knowledge regimes and normalization present in the constructing of prisoners as agents to be reformed, patients as entities to be healed through clinical examination, and sexuality as a core dimension of the person to be regulated, repressed or liberated (Foucault, 1973; 1978; 1979). Significantly, subjection not only derives from external domination, but is also the 'willed effect of the subject' (Butler, 1997: 14). In this respect, subjection is similar to the psychoanalytic understanding of unconscious processes, but the influence of structuralism upon this concept means that subjection tends to signify the subject's enactment of a position and that agency (or will) corresponds to an interpellated identity.

The concept of subjection is undoubtedly a critical category and it is relevant to the more insidious forms of social control that developed in modernity, especially those associated with professional discourses concerning the subject and large-scale institutions concerned with regulating the social body, like health, law and education. The Marxian notions of personification as alienation and the subsumption of labour under capital refer to similar processes of subjectivity's regulation and control, yet subjection implies a deeper bind, because it proposes that subjects are constituted through personification and similar identity-constructions.

Although they need not be viewed as contradictory and mutually exclusive, there are important normative and methodological differences between the concepts of subjection and alienation. Subjection is based on the logic of identification, even though it is generally critical of the constraints or governance that identification entails, whereas alienation is directed towards discordance and contradiction. Normative differences correspond to this contrast: the intertwining of subjectivity and power in the concept of subjection suggests that while autonomy is constituted in its opposition to heteronomy, this opposition or resistance is dependent on that which it resists. This is why the concept of subjection induces some scepticism toward the normative project of radically transforming heteronomous social relations in order to abolish alienation. By contrast, the contradictory character of alienation implies that action has a greater degree of latitude than in the case of subjection. The power of institutions is less intrinsic to the subject and the concept of alienation emphasizes the dependence of institutions on the initiative of action, such as Marx conveyed in metaphors of dead and living labour.

The conceptual equivalents for alienation have often been deployed in the articulation of experiences of post-colonial estrangement. Post-colonial estrangement derives, of course, from the prior alienation of dispossession and cultural destruction. It is also addressed to the liminal and subordinated identities of migrants from former colonies. Post-colonial reinterpretations of alienation have particularly highlighted the salience of race in shaping social relations of inequality and subordination. The structural violence of colonial appropriation not only entailed the alienation of producers from their objectification, it involved the depreciation of the colonized subjectivity as a justification for exploitation. Where the colonized internalized this colonial ideology, the outcome was sometimes the intense alienation of self-hatred (Sayad, 2004). Similarly, the post-colonial estrangement of migrants has often been depicted in terms of the dislocation of identity, such as in being not fully integrated into a new society and yet being disconnected from the society of origin. Of course, this dislocation is material as well as symbolic or cultural, being grounded in such things as diminished citizenship rights, precarious employment and marginal living conditions. In many post-colonial contexts, estrangement is the product of the over-determination of subjectivity by the trauma of colonial violence, with this experience being carried into the present in the collective memory and subjects' bodies (Biehl et al., 2007; Fassin, 2007).

The ontological insecurity that colonialism generated may have provoked compensatory identifications with the imagined community of the nation; however, accounts of post-colonial estrangement have regularly focused on the subsequent disappointment with the new political order and the tendency for national integration into the global system to lead to a reiteration of alienation. Similarly, migrants from former colonies have had the alienating experience of their rights as citizens being undermined by the substantive marginalizing of racial and ethnic communities. In both cases, there is a considerable mismatch between the anticipated future and the experienced post-colonial reality. These kinds of discrepancies are powerful sources of indignation. Boltanski and Chiapello (2005) detail how the discourse of alienation in the 1960s resonated with the growing discrepancy between increasing educational qualifications and the limited employment options. More recently, a similar discrepancy has played out on a transnational level. The corresponding indignation and dislocation is sometimes referred to in order to explain why foreign educated professionals join fundamentalist movements (Eisenstadt, 1999a; Gambetta and Hertog, 2009). Significantly, colonialism's systematic denial of meaningful participation, even as an ideal, provides a negative clarification of how integral *participation* is to the concept of alienation. It also intimates at why other concepts, like dehumanization and exclusion, may provide more precise explications of aspects of colonial and post-colonial subordination and suffering.

Even though it is intended as a reinterpretation of the notion of reification, Honneth (2008) has recently developed a social ontological interpretation of the practice of dehumanization. Honneth's conception of reification expands on the long-standing view of alienation as interpersonal estrangement and it is based on disclosing a negation of a basic supposition of communication. Honneth contends that reification is the forgetfulness, or practical denial, of recognition. Recognition involves appreciating the claims made by others upon oneself and the capacity to respond in an appropriate manner. For Honneth, reification is not simply an outcome of a moral decision to treat another person in an instrumental manner; rather reification entails the suppression of a core dimension of the anthropology of human beings, one that is a precondition for adopting a moral standpoint. That is, Honneth claims that the development of cognition is dependent on prior recognition and the ability to learn through interaction with others. The specific moral perspective that an individual acquires through socialization is overlain upon this primary structure of recognition. This underlying recognition entails an intrinsic sense of connection with other human beings. By equating humans with insensate beings or things, reification forgets this interdependency and denies (explicitly or implicitly) recognition. It is clear that Honneth's conception clarifies an important attribute of social prejudice and that it is relevant to Hannah Arendt's (1992) question of how genocide overcomes basic animal pity. Similarly, Honneth delineates a significant source of social cooperation and a deep-seated reason for the appreciation of cooperation in social life. In this sense, the denial of recognition directly translates into the alienated forgetfulness of cooperation.

Nonetheless, Honneth's conception does not do justice to the explanatory intentions of Lukács's original interpretation of reification and those of the concept of alienation to which it is often related. Lukács sought to comprehend how reification is generated by the dynamics of capitalism. He argued that the subjective experience of these dynamics as independent processes was related to the apparent constitution of capitalism as integrated social system. Honneth's conception, by contrast, contains neither a detailed account of the structural conditions that underpin the perpetuation of alienation nor a developed explanation of the contribution that reification or alienation make to the reproduction of these condition. Of course, it is possible to infer these from Honneth's more general theory of recognition, but his reification essay's concern with the diversion from the antecedent mode of recognition makes it limited in its explanation of specific institutional forms. This limitation may be due to the fact that the historical perspective that was central to Lukács's notion of reification and Marx's conception of alienation is largely absent from Honneth's reinterpretation. Marx and Lukács aimed

> to locate capitalism in the continuity of the historical process, to uncover thereby the historical character of its self-enclosed unity and self- propelling progress – in the sense of showing its transitoriness, the possibility of its practical overcoming. (Márkus, 1982: 153)

Despite the differences in explanatory frameworks, Honneth's interpretation of reification clarifies a requirement of the reconceptualization of alienation. Honneth's depiction of the denial of recognition is meant to disclose attitudes and practices that are not only damaging towards others but also to one's own self. The concept of alienation should identify analogous destructive or damaging practices. It is not sufficient – as Honneth's remarks on the overlaps between Lukács's theory and Simmel's notion of the separation between objective and subjective culture makes plain – to conceive of alienation as separation, such as between the subject and the object, or the subject and other subjects (Honneth, 2008). Rather, as an analytical category, the concept of alienation needs to expose some damage to the subject that corresponds to it. Indeed, it makes sense to describe the experience of extreme forms of separation as reification, because they seem to impose a contemplative standpoint upon subjects that is similar to the one that Lukács described. These are processes that can be radically challenged, but they present themselves as eluding the capacity of subjects to intervene, or where intervention may compound the process, such as the environmental crisis or the second order alienation of global finance and its self-referential system of value. Honneth previously grounded progressive social change in the ability to generalize from the experience of recognition and the shift it enables to more universalistic moral standpoints. In my opinion, this capacity is relevant to challenging those social processes that impose a contemplative perspective through their extreme forms of separation. Reification would then be the refusal of this ability to generalize that is derived from recognition, since it enables the extension of the idea of human equivalence to larger categories of persons and marks a shift from contemplation to active engagement.

This revision has the advantage, in my view, of highlighting how the reification involved in the equation of a person and a thing is a social imaginary construct that becomes real through its institution. The notion of alienation as thwarted participation, which the next section elaborates, has significant affinities nevertheless with Honneth and Hartmann's definition of the paradoxes of contemporary capitalist modernization: it espouses normative claims to autonomy that it practically undermines (Honneth and Hartmann, 2012). The critical analysis of the conceptual equivalents that displaced the concept of alienation demonstrates the relevance of subjects' reflexive interpretation of their practices to experience. The revised concept of alienation needs to include then some explication of individuals' interpretation and how it shapes action. It could be argued that while the objectification model presupposed this dimension of experience, it did not foreground the specification of the meanings that orient practices.

At the same time, in making this revision it is necessary to take into account how the most influential versions of linguistic alienation have been subject to parallel criticisms: Honneth (1995b) contends that while Habermas' pragmatic theory of communication provide insights into misunderstanding it does not correspond to subjects' experiences of oppression and their motivations for struggle. Similarly, Joas (1993) claims that the deficiencies of Habermas' theory derive from its focus on the coordination of action, rather than the actual processes of undertaking social action. Likewise, Boltanski (2011) argues that Bourdieu's conceptualizations of habitus and symbolic power accentuate the background and preconditions of action, rather than the situations of practical enactment and transaction. The action contexts and acting processes, he argues, should not be simply assimilated to prior understandings. Like Honneth and Joas, Boltanski claims that action contains the possibility of challenging and creatively modifying interpretations. Indeed,

> the notion of action is only really meaningful against a backdrop of uncertainty, or at least with reference to a plurality of possible options. (Boltanski, 2011: 22)

Now, these criticisms and refinements imply that the concept of alienation should be initially grounded in an explication of the practical processes of social action and the dialectic of control that conditions the reproduction of institutions through social action. In this way, alienation should reveal itself in social practices. The next section explains how conceptual modifications are necessary to grasp how contemporary institutions perpetuate alienation.

Towards a Reconceptualization of Alienation

The review of the original conception of alienation, the critique of the standpoint of objectification, and the analysis of the categorical equivalents for alienation lead to the following conclusions that will guide this reconceptualization and clarification of alienation's instantiation in the contemporary constellation of capitalist modernity. The concept of alienation has to be initially conceived as a category of social action and it pertains to the structuration of social institutions. The strength of the objectification perspective consisted in its focus on social reproduction and this made its framework of explanation somewhat superior to several conceptual alternatives, despite the criticisms of its limitations with respect to cultural significations and its inadequacies with respect to how estrangement intersects with the suppression and marginalizing of identities. It is necessary to explain then how action is a medium for the reproduction of institutions and how its outcomes condition future alienated practices.

There are two reasons in particular for this structuration: first, the institutions concerned should be shown to have an appropriative relationship to action, since action serves their reproduction. Second, there is an explicit or implicit compulsion that conditions the practices involved in alienation. For this reason, contexts of alienation involve a 'dialectic of control' and this dialectic reveals some of the contradictions of institutional orders, particularly between the semantics of incorporation and the institutional limits to realizing autonomy. In addition, the comparison with similar critical diagnostic frameworks suggests that the concept of alienation should not be limited to highlighting processes of separation and the inability of subjects to perceive or appropriate the outcomes of their actions, but rather that the concept of alienation should disclose some sense in which it is damaging to the subject.

The proposed reconceptualization of alienation is intended to be applicable to a broad range of institutional contexts, although the situation of work remains a major domain of alienation. It could be argued that a distinctive feature of contemporary capitalist modernity is the degree of reflexivity concerning alienation. At least at the level of the ideological self-representation of advanced capitalist organizations, managerial practices have somewhat sought to reform themselves in ways that obviate the previous subjective experiences of alienation, especially those associated with mundane and repetitive work. Post-Fordist management appears to valorize participation and modes of self-organization relative to the former hierarchical structures of managerial authority. However, the internal logic of the capitalist institution limits such managerial reforms and it is rather the modality of alienation that is reconfigured. The ensuing reconceptualization of alienation is informed by the significant questioning of the ideological self-representation of new capitalism. Boltanski and Chiapello (2005) contend that the managerial reforms of new capitalism effectively replaced the social relations of industrial alienation with those of market alienation. Similarly, Richard Sennett (1998) has highlighted the disorientation that is associated with flexible and insecure modes of new capitalist work organization. Further, from a global perspective, the alienating work of Fordist production has in no sense disappeared and it has probably expanded with the extension of markets for labour. Nevertheless, the post-Fordist modes of alienation differ insofar as they contradict the promotion of subjective involvement and often manifest in relation to the very normative expectations of meaningful participation.

The reflexivity concerning alienation is by no means limited to work contexts and some version of participatory involvement is to be found in diverse social spheres. The problem of political disaffection and the subordination of the public to expertise and bureaucratic administration have given rise to attempts to facilitate active citizenship. Active citizenship is presented as not only increasing the legitimacy of political decision-making and to some extent enabling the devolving of authority to the community but also as beneficial for the subjectivity of the citizen and the development of citizens' capacities for self-determination and self-realization. Similarly, the alter-globalization movement, and related instances of contestation, like the Occupy protests, have sought to organize themselves on the basis of direct and radical democratic forms of participation, such as through open discussion in general assemblies and the rejection of delegation. Pleyers argues that strands of the alter-globalization movement institute spaces of open participation in order to give subjects experiences of another reality to that of capitalism. Now, experience is something that these segments of alter-globalization believe cannot be delegated and they seek to instantiate opportunities for individual creativity and self-expression (Pleyers, 2010). Likewise, influenced by critiques of the pervasiveness of the capitalist commodity form and the desirability of increasing community involvement, the last two decades have seen a significant expansion in participatory art, which is sometimes called 'the social turn' (Bishop, 2012). It seeks to overcome the disconnection from experience of art institutions and the passive position of the spectator through the public's collaboration in the creation of the artworks. Aesthetic reflexivity can extend to facilitating participation in order to generate experiences of alienation, since alienation under these conditions is taken as a means of social disclosure and subjective revelation.

The intention of these contemporary responses to potential alienation is relatively clear: the absence of participation not only makes artistic practices, citizenship, movements, or organizations less legitimate but also functionally deficient with respect to realizing their purpose or objectives. In one sense, these developments represent attempts to satisfy the norm of participation in modernity and a certain acceptance of critiques of divergences from it. The politicization of alienation in modernity has recurrently given rise to attempts to instantiate participatory democratic forms of organization and social relations, such as in relation to work organization during major revolutionary contestations (Arendt, 1973; Castoriadis, 1997a; 1997b). Charles Taylor describes this modern politics of 'disalienation' as having developed during The

French Revolution (Taylor, 2004; 2007; Browne, 2009a). It reflected the influence of Jean-Jacques Rousseau's argument concerning the democratic form of the *general will* and the correspondence it instantiated between the interests of the individual and those of the collective. Because individual autonomy is realized through direct participation in the *general will*, the practices of delegation or representation constitute forms of alienation from this perspective. Of course, modern capitalist institutions do not satisfy this ideal and they cannot satisfy it; nevertheless, the accentuation of participation generally entails normative justifications that make strong claims about the convergence between the general interests of the institution and those of the individual. In other words, these normative justifications claim that the institution enables (or seeks to enable) individual autonomy and self-realization. One could, after Luc Boltanski, describe this normative justification as a 'hermeneutic contradiction' (Boltanski, 2011). It simultaneously admits the institution's dependence on people's action and veils the institution's compulsion, or even coercive relation to this action.

> What is designated here by the term 'hermeneutic contradiction' is therefore not merely an analytical device. This contradiction is constantly in the consciousness of actors or, at least, on its edges and liable to be resuscitated every time an incident – be it a dispute or simple maladjustment between the elements that make up the environment – reawakens doubts about the content of reality. But it would be a mistake to confine this unease to the psychological register of belief. It is above all in the domain of action that it manifests itself. (Boltanski, 2011: 86)

The contradiction between contemporary institutions' accentuation of participation and the actual conditions of action is equally present in the denial of the new forms of the earlier sources of alienation, like hierarchy, monotony, and interpersonal estrangement. Indeed, the other major normative justification for increasing participation is that of the creativity of individuals. It intersects in several ways with the justification based on the supposed convergence between an institution's interest and those of the individual, or what I have described as a modified version of the democratic form of the *general will*. On the one hand, these two justifications have a formal similarity, insofar as the creativity of subjects simultaneously enables individual self-actualization and satisfies institutions' conditions of reproduction and alleged need for innovation. Significantly, the notion of self-expression as the basis of an authentic identity, which originated with the Romantic Movement, has become increasingly widespread (Taylor, 1991). Self-expression is now often seen as a prerequisite of autonomy. On the other hand, individual creativity cannot be delegated or transferred; rather creativity is something that is contingent on participation. With the exception of certain conceptions of aesthetic – and perhaps also sexual – experience, alienation is generally considered to be a state that is antithetical to creativity.

There are contradictions similarly present in contemporary institutions' promotion of participation in order to enable creativity. First, the sense of creativity that is supposedly yielded by participation is often defined in ways that are consistent with the managerial interest in obligatory performance. In other words, the normative justification that is based on valuing creativity often amounts to simply that of a semantic redefinition of quantifiable outputs. Second, whilst it could appear that the post-industrial economy is opposed to alienation, this appearance is contradicted by the fact that the majority of the 'new' economy's occupations do not generate significant innovations and the tasks involved do not offer that much greater scope for creativity than those of earlier industrial occupations (Murphy, 2012). It may be rather that what is important to the new economy is not so much the creative practices themselves as the diffusion of the 'bohemian' attitude or 'artistic' sensibility. Ironically, the bohemian attitude may be the one most suited to the contemporary capitalist context of increasing insecure, casualized and intermittent work.

Despite the rather problematic semantic redefinitions and institutionalized contradictions, the normative requirement of enhancing participation in order to facilitate creativity constitutes a substantial basis for immanent critique. Importantly, to reiterate an aspect of the critique of alienation from Marx through Castoriadis to Boltanski, alienation is consistently considered to entail a lack of genuine or effective recognition of subjects' creativity and simultaneously an appropriation or exploitation of creative action. Marx traced this dialectic of denial and appropriation, as we have seen, to the capitalist division of labour and other institutional orders contain some equivalent asymmetrical relation. Similarly, the dynamic of compelled yet thwarted participation means that the norm that institutions espouse concerning creativity is unable to be realized. Finally, the notions of creative action as an expression of the autonomy of the subject and what has sometimes been defined as the consummation of action, that is, the realization of objectives and the integration of the various dimensions of action in the process of its fulfilment, represent alternatives to alienated practices and the compartmentalizing of action according to the schematic alternatives of either normative or instrumental action (see Joas, 1996).

These contradictory relationships demonstrate why the concept of alienation is double-sided, or concerns the duality of the institution and action. As an analytical category, alienation cannot be limited to the subjective perspective of social actors, even though it finds expression in affective states like dissatisfaction, frustration, or even depression. Whilst the individual's subjective perspective may not be sufficient, it is undoubtedly a necessary prerequisite for the application of the category of alienation. The concept of alienation does not have any referent without the correlative subjective experience. In this sense, the subjective experience of alienation precedes its theoretical conceptualization, although individual subjects are likely to misunderstand the sources of alienation.

The concept of alienation equally requires the specification of social institutions' objective dynamics, since these dynamics condition subjects' action and experience. In my opinion, the category of alienation should be limited to contexts in which institutions can be shown to have an appropriative relation to action. Appropriation is probably the most significant source of the contradiction intrinsic to alienation, because institutions have to compel or facilitate action in order to be able to appropriate action and its outcomes. Marx's notion of alienation concerned the capitalist appropriation of labour and its objectification, but other institutions involve different orders of appropriation. In the case of these institutions, the appropriation of action and its outcomes may be oriented by values other than that of capital accumulation and dependent on mechanisms other than commodity exchange. For instance, it has already been noted how political citizenship can constitute a significant domain of alienation and how the political order can be appropriative. Perhaps, the entire imaginary institution of society and its indeterminate interconnecting of various 'second order institutions', like family, school system, labour market, and civil society, constitute the broader and only partially recognized sources of compulsion and appropriation.

The criteria of appropriation should enable an analytical differentiation of alienation from seemingly similar subjective experiences and affective states. In other words, some dissatisfying subjective experiences do not meet alienation's criteria and other analytical categories would be more suitable. For example, there is probably a considerable affinity between alienation and the types of dissatisfaction that students regularly feel in learning new information and acquiring new skills, since this learning generally entails some gap between the subjective involvement and what is achieved. However, the concept of alienation applies more to those contexts in which education institutions diverge from their purported purpose of developing students' capacities and prioritize instead other objectives, like contractual relations and financial gain. In the case of education institutions, it may be the failure of the institution in some sense, rather than its effective functioning, that conditions alienation and thwarts students' meaningful participation. It is worth emphasizing this sense of divergence and distortion, because two major instances of social contestation – May 68 in France and the 2011 Egyptian uprising – have been partly explained in terms of the relationship between the alienation of students and the deficiencies of education systems. Alienation reflected the discrepancy between the rising expectations of an increasingly educated youth and the limited opportunities in those societies at the time for either employment or rewarding work commensurate with qualifications. Although it has focussed more on the dynamics of classroom interaction, the elimination of alienation has sometimes been an objective of pedagogical practices. Similar to how the festivals that were staged during the French Revolution sought to overcome the division between the performer and the spectator, the educational practices that opposed alienation endeavoured to overcome as far as possible the division between the teacher and the student. In other words, it was presumed that genuine learning is enabled by full and equal participation, rather than by a system of external imposition.

The concept of alienation should further disclose how institutions' objective dynamic of appropriation is damaging to the subjectivity of social agents. This is why education represents only a conditional instance of alienation and one where alienation ensues from the distortion of this institution's purpose, because education should serve the life-project of the individual. In this sense, the typical student dissatisfaction is temporary and even necessary to the process of acquiring new capacities. Of course, whether an education institution is fulfilling its objective may be difficult to assess whilst a student and, no doubt, education is a major context of *subjection*. Still, the reasons why the category of alienation is qualified in its applicability to education are relevant to what is meant by alienation being damaging to subjectivity. Alienation is destructive of the life-projects of individuals. Specifically, the actions of individuals that should enable the realization of their life-projects actually undermine them or constitute obstacles to their realization. This conception of destructive of subjectivity can readily encompass those more immediately experienced forms of alienation, like drudgery and repetitive work. It is nevertheless tailored to elucidating the contemporary damage to subjectivity that derives from contradicting the normative claim of the integrity between institutions' interests and individuals' actions. In fact, there is something pathological about taking this normative justification too seriously and believing that contemporary institutions can facilitate without contradiction individuals' life-projects. For there are simply too many mixed messages and attempts to enact the norm of participation will lead to the discovery of boundaries that circumscribe and preclude effective participation. This is why the counter-argument that institutions have to overcome the apathy of people, such as in relation to the political order or aesthetic sphere, ignores how apathy develops in response to the lack of meaningful participation and the fraudulent attempts to instigate it.

Many commentators have drawn attention to contemporary capitalist modernity's double meanings and, more technically, the dialectic of the semantic and the pragmatic that pervades organizations and institutions (Boltanski, 2011; Sennett, 2006). Christophe Dejours (2012: 219), for instance, speaks of work organizations' 'gap between prescription and reality' and the pathology of how the 'very orders which are supposed to organize work sometimes wind up disorganizing it' (Dejours, 2012: 220). Sennett likewise attributes a 'corrosion of character' to new capitalism's undermining the subjective commitments required for its reproduction and its lack of legibility. In Sennett's opinion, new capitalism's fractured temporality and individualistic conception of agency are detrimental to the social relations necessary for the construction of meaningful life-projects (Sennett, 1998). It can be argued that the contradictions of new capitalism are internalized by individuals, because they are expected to act on the basis of normative principles that would facilitate their life-projects and yet the rules that actually organize their activities are indifferent to this consideration. This duplicity can equally be seen in how new capitalism claims to expand individual autonomy whilst actually instituting changes that increase individual insecurity and the competition between individuals, such as through reclassifying activities, making contracts impermanent, and introducing individualized modes of assessment (Boltanski and Chiapello,

2005). In an analysis of a case of shipyard 'restructuring', Joseph Blum (2000) shows how similar mechanisms of expanding insecurity and competition have been applied to traditional industrial and manufacturing occupations. Indeed, they are probably more consequential in these sectors of advanced capitalist societies because of their aggregate decline in employment.

New capitalism's conditions of participation, which are regularly presented as enabling self-determination and creative expression, actually make the realization of individuals' life-projects less tenable. In particular, the demand of participation under these conditions can damage the relationship that subjects have to their own actions and their confidence in the adequacy of their capacities relative to the expectations placed upon them. Individuals regularly experience the discrepancy between their intentions and the outcomes of their actions as evidence of subjective deficiencies, since emphasis is placed on their initiative. This paradox is one of the major reasons why contemporary alienation is destructive. Dejours finds that subjects believe that they are unable to change the work context and that their situation is permanent or enduring, even though contemporary institutions are supposedly flexible and claim to facilitate participation in transformation.

> It is not so much the extent of mental or psychic constraints in work which lets suffering appear (even though, obviously, it is an important factor), but rather the impossibility of any evolution towards its lessening. The certainty that the level of dissatisfaction can no longer diminish marks the entrance in suffering. (Dejours as quoted in Deranty, 2008: 449)

There is another important subjective reaction to alienation. It represents an alternative to the suffering ensuing from the damages to subjectivity and a means of sometimes giving expression to experiences of thwarted participation and institutions' failure to conform to their normative representation. That is, the experience of alienation tends to provoke forms of resistance, from overt modes of contestation, like political and industrial action, to more latent acts of resistance, such as in covert non-compliance with regulations, sabotaging aspects of production, or even simply subjective disengagement in relation to obliged participation. Of course, some modes of latent resistance express individuals' sense of malaise and are, in this respect, indicative of the damages to subjectivity. Yet, what is most important about resistance is the fact that it demonstrates how alienation entails a dialectic of control. Alienation involves social struggles and its complexion is conditioned by social struggles. Institutions, as has been noted already, have an interest in appropriating action and its outcomes, whilst subjects contest various dimensions of alienation, from the degree of compulsion that is involved, through the intensity of the action process, the negation of their capacities for self-determination, to the legitimacy of the dynamic of appropriation. The dialectic of control is anchored in the dependency of institutions on actions that they cannot generate themselves for their reproduction. Significantly, explicating this facet of alienation presupposes an analysis of the contested interaction between the objectivity of institutions and the subjectivity of social actors.

Boltanski and Chiapello (2005) have importantly shown how the dialectic of control shapes not just the immediate situations of conflict over alienation but also the longer-term relation between action and the capitalist institution. In their opinion, the substantial contestation over alienation during the late-1960s and 1970s led to a series of changes that gave rise to the 'new spirit of capitalism'. Specifically, the contestation precipitated major changes in managerial practices, which were intended to alleviate conflicts over industrial alienation, and the constitution of a new legitimating 'mythology' of capitalism. The contestation was particularly influenced by the themes of the 'artistic critique' of capitalism, such as the critique of capitalism's denial of creativity, self-expression, authenticity, and flexibility. These themes somewhat distinguished the artistic critique from that of the 'social critique' which had been advanced by the workers' movement, and which largely prioritized the critique of material inequalities and the injustices that derived from the class structure. During the period of intense contestation, there was a convergence between these two critiques of capitalism and the restructuring of the capitalist spirit partly resulted from an incorporating of the themes of the artistic critique. Yet, the meanings of significations like flexibility and self-organization were modified in the process and they were rendered compatible with the institution of contractual relations in the market. Boltanski and Chiapello argue that the 'project' *cité* or polity emerged as the new regime of justification and the 'network' became the model of the new capitalist organization. In short, the network supposedly represents an alternative to the former hierarchical and authoritarian model of industrial management and in the project polity 'engagement is conceived as voluntary' (Boltanski and Chiapello, 2005: 110). According to the new capitalist spirit's self-representation, networks do not have an existence external to their constituent participants and projects' limited duration prevents the consolidation of bureaucratic domination and standardized practices.

It is not difficult to understand the appeal of the 'project' polity and the network model, especially compared to the preceding forms of industrial organization. The fact that there is a continuing dialectic of control evidences the substantial discrepancies between new capitalism's self-representations and its actual institution. Indeed, the pathological quality of new capitalism's double meanings has already been highlighted. Boltanski and Chiapello contend that capitalism's conflicts were subject to *displacement*, but this means they have been moderated and modulated rather than resolved. Alienation is connected to the contradiction that capitalism depends on 'mobilizations' that it cannot generate itself (Boltanski and Chiapello, 2005: 53). At the same time, it thwarts the participation that enables its reproduction, since full participation would presuppose a reorganization of the capitalist institution. Alienation expresses a substantial imbalance in the transaction or conversion between the subjectivity of social actors and the objectivity of institutions.

The paradox of alienation is how institutions' appropriation of subjects' actions and the outcomes of these actions are constitutive of subjects' dependence on the institutions that depend on their actions. The interdependency of capitalism's 'involuntary socialization' means that alienation contains the possibility of its immanent negation. Alienation always concerns the relationship between social practices' potential and their actual conditions. It is not a static phenomenon and alienation is relative to the potential for autonomy and creativity that is present but unfulfilled. However, what has changed in the present phase of capitalist modernity is the way in which this discrepancy between the potential and the actual has become a major source of the damages to individual life-projects. Now, partly as a result of new capitalism's future-oriented temporality, which has been reinforced by financialization and technological changes, contemporary capitalist institutions regularly derive legitimacy from their potential, rather than the actuality of their present form and functioning. It is certainly not coincidental that Boltanski and Chiapello define the new spirit of capitalism's regime of justification as the '*project*' polity or *cité*. In a different way, Rosa has highlighted the connection between acceleration and alienation (Rosa, 2010; 2013).

Despite its connection to the critique of new capitalism's failure to meet the normative expectations that it generates, my reconstructed conception of alienation is based on a social ontology. It presumes that the transaction or conversion between the subjectivity of social actors and the objectivity of institutions is a general feature of all forms of social life. Further, social action is considered to be generative of institutions and alienated action enables the reproduction of institutions. Like Marx's notion of objectification, my reconceptualization considers that the relationship that subjects have to their own actions is critical to their experience of alienation. Yet, my conception emphasizes to a greater extent the interpretative character of subjects' relations to their actions and the sense in which meanings form part of the dialectic of control that is operative in contexts of alienation. This should be evident from the discussion of the significance of normative expectations and the discrepancy between actors' experience and the semantics of social institutions. The definition of alienation, as compelled yet thwarted participation, equally enables an appreciation of how alienation coincides with class and other social relations of inequality. There can be little doubt that the manner and degree of compulsion and constraint constitute important indexes of social relations of subordination and inequality.

Two Contrasting Forms of Malaise

Although my reconceptualization of alienation is intended to be consistent with subjects' experiences of suffering and discontent, there are contemporary forms of malaise that could appear similar to alienation but which should be differentiated from it. There are two such particularly significant forms of malaise in the contemporary period: first, there is the thwarted participation of those segments of the population that are external to major institutions of advanced capitalist societies, institutions like the labour market and the public-political sphere. The second malaise tends to be most visibly expressed by so-called religious fundamentalism and political Islam. The latter has recently, of course, been a significant force of mobilizing certain experiences of discontent. In my opinion, the contrast with these two types of malaise throws into relief some of the distinctive elements of my conceptualization of alienation and alternatives to it. Unlike theological notions of malaise, my conception of alienation is entirely social-historical. It is founded on the modernist ideal of the autonomous constitution of society. My reconceptualization is likewise intended to preclude the misuse of the category of alienation; because highly consequential implications have been drawn from the contention that alienation precludes the possibility of authenticity (see Bourdieu, 1991a; 1991b; Taylor, 1991; Jaeggi, 2014).

There can be little doubt that in advanced capitalist societies the long-term unemployed and other categories of marginal individuals are alienated in the lay, or everyday, sense of the term. It is certainly the case that absence of employment or social rights thwarts their participation and that these states are extremely damaging to subjectivity. Yet, these are social positions that differ in some respects from my conception of alienation. One of the most significant features of these social positions of exclusion and marginality in advanced capitalist societies is how institutions appear not to depend on the appropriation of these subjects' actions for their reproduction. In other words, these positions regularly lack the conditions of integration or participation. The independence from these subjects of institutions means that alienation, that is, compelled yet thwarted participation, does not reveal itself directly in the relationship that they have to actions that serve the reproduction of institutions. For this reason, these positions involve a somewhat different dialectic of control. Although it might be argued that the contradiction of alienation is located in the relationship between institutions that these individuals experience, for instance, the state may compel the long-term unemployed to participate in labour market training programmes and yet their participation may be then thwarted by the lack of employment owing to regional or industrial decline.

I want to propose that these positions should be conceptualized in terms of a revised conception of reification; one that relates such experiences of exclusion and marginality to the dynamic of system integration at the expense of social disintegration. Reification better characterizes the standpoint that develops amongst these subjects, because they are affected in a different way by the social processes that they have no, or limited control, over. It is certainly equally the case that alienated individuals, in my terms, experience reification; the difference is that the sense of interdependency that conditions alienation is largely absent in the case of such marginalized and excluded individuals. They basically experience only the separation of institutions from them and not so much the dynamics of appropriation. To be precise, the normative promise of institution is not extended to the individuals in these positions and this has major implications for how the marginalized understand their life-projects. In actual fact, there is never a complete marginalizing, but rather an exclusion from a salient dimension of social integration. This is why the next chapter defines such marginality and exclusion as *half-positions*: where some level of involvement is compromised by the subject's exclusion at another level.

The conception of alienation that I have proposed should be similarly distinguished from comparable religious or theological notions. The multiple modernities perspective has highlighted the enduring 'civilizational' complexion of religious articulations of the distinction between immanence and transcendence (Eisenstadt, 2000). This distinction is regularly framed in terms of the problem of alienation: with transcendence overcoming some immanent state of alienation, such as through the attainment of reconciliation with God or the world of being in general. It is probably the case that residues of these theologies can be found in secular conceptions of alienation and that the latter draws on similar metaphors to define states contrary to alienation, like those of reconciliation, fulfilment and actualization. In a general sense, the religious theologies of human alienation respond to generic problems of human existences, such as the requirement of meaning, the need for a normative framework, and the incertitude of human experience. Yet, these theological conceptions usually represent a metaphysical perspective that situates the overcoming of alienation in a domain beyond that of social practices. Further, theological conceptions of alienation have been employed to explain a lack of authenticity among some communities and to characterize the alienated state of individuals that diverge from particular interpretations of religious beliefs and practices. One can find variations of these interpretations amongst different religious communities, but in recent decades specific theological conceptions of alienation have served to mobilize discontent and justify acts of extreme violence.

Gilles Kepel (2006) has drawn attention to how an interpretation of the alienation of certain categories of Muslims from Islam was used to legitimate acts of violence, since these acts would have otherwise explicitly contradicted the religious norms and theology. Similarly, modern political movements have not been exempt from employing quasi-theological conceptions of alienation and considering the deviation, or departure, of subjects from a political programme that supposedly represents their interests as evidence of alienation. Shmuel N. Eisenstadt argues that this assessment reflects the totalizing and Jacobin character of many revolutionary movements in modernity (Eisenstadt, 1999a). It is not difficult to perceive how these political and religious interpretations of alienation can be aligned with an elitist position and processes of disqualifying others' practices as inauthentic. Political and religious movements have sometimes embraced the rather dangerous proposition that alienated groups and individuals cannot reform themselves through their own actions.

The conception of alienation that I have proposed should preclude the misuse and instrumentalizing of this category on the basis of metaphysical notions and an extra-social political position. It is a conception that is logically opposed to the substitution of a political or religious agency for that of the social actors that are alienated, because this process of substitution meets the criteria of alienation that I have proposed, including that of the appropriation, or properly misappropriation in this case, of agency. The dialectic of *compelled yet thwarted participation* nevertheless points to substantive conditions for social transformation and how practices contain an immanent potential for overcoming alienation in generating social institutions.

Conclusion

The concept of alienation that I have proposed simultaneously gives expression to the 'pretheoretical' experience of subjects and serves to analytically delineate the complexion of the social context of alienation. Alienation constitutes a state that harbours a potential for immanent transformation, since it discloses a potential for social reorganization that is present in the processes of social reproduction. No doubt my conception of alienation, that is, compelled yet thwarted participation, is strongly conditioned by the context of the third phase of capitalist modernity (Wagner, 1994; Domingues, 2012). At least at the level of their legitimation, institutions in the third phase of modernity exhibit an increased reflexivity in relation to the detrimental consequences of alienation. Institutions' power to appropriate action and the outcomes of action appear to require normative justifications that value participation, self-actualization, and creativity (Boltanski and Chiapello, 2005). Still, the fact of appropriation and structures that effectively limit social actors' control contradict these normative justifications. Indeed, I have argued that this discrepancy is a major source of damages to actors' subjectivity. The self-relation of subjects was a substantial component of Marx's critique of alienation from the standpoint of the paradigm of objectification. My conception sustains this concern whilst more strongly emphasizing the interpretative dimension of this self-relation and how action stands in relation to individuals' life-projects. Similarly, the action-theoretical conceptualization of alienation distinguishes it from many of those categories that have developed to explain similar experiences, such as that of subjection; and which are often informed by other theoretical perspectives, like psychoanalysis, linguistic and post-colonial studies.

The critique of alienation nevertheless depends on the envisaging of another relationship between social institutions and social action. For this reason, the ideal of creative and self-determining action remains an emancipatory alternative to alienation, because it is suggestive of how action can simultaneously alter subjectivity and institutions. This is one of the reasons why the democratic form of the 'general will' signifies a vision of how society can be constituted in ways contrary to alienation. The 'general will' represents a normative vision of participation that has been somewhat appropriated by contemporary institutions, even though it is contrary to the conditions that sustain these institutions. I have drawn attention to this political philosophical alternative to alienation in order to emphasize the depth to which the ideal of the mutuality of individual and collective autonomy is present in modernity. It is this ideal that originally set the terms in which the contestation over alienation emerged. Marx's projection of the alternative to alienation of autonomous, creative action is a society organized on the basis of universal cooperation may appear to be simply a remnant of romantic nostalgia, but it can continue to serve to distinguish the potential that is being created and the actuality that limits its realization.

3

SYSTEM INTEGRATION AND SOCIAL DISINTEGRATION

Introduction

The Critical Theory of the Frankfurt School originated during a period of the protracted crisis of capitalism and its critique reflected the diminishing prospects of an emancipatory transformation. Critical Theory consequently sought to expose the connections between the rationalization of modernity and the social pathologies of capitalist reification. This concern with the dialectics of rationalization remains a constitutive dimension of the programme of Critical Theory. Habermas sought to revise the theory of reification with the explanatory thesis of the 'internal colonisation of the lifeworld' (Habermas, 1987a). My analysis of contemporary reification draws on the framework of Habermas' thesis, but it radically revises this conception in light of the contradictory tendencies of globalization and the subjective experiences of injustice and heteronomy associated with them. In the preceding chapter, I suggested that reification may be evident in an inability to generalize the principles of mutual recognition. The ensuing analysis highlights long-standing and contemporary structural conditions that hinder mutual recognition. In their current configurations, these structural conditions crystallize an inverted cosmopolitanism and institutionalize borders to effective social participation. The metaphorical reference to colonization may be relevant to apprehending the ensuing conflicts and demands for retribution.

The contemporary phase of global modernity has extended social interconnections, especially beyond the national frame. However, new forms of exclusion, subordination and marginality have resulted from the processes that enable the extension of social relations. This paradoxical dynamic of system integration and social disintegration is one of the contemporary forms in which the contradictions of the capitalist system are displaced onto other social institutions. The result, I argue, is fractures in the institutional means of social integration that developed during the preceding phases of modernity and conflicts that are conditioned by the contemporary consolidation of types of half-positions. These half-positions lie at the borders between the lifeworld of social actors, on the one hand, and the state and the market economy, on the other. Half-positions are prototypically those of workers without the full rights and entitlements of citizenship, and citizens without the material resources and social recognition of wage labour. Half-positions are, in effect, the product of exclusionary integration and this tendency of exclusionary integration is reinforced by the fact that race and ethnicity are often salient to the determination of those in half-positions. In this respect, Fraser (2009) is right to argue that a Critical Theory of globalization should explicate the justice claims over *who* is represented politically. Yet, my analysis shows that whilst Fraser's normative position is relevant to addressing certain dimensions of the subordination and injustice of half-positions, it does not encompass some significant features half-positions' modes of contestation.

The contestation that ensues from exclusionary integration of half-positions is related to two other significant forms of conflict in global modernity, but it also exhibits specific attributes that distinguish it from them. First, there is conflict between global capitalism and democracy, which overlays the dynamic of class conflict and that tends to generate reflexive modes of contestation, from the practices of the alter-globalization movement and anti-austerity protests to the mobilizations based on nationalist ideologies and the antinomian strands of major religions (Eisenstadt, 1999a; 1999b; Browne, 2002; 2009a; Domingues, 2012). In my opinion, the conflict between globalization and democracy concerns the potential for collective self-determination, and this is why this conflict often manifests itself in terms of competing agencies' attempts to shape and control the direction of modernity (Wagner, 2012). In fact, the conflicts associated with half-positions are in large measure a by-product of this conflict and they are a displaced version of its central dynamic. Nevertheless, the exclusionary nature of half-positions means that this category of individuals are more affected by the specific articulation of the conflict between democracy and globalization than they are capable of shaping its dynamic. This is one of the reasons why the contestation of half-positions needs to be understood in terms of distinctive experiences of reification and real abstractions (see Domingues, 2006).

Second, there is the conflict intrinsic to the relationship that institutions have to the social action that serves their reproduction. Institutions depend on the creativity of subjects and yet limit subjects' control over their own activity (Castoriadis, 1987; Boltanski and Chiapello, 2005). In other words, it is the conflict based in alienation. The half-positions of workers without citizenship and citizens without work are, to be sure, implicated in this conflict of compelled but thwarted participation. Yet, despite significant overlaps with the conflicts over alienation, the contestation of half-positions can be differentiated from it. The social integration necessary to participate is often what is precisely at stake in half-positions and a half-position entails some disassociation from mechanisms of social involvement, like the legally defined positions of either wage labour or citizenship. There are many analyses of vulnerability

(Misztal, 2011), 'disaffiliation' (Castel, 2003), 'precarity' (Standing, 2011), and 'marginality' (Wacquant, 2008) that draw attention to the emergence in capitalist nation states of significant categories of individuals that are seemingly superfluous from the standpoint of the labour market and the neo-liberal state (Bauman, 2004). The structural changes of the contemporary phase of global modernity are then generating a variety of antagonisms and injustices; however, the 2005 French Riots will be taken as a major exemplar of the conflicts emanating from half-positions. The rioters' acts of resistance, I argue, were conditioned by their exclusion from the dominant public sphere and the principal justice claim connected to their actions was that of retribution.

The consolidation of half-positions is particularly due to the character and limitations of the principal coordinating mechanisms of the third phase of modernity, especially the network mode of organization and the market. José Maurício Domingues argues that these forms of coordination have to varying degrees replaced the second phase of modernity's more state-organized coordination through principles of hierarchy and command, although modernity's third phase is actually a 'mixed articulation' of these different modes of coordination. The elements of earlier phases of modernity are not so much 'erased' in a process of succession as rearranged and realigned in a more layered and complex pattern (Domingues, 2012: 26). Half-positions reflect the disjunctions between these different forms of coordination, since the institutional inclusion as a citizen, may not, for example, be replicated at the level of wage-labour. Similarly, the unemployed may simultaneously confront expectations of voluntary collaboration as a basis of social membership and other state agencies' authoritative commands, especially those of the police and the judiciary. Indeed, disjunctions between modes of coordination are relevant to the often indefinite objectives of the contestation deriving from half-positions, because the source of deprivation may be spatially distant global processes that are only indirectly encountered and the more directly experienced local context is conditioned by the interface with other institutions, like the family, the school system, the urban housing estate, welfare organizations, voluntary associations, police and informal social networks. Although half-positions have distinctive features, their consolidation crystallizes broad trends towards social disintegration. Robert Castel sought to define the social question's metamorphosis during the third phase of modernity in somewhat similar terms. Castel argued that the resurgence of market coordination was calling into question the capacity of society 'to exist as a collectivity linked by relations of interdependency' (Castel, 2003: xix–xx).

Exclusionary Integration: Genealogies and Misalignment in the Third Modernity

The notion of half-positions presumes that the integration of individuals and groups in capitalist societies depends on the combination of wage labour and citizenship. In fact, the insufficiency of one of these positions in the absence of the other was integral to T. H. Marshall's conception of social citizenship. Marshall (1950) described a conflict in capitalist societies between the 'warring principles' of 'market inequality and class divisions on the one side, and citizenship's egalitarian and universalistic principles on the other' (Somers, 2008: 82). Citizenship formed the basis of individuals' participation in public life and mitigated some of the effects of class inequalities. Significantly, Margaret Somer's historical genealogy of citizenship and Robert Castel's historical genealogy of wage labour each details how citizenship and wage labour have been institutionally elaborated in relation to each other (Castel, 2003; Somers, 2008). On the one hand, the social rights of citizenship represent a set of protections against the inequalities and vulnerabilities that are present in the market determination of wage labour. On the other hand, struggles over wage labour were critical to the extension of the social rights of citizenship. Wage labour provided a substantive means of participation and supplemented the formal equal liberty of citizenship. The circumstances of groups that were historically excluded from either citizenship or wage labour, particularly women and males without property, reveals the interconnection between these two channels of integration and the 'complex inequalities', to use Sylvia Walby's term, that ensues from the variation between them (Walby, 2009).

Somers and Castel's respective historical genealogies of citizenship and wage labour are each significantly informed by Karl Polanyi's argument about the 'double movement' by society, which was conveyed by groups and movements, against the disembedding of the market during the first phase of liberal modernity (Polanyi, 1957[1944]). It is worth noting that Polanyi considered that the system of protection that the European 'double movement' generated against the destructive dynamic of the disembedded and self-regulating market system was not attainable in colonial contexts, because colonies 'lacked the prerequisite, political government' (Polanyi, 1957: 192). In Polanyi's opinion, the revolts against imperialism during this period were mainly attempts by the colonized populations 'to achieve the political status necessary to shelter themselves from the social dislocation caused by European trade policies' (Polanyi, 1957: 192). Polanyi argued that the market society of the first liberal phase of modernity was unsustainable. It was, as Castel (2003: 410) reiterates, 'only able to take hold in the first place because it was embedded in a social system where traditional patronage and "organic" forms of solidarity remained strong' and the related familial and communal protections initially 'blunted its potentially destabilizing effects'. Market society's protracted crisis culminated in the assertion of social regulation, but social protections had to be established on new bases due to the dissolution of previous social bonds. The capitalist expropriation of land and the commodification of labour had created a society dependent on wage labour and the movement of people from rural regions to industrial centres (Castel, 2003; Polanyi, 1957). The elaboration of the social rights of citizenship and the establishment of systems of regulation that qualified the market determination of wage labour's conditions were largely consolidated during the second phase of 'organized modernity', especially with the institution of the post-Second World War democratic welfare state capitalism (see Wagner, 1994; Streeck, 2011).

Democratic capitalism represented a social model in which the welfare state alleviated inequalities to varying degrees in different national contexts on the basis of taxation revenues and provided the market with some degree of coordination. Critical Social Theory largely considered democratic welfare state capitalism a class compromise and argued that capitalism's contradictions were not resolved. Rather, the contradictions of capitalism were either transferred onto the state administration or manifested themselves in the displaced form of crises of social identity. Although Habermas' original conception of late-capitalism undoubtedly overestimated the extent to which the welfare state had irrevocably transformed the conditions of capitalist accumulation. Habermas' more recent analysis of 'the postnational constellation' draws on Polanyi in order to highlight the persistent competing dynamics of the opening to markets and the closure of national protection against them (Habermas, 2001a). In a sense, the denationalizing character of globalization is primarily the disembedding of the various forms of market-based exchange from the broad conditions of social integration.

The third phase of modernity involves, what Domingues (2012) describes as, a more flexible and polarizing global dynamic of capitalist accumulation. It is a dynamic that reinforces the misalignment in the institutional channels of social integration; for instance, the third phase of modernity intensifies the differences in the temporalities and spatial extensions of capitalist markets and bureaucratic administration (see Sassen, 2008: 390–5). One of the consequences of the fracturing of the channels of integration is that individuals occupying half-positions encounter 'internal borders' that limit participation and membership (Balibar, 2004; Bosniak, 2006; Somers, 2008). In all cases, half-positions entail some reduction in the ability to effectively access those forms of social protection that had limited the subjective experience of structural transformations and social subordination. This is particularly important because the contestation of half-positions is shaped by experiences of how legitimate expectations of equal treatment are not upheld and the exclusion of those in half-positions from the dominant public sphere.

The exclusionary integration of half-positions discloses the fragility of the democratic regulation of capitalist inequalities through the social protections of citizenship. There have generally been significant exceptions to the normative universalism of citizenship. In most cases in the capitalist periphery the elaboration of citizenship as a system of social protections remains at best prospective and even in the capitalist core there are important variations. These discrepancies in the institutional systems of social protection have had long-term consequences. It has already been noted how second modernity gave rise to improvements in the conditions of wage labour and citizenship, although these changes were the result of different, though related, features of modernity. The limiting of inequalities was generally a direct result of emancipatory social struggles, but the institutionalizing of fairer distributions of resources was often closely tied to a nation state's response to economic crisis or the project of 'nation building'. The 'New Deal' in the USA, the so called 'national settlement' that took place shortly after the federation of Australia at the beginning of the twentieth century, and the post-Second World War welfare state in the UK are instances of such developments. However, these progressive reforms incorporated aspects of exclusionary integration. Notably, the occupational categories of farm labourers and domestic servants were exempted from many of the New Deal's industrial regulations (Lieberman, 1998; Katznelson, 2005). This detrimentally affected the many African-Americans who were employed in these poorly renumerated areas of employment. In the Australian case, the limiting of inequality amongst male employees went together with discriminatory, racially based immigration policies and the denial of an equal status as citizens to the indigenous population (Lake, 2008; Beilharz, 2008).

The compromises that limited reformist initiatives were inconsistent with the universal principles that were mobilized to justify social citizenship, and these historical instances of exclusionary integration continue to impinge on contemporary situations. Margaret Somers (2008) argues that exemptions from the New Deal labour regulations influenced the living conditions of the African-American population affected by the Hurricane Katrina emergency. In this way, the contemporary 'market fundamentalist' policies of limiting the social state intersects with the longer history of racial inequality. The dynamic of exclusionary integration in third phase of modernity is predominantly a consequence of, what I will term, the globalization of the lifeworld. That is, the *globalization of lifeworld* refers to the contradictory tendencies resulting from the relative decoupling of processes of economic and political system integration from those of social integration. In short, the coordination of the disembedded market system can simultaneously have the opposite consequence of disorganizing the institutions of social integration, including the political institutions to which citizenship is affiliated. Yet, the decoupling of system integration from social integration is never total and the renewal of the self-regulating market is an ideological project. Saskia Sassen is right to argue that 'global systems insert themselves in national domains where they once were non-existent', but that nation states have facilitated globalizing processes (Sassen, 2008: 227).

The developments in global system integration that have altered the parameters of the relationship between the state and the economy in capitalist societies are well known: the expansion in the wealth and power of financial markets, with the institutionalization of trade in national currencies following the breakdown of the Bretton-Woods system and the deregulation of finance, the growth in the number and size of multinational corporations in recent decades, with the corresponding increase in the proportion of economic activity that is intra-firm; as well as the clustering of subsidiary business services, the internationalization of the division of labour and the development of supranational regimes of economic governance, with the influence to compel states to adjust social and economic policies (Held et al., 1999; Beck, 2005; Sassen, 2008). The growing autonomy of the capitalist economy is equally evidenced by the fact that capital's increased mobility compared to labour has coincided with a decline in many nation states of the proportion of state revenue that is derived from business taxation. There is another significant, though sometimes overlooked, implication of these new regimes of system integration. The strategic adaptation of nation states to the 'external' conditions of coordinated market competition increases the unevenness of the 'internal' economy. In short, as the notion of comparative advantage itself implies, most 'countries succeed in a few industrial sectors but not very well in most' (Hollingsworth and Boyer, 1998: 38). These divergences in industrial capacity regularly accentuate differences between regions and cities, as well as often coinciding with the socio-economic divisions in the labour and housing markets (Sassen, 2006).

The half-position of wage-labour that lacks the full entitlement of citizenship applies to the situation of such categories as guest workers and illegal migrants. Of course, the connections that wage labour with reduced citizenship entitlements have to processes of global system integration is most evident in the creation of so-called 'free zones' that are exempt from many of the social protections of national labour regulations and national taxation obligations (Ong, 2006). Free economic zones are very concrete instances of the tendencies of diminishing the citizenship dimension of work and 'denationalizing' the economy. Yet the erosion of the citizenship dimension of wage labour has occurred in core capitalist states and it is a broader tendency of 'flexible accumulation'. Boltanski and Chiapello (2005) describe this as the 'dismantling of the world of work' in the third phase of capitalism. It has included the dismantling of some of the social protections of labour legislation on the grounds of deregulation and flexibility, the increase in the scale of part-time and precarious employment, the use of sub-contracting and outsourcing, and new ways of segmenting the workforce on the basis of qualification, gender, ethnicity and age, for instance, 'seniority has become a factor less of security than insecurity' (Boltanski and Chiapello, 2005: 238). These processes have generally coincided with significant declines in the percentage of the workforce that are members of trade unions.

Beside the regulation of the labour market and the social protections that went together with citizenship, citizenship implies a certain valuing of subjectivity. The latter distinguishes the citizen's experiencing the 'dismantling' of work conditions from that of those groups that are in a formal sense in the *half-position* of workers without citizenship, particularly in terms of the potential modes of contestation and, in Nancy Fraser's terms, 'representation' in the political sphere (Fraser, 2009). Indeed, in Europe and North America the integration of non-citizens through wage labour has been countered by the coercive state power that has been directed towards non-citizens, particularly through enhanced 'security controls', legislative changes, and curtailing the informal means of participation in a community (Balibar, 2004; Bosniak, 2006; Sassen, 2008). Étienne Balibar provocatively considers that there are certain parallels with South African apartheid in the recent coercion that European states applied to

> the important group of workers who 'reproduce' their lives on one side of the border and 'produce' on the other side, and thus more precisely are *neither insiders nor outsiders*, or (for many of us) are *insiders officially considered outsiders*. (Balibar, 2004: 123; emphasis in the original)

It can be argued then that a contradiction has emerged in global modernity between the normative justification of law based on appeals to cosmopolitan justice and human rights, on the one hand, and the simplification in many Northern and Southern nation states of law into an instrument of control in order to deal with social disorder and developments construed as originating outside the boundaries of the nation, on the other hand (Habermas, 2006; Comaroff and Comaroff, 2006). That is, law becomes for those in half-positions a means of forced coordination, rather than an institution whose legitimacy is generated by public communication and the participation of those affected. In this way, the state's coercive powers increasingly mediate the disintegrative consequences of the globalization of the lifeworld (Wacquant, 2008; 2012).

Similarly, the half-position of citizens that lack the full entitlements of employment is closely related to the limits of welfare state intervention, patterns of unemployment in contexts of 'deindustrialization', as well as being related to increases in insecure forms of employment and the consolidated effects of segmented labour markets. The general underlying tendency in capitalist welfare states is that of the economy's inability to meet the former expectations of full employment and the strong segmentation of labour markets. One of the things that the 2005 French riots highlights is a generational shift in this case of half-positions. Many of the rioters were in the half-position of being citizens without work, whereas their immigrant parents had occupied the contrasting half-position of workers without the rights of citizenship. In capitalist welfare states, half-positions' diminished circumstances are exacerbated by changes in the third phase of modernity's modes of coordination and the transference of former public entitlements into private functions that require individual, familial or communal network solutions, whether in the form of voluntary work or household expenditure (Bourdieu, 1999). The conditions of welfare recipients have likewise altered over the past decades in these nation states. Despite labour market failures, the introduction of 'workfare' and 're-commodification' extended the contractual principles of market exchange (Gray, 2004). Somers (2008: 8) argues that when the 'contractualizing' of citizenship intersects with entrenched inequalities, such as those of race, it can lead to situations that are similar to that which Hannah Arendt (1979) described as the losing of the 'right to have rights'.

Given these changes in the relationship between the different modalities of integration, the historical experience of colonization is in some respects a precursor to the pathologies of the globalization of the lifeworld. The conversion of social integration to the external conditions of system integration is a distinguishing feature of colonialism (Pels, 1997). The transnationalism of colonial systems produced fractured relations of social integration, especially given the systematically distorted relations of recognition between colonizers and colonized (Fanon, 1986). Although there are considerable variations in colonial formations, the imbalance between the metropolis and the periphery underpinned the exploitive relations of colonization. It determined the direction of the capitalist world system's commodity chains and established the preconditions for economic dependency. For the colonized, colonialism represented a system of partial involvement and unequal participation; the rights of citizenship were unevenly distributed. In colonial contexts, differences in social integration were used as a weight against the factual involvements of colonized populations at the level of system integration (Asad, 1991). It is possible to discern continuities with contemporary global integration in these colonial ruptures with equivalence and the equality of conditions. There can be little doubt that the disparity between economic circumstances underpins the integration of individuals as consumers in contemporary capitalist nation states.

The distribution of half-positions is uneven and it is the concentration of half-positions amongst marginalized populations that one finds further parallels with colonial relations of system integration and social disintegration. Half-positions are, in a sense, an inversion of the cosmopolitan potential of globalization, particularly because they tend, though not exclusively, to coalesce around the ascribed categories of race and ethnicity. Yet, despite their contradictory nature and attendant potential to undermine the symbolic reproduction of the lifeworld, many half-positions are highly functional from the standpoint of system integration. The uncoupling of work from the rights of citizenship can be the very source of the value of the individual from the perspective of an employer and indirectly that of a consumer (Kearney, 1998: 128; Gray, 2004). Of course, this valuing then depends on sustaining marginality and the exclusion from citizenship. For this reason, the half-position is mapped directly onto subjectivity, rather than effectively mediated by the other channel of integration. Now, it is my argument that this dialectic of integration and disintegration *induces displaced reactions* to the experiences of reification and alienation. The binds that can develop for those occupying half-positions can result in frustrations that infuse episodes of violent contestation. Balibar likewise points to how the experience of 'internal exclusion' shaped the 2005 French riots and the rioters' destruction of the 'thing' 'from which they are contradictorily *excluded* as non-citizens', 'but of which they are themselves a part, that in a way is part of themselves and their identity' (Balibar, 2007: 51).

The displaced reactions to the globalization of the lifeworld are not limited to violent and disorderly modes of contestation; ideological confusions and distrust of social institutions are probably more common responses. In fact, this is one of the reasons why there are opposed types of social disintegration ensuing from increasing system integration. On the one hand, there are the subjective experiences *of* those occupying half-positions and its implications for social contestation will be explored in more detail. The antithetical relations to oneself and others that are generated by this exclusionary integration have already been highlighted. On the other hand, there are the anomic reactions to half-positions coalescing with race and ethnicity. These reactions can amount to an endorsement of social exclusion, as is evident in the types of resentment that are directed towards refugees and marginal groups (Hage, 2003). The reactions *against* those in half-positions sometimes reflects a divide between majority and minority cultures, with the former appealing to some association between the institution of the nation state and the idea of the nation as the foundation of social integration. It is this conception of social integration that the denationalizing dynamic of globalization challenges and which can in turn lead to the socially regressive contestation that seeks to establish internal borders.

The recent xenophobic and racist reactions to minorities, immigrants and supranational institutions in many nation states can be viewed as simply the more visible and extreme versions of dominant classes' or popular majorities' attempts to monopolize the influence over the institutional anchoring of social integration. That is, the dominant classes or popular majorities endeavour to exclude themselves from the *colonizing* aspects of the globalization of the lifeworld and to confine its effects to the minorities in half-positions, thereby reinforcing them. If this analysis is correct, then it could explain the growth of so called 'welfare chauvinism', that is, policies making it more difficult for migrants to access social rights and welfare benefits, whilst preserving them for nationals (Banting, 2000: 25; Huysmans, 2006). It is important to note that the social disintegration that coincides with the globalization of the lifeworld is not exclusive to the circumstances of migrants. Rather, it is relatively explicit in relation to immigrants because of citizenship's formal determination and migrants having been the negative object of displaced reactions to system integrating processes. Half-positions result from the uneven and polarizing developments in global, national and regional economies and the state's incapacity – or unwillingness – to prevent, in Bauman's (2011) terms, 'collateral damages'. The next section develops the claim that half-positions lead to forms of mobilization that differ from the more typical format of modern social and political movements. The 2005 French Riots were significant in terms of the scale of their unplanned coordination and the participants' reaction to the experiences of exclusionary integration (see Browne and Mar, 2010).

Social Disintegration and Social Contestation: Reification, Racism and Retribution

There are several reasons why the 2005 riots in France illustrate the thesis that the current processes of system integration involve tendencies of social disintegration. The riots had considerable symbolic resonance and were often viewed as symptomatic of the social malaise of globalization (Balibar, 2007).

The participants were largely the children of immigrants from former French colonies and exemplify the coalescing of half-positions. The riots were undoubtedly a form of symbolic action and laden with meaning, yet it is difficult to attribute a particular objective to them. In other words, the riots lacked the political elaboration of more traditional contentious politics, like those of the anti-racism movements and student protests (Lentin, 2004; Wieviorka, 2005; Lagrange and Oberti, 2006). In my opinion, the riots' imprecision of meaning is connected to experiences of reification and the displacement of contestation from the sources of inequalities to the institution of authoritative control and regulation. The perceived illegitimacy of intensive police intrusions formed the backdrop to the 2005 French riots, which were triggered by the death of two youths from an electrical surge whilst hiding in a power substation in the belief that the police were searching for them. The riots probably refract quite mediated and indirect experiences, given half-positions accumulate damages owing to weaker social protection (Offe, 1996: 33).

Underlying the riots were substantial and protracted structural problems of system integration. In particular, segments of the French immigrant population have experienced sustained rates of high unemployment, itself a reflection of the decline in traditional manufacturing industries and the introduction of less labour-intensive methods of production. As a consequence, the archetypical half-position has undergone something of a generational change, from migrant labourers without the full rights of citizenship to French citizens without the material resources and social recognition of employment. Likewise, the riots appeared to signify the declining capacity of the French state to deal with problems of system integration. The state's policy options seemed to diminish as a consequence of fiscal problems that were simultaneously veiled by attributing demands for restraint to the European monetary union (Smith, 2004). Similarly, over the previous decade the social policy of the French state shifted from active job creation through public and private industry sponsorship to the more market enhancing position of funding labour market training programmes (Levy, 1999; 2005; Palier, 2005). Despite the considerable resources that have been deployed, these programmes are limited in their capacity to transform the exclusion and lack of opportunity of the children of migrants from the outer suburban *cités* and *banlieues*. A diffuse background of racism and the stigmatizing of the *banlieues*' inhabitants generated the sense of injustice that propelled the riots' retributive actions. In this context, racism often takes the precise form of systematically distorted communication. That is, the raising of validity claims concerning the rights of membership of French society for which there are neither the institutional conditions for their realization, nor the means for accessing them owing to the occupancy of half-positions (Habermas, 1970a; 1970b; 1984; Castel, 2006).

The devaluation of local place can likewise compound the damages of half-positions and reinforce the public discourses of the failures of integration. In the public imagination, the *banlieues* are associated with the past 'modernist' projects and the negative effects of bureaucratic planning (Castells, 1983;

Wacquant, 2008). There are certain analogies with colonial disjunctions in these experiences of urban exclusion and the stigmatizing of the housing projects as materializing the periphery. The globalizing context may have altered the system problems that generate the colonization, in Habermas' terms, of lifeworlds by commodities and the state administration, yet this dynamic's salience to the 2005 riots is disclosed by the violence being principally enacted on private property in the form of automobiles and public property in the form of schools. Although these two types of property were undoubtedly defaced due to their accessibility, they resonate with half-positions' contradictory interchanges: automobiles signify the desired but exclusionary integration of consumerism and school is the institution that transmits cultural norms and values whilst generally allocating subordinate positions in the division of labour to the children of migrants.

There is no inevitable connection between half-positions and the enactment of violence. In fact, half-positions more generally lead to resignation and demoralization. The 'hidden injuries' of half-positions are connected to the 'in-between' situation of social integration that is conditional on consent or acquiescence to a position that is relatively subordinated and largely precludes the public expression of aspects of identity (Sennett and Cobb, 1973: 118; Cowlishaw, 2004). Hidden injuries are the *debilitating self-relations* that can develop from occupying half-positions and experiencing a constant denial of reciprocity in social interaction. On the one hand, this kind of disrespect may engender destructive forms of collective behaviour when conflicts that are normally veiled by everyday moral orders and the 'unarticulated condemnations' of social subordination are brought into the open by events which undermine the legitimacy of the coercive powers of the state (see Honneth, 2007: 93). It is in precisely these terms that the contestation of the 2005 French riots can be viewed and I will highlight two features that an investigation into the riots disclosed: retribution and creative disrespect (Browne and Mar, 2010).

The 2005 French riots were a form of retribution for the perceived and experienced damages of material and symbolic denigration. Retribution is a kind of moral claim that is moulded by expectations that full membership, whether as a citizen or paid employee, cannot be taken for granted. Further, that even the tacit rules regulating the subordinated groups' relations to the institutional authority of the police have been transgressed and violated. This is not to deny that one could discern some order of claims for redistribution and recognition in the riots, but the action of retribution accentuates a lack of mutuality and it responds to the affective experience of humiliation. Retribution belongs to a moral economy that markedly differs from those of 'individual rights' and procedural claims to justice: it is a form of popular will and reflects limited means of redress. In particular, the primary aspect of retribution is to affirm the collective pride of the aggrieved group by challenging the expectations of the state concerning compliance with its authority. The riots did, however, involve actions of creative disrespect. That is, performative actions which give expression to a frustrated social agency in the absence of other means of effective access to the public sphere. These actions are creative in their making explicit the contestation over values and legitimacy.

Creative disrespect arises out of the attempt of a collective to reassert some form of self-control in relation to institutionalized subordination. For this reason, violent provocations and ritualized performances, like burning cars, taunting police and even exaggerating a racially stigmatized identity, are modes of self-assertion and ways of demarcating the limits to the intervention by authorities (see Cowlishaw, 2004). These actions may not be effective politics from a strategic point of view, but they are nevertheless modes of taking initiative outside the dominant public sphere and the official channels of representing grievances. Creative disrespect is a mode of communication by means other than those of discursive speech. Rather than traditional dialogue, it can take the traumatic form of re-enacting some of the binds of half-position. Creative disrespect may involve making claims for dignity and respect in ways that are at the borders of legality and that may compound social exclusion, as in the case of riotous actions and modes of self-mutilation as a method of protest. The latter is not uncommon amongst highly traumatized groups and individuals (see Good et al., 2008).

Conclusion: The Globalization of the Lifeworld and its Variegated Displacements

The dynamic of exclusionary integration has been a constant feature of modernity, however the manner of its articulation has acquired some new dimensions in modernity's third phase. In my opinion, the tendencies that result in the consolidation of the half-positions of workers without citizenship and citizens without work represent a major contemporary form of reification. The reifying experience of being subject to processes that appear independently of your actions and those institutions that supposedly provide some measure of social protection has generated displaced reactions and contemporary forms of disorderly contestation. The tendencies of disembedding and real abstraction that result in half-positions are not exclusive to developed nation states, although the connection to the deterioration of the basis of citizenship's social rights in the welfare state is distinctive to them and reflects differences in the normative expectations that have underpinned social integration. Despite the enormous disparities in material conditions, Partha Chatterjee (2004) highlights an analogous mode of exclusive integration in contemporary India. Chatterjee argues that the current phase of primitive accumulation involves a substantial and almost complete disembedding of the peasantry, yet there is not sufficient work available in the labour market for this dispossessed population. In his opinion, a portion of the dispossessed are now in the intermediate position of being part of 'political society', that is, subject to intense state regulation whilst 'not regarded by the state as proper citizens possessing rights and belonging to the properly constituted civil society' (Chatterjee, 2008: 58).

The analysis of the 2005 French riots served to highlight the disintegrative consequences of the globalization of the lifeworld and the types of social contestation that diverge from the more standard forms of social movement contention and their objectives. In the case of the 2005 riots, the pathological effects of half-positions was evident in the violent reaction to stigmatized personalities, the anomic relations to the institution of law that functions as a medium of forced coercion, and the cultural breakdown that is conditioned by the tension between a commitment to universalism and a restrictive interpretation of national identity in the public sphere. No doubt there is a specific intensity to the 2005 French riots, yet my allusions to parallel analyses suggest that conflicts over half-positions may become more pronounced in modernity's third phase. Indeed, structural adjustment regimes and austerity programmes only seem to consolidate the misalignment in the institutional channels of integration. Finally, my analysis suggests that whilst much contemporary Critical Theory underestimates social complexity, the older assumption that the structural contradictions of capitalist modernity have not been resolved and that they manifest themselves in displaced forms remains relevant.

4

THE END OF IMMANENT CRITIQUE?

Introduction

It is often suggested that critical social theory depends on the methodology of immanent critique (Antonio, 1981). In its simplest terms, immanent critique delineates 'the difference between how men and things are and how they could be' (Habermas, 1982: 231; Adorno, 1973b: 167). When it is framed by such a distinction, immanent critique can only either be incomplete or a methodology that is abandoned; it could be misapplied but not really refuted. The possible end of immanent critique has two main sources: internal developments within critical theory eventuated in Habermas' abandoning immanent critique in favour of other methodologies (Habermas, 1971; 1976; 1984; 1987a; 1987b). He claimed that the altered ideological constellation of late-capitalism suspends its preconditions; a change to the paradigm of communication was necessary to secure critical theory's normative foundations. Second, Critical Theory is an interdisciplinary approach, drawing on the most advanced perspectives in philosophy and the social sciences. However, assimilating the diagnostic frameworks of influential theories of contemporary society may undermine Critical Theory's distinctive normative and empirical orientation. The following analysis will focus on how the logics of perspectives on the present, particularly postmodernism, the risk society and globalization, appear at variance with the methodology of immanent critique.

These two sources of the prospective displacement and incoherence of immanent critique are not divorced. Changes in Critical Theory's methodology and normative background underscore an increasing distance between philosophical foundations and the empirical analysis of social developments. The deficiencies of the Frankfurt School's and subsequently Habermas' theory of contemporary capitalist society give rise to a need to incorporate aspects of other representative conceptualizations of the contemporary period. There are nevertheless substantial obstacles to any constructive synthesis. Postmodernist rejections of normative universalism and epistemological foundations constitute less of a challenge than the intuition that modernist arguments fail to grasp the consequences of ambivalence. This postmodern intuition leads to the view that the very social processes that generate the possibility of emancipatory change equally render improbable the normatively founded aspiration of liberation. In the case of the risk society thesis, a methodological affinity with immanent critique leads to paradoxical conclusions: the potential defines the actual in the contemporary risk society, but to the extent that immanent social developments are over-determined by their unintended consequences. Similarly, some discourses of globalization are close to the normative orientation of Critical Theory, yet even they cannot avoid raising questions about the parameters of critique and its diverse applications. Globalization, properly understood, poses the analytical problem of comprehending the stability and change that results from the interaction of social processes having different origins and trajectories. The continuity of the meaning of immanent critique is therefore in doubt, being itself subject to the transformative logic of globalization.

In order to effectively delineate these contemporary theories' discord with immanent critique it is first necessary to clarify those features of this methodology that distinguish it from other forms of criticisms. This explication suggests that it is not so much immanent critique in general that is threatened with the possibility of ending, rather a variant particular to critical theory. A number of immanent critique's principles have become widely accepted in social theory; it can be argued that there are no meaningful alternatives today. Honneth comments that 'it is customary to suspect that any use of a transcendent standard forces one to adopt a perspective that is too alien, too external to the criticized society to find any application within it' (Honneth, 2000: 117). Even so, the rejection of transcendent standards hardly eliminates the problem that contemporary conceptions of immanence are often based on suppositions contrary to Critical Theory's commitment to rationality and normative universalism.

Immanent Critique: Method and History

A number of contemporary theorists have asserted that western modernity has its origins in the adoption of immanent perspectives and the possibilities this created for critical reflection on a reality that was recognized to be amenable to transformation (Lefort, 1988; Gauchet, 1998; Hardt and Negri, 2000). These sketches draw attention to the background cultural horizon that influenced immanent critique without giving it precise definition. The critique of unjust and oppressive social relations is neither unique to Critical Theory, nor the defining feature of its orientation. Critical Theory seeks to identify the potentials for emancipation immanent in the needs of subjects and aims to provide an analysis of contemporary society that apprehends its developmental possibilities. Marx first expressed this orientation in the contention that 'the construction of a socialist society' is, in Giddens' (1981: 233) words, an 'immanent negative principle of the continued reproduction of capitalism itself'. Marx's dialectical logic not only required enlightened political practice, it presupposed a sociological understanding of the historical process. Based on its reflexivity concerning its social-historical constitution and ties to subjects' practices, the differences between immanent critique and the standard types of external criticism, like those of empirical and logical refutation, are relatively straightforward. In short, the methods of standard criticism are not discarded, only subordinated to other considerations.

Despite its embedding in the social-historical process it analyses, Critical Theory's interest in the sociological translation and historical realization of philosophical categories distinguishes it from generic forms of social criticism. Critical Theory aspires to a synthesis of normative principles and empirical analysis; theory plays a constitutive role in its understanding of critique. According to Calhoun:

> Immanence by itself was not enough; one could not just trust to history to realize the possibilities embodied in the forms of culture or in material social relations. (Calhoun, 1995: 23)

From Marx's writings onwards, Critical Theory is also the critique of theory as ideology. In this way, Kant's conception of critique as the determination of the limits of reason is continued in critiques of the social foundations and legitimizing implications of traditional philosophy and later positivist social sciences. Of course, this determination is not accomplished through a transcendental deduction; Critical Theory specifies the limits of knowledge by explaining the limitations of the present organization of society. It either prevents the proper actualization of reason or entails the expression of knowledge in ideological form. The assumption that there is a subject and agency of historical change strengthens this position. In this respect, Hegel's philosophy employed a version of immanent critique that anticipated later methodological refinements. His *Phenomenology of Spirit* assumes that each stage in the development of consciousness contains internal limitations that condition its negation and therefore a potentially superior rationality (Hegel, 1977). Horkheimer's conception of Critical Theory rejected idealism but retained the logical framework of Hegel's interpretation of history. Immanent critique confronts, Horkheimer stated,

> the existent, in its historical context, with the claim of its conceptual principles, in order to criticise the relation between the two and thus transcend them. (Horkheimer, 1974: 182)

The critical theorists considered Hegel's resolutions of social contradictions metaphysical. In Adorno's opinion, immanent critique should explore the strains and tensions within bourgeois culture and in its relation to its material reproduction.

> What distinguishes dialectical from cultural criticism is that it heightens cultural criticism until the notion of culture is itself negated, fulfilled and surmounted in one. (Adorno, 1981: 29)

The historical grounding of analysis and contribution to the reflexive liberation of subjects differentiate immanent critique from what can be loosely categorized as context-dependent internal criticism and context-independent models of normative criticism. There is a basic methodological contrast between the latter and immanent critique. The values immanent critique employs belong to the reality it criticizes; they should neither be imposed nor arbitrary (Held, 1980). Internal criticism shares immanent critique's interest in disclosing how the principles and values of a culture are denied and negated by social structures (Walzer, 1987). It appeals to the standards and norms present in traditions and documents, like bills of rights, constitutions and even international treaties, to criticize institutionalized arrangements inconsistent with them. However, internal criticism neither grounds critique in a sociological explanation of the necessity of this distortion within the current social order, nor does it base itself on claims to universal validity. Despite the apparent overlaps, an account of the dynamics of change is less central to the configuration of internal criticism. The understandings of social transformation are not equivalent. Internal criticism often highlights the injustice located in the discrepancy between claim and reality, but it strictly limits criticism to the application of norms that already have current validity and are accepted in local contexts. Owing to its comparatively fixed horizon, Adorno (1981: 31) believed that internal criticism is structurally limited and conditioned by ideology. One need not agree with Adorno's view that the antithesis of immanence and transcendence is false to recognize that Critical Theory has a far more selective and indeed critical relationship to the normative principles that are present, though unfulfilled, in particular contexts. This explains Critical Theory's synthetic incorporating of the normative principles that it considers the most advanced and possess universal validity, even though they may originate from supposedly context-independent criticism.

Honneth (1994) contends that critical theory distinctively locates its own perspective in the pre-theoretical standpoint of the subjects themselves and that without this 'left-Hegelian' principle of 'immanent-transcendence' it would be simply another form of criticism. This requirement is a corrective to the neglect of subjects' capacities for innovative action that is typical of notions of ending, yet it may not prevent a version of immanent critique lacking practical-political relevance and being thereby redundant. A more profound difficulty is the problem of whether critique can connect its analysis of large-scale developmental tendencies to the consciousness of actors in a way that is reflexively liberating (Bohman, 1999: 65). The Frankfurt School's Critical Theory has regularly been faulted for failing to satisfy this requirement. For many commentators, the Frankfurt School's representations of a closed system of capitalist domination seemed not just to lack any immediate practical-political relevance, but effectively undercut the prospect of emancipation entirely (Wellmer, 1985; Benhabib, 1986). These representations evidenced their dissolution of confidence in the two volitional tendencies immanent critique sought to discern: the emancipatory practice of an emerging collective subject and systemic processes enabling the rational resolution of capitalist crises. The integration of the working class into the capitalist order undermined the former tendency, while twentieth century political forms demonstrated that a more rational institution of society is far from a logical outcome of capitalist crises.

Habermas would link his arguments for a change to the communication paradigm with those rejecting immanent critique, criticizing the Frankfurt School's interdisciplinary research programme for its residual ties to a philosophy of history. In his opinion, their critique of instrumental reason floundered because it depended on translating arguments about an 'objective teleology in history' into 'pseudo-normative propositions' (Habermas, 1987a: 382; 1982: 230–232). Habermas argued that independent normative criteria were necessary because immanent critique had lost its point of reference; the labour theory of value no longer applied and contemporary technocratic ideology disavowed normative justification (Habermas, 1971). Habermas' critical theory is founded instead on the rational reconstruction of those norms actors presuppose whenever they enter into processes of communicative action oriented towards mutual understanding (Habermas, 1984; 1987b; 1990). Its discourse ethic employs a somewhat different methodology and requires direct validation as a normative theory of justice. Rational reconstruction does seek to interrelate normative philosophy and empirical sociology, however it does not fuse them in the manner of immanent critique. *The Theory of Communicative Action* justifies the formal structures of rationality in an 'ahistorical manner' before relating them to the historical processes of their actual development (Habermas, 1984; 1987a). In this work, a critique of a distorted pattern of modernization replaces the immanent critique of the contradictory developmental tendencies of modernization as a whole.

Despite its significant theoretical innovations, the syntheses of Habermas' theory of communicative action were neither equivalent to those of immanent critique nor intrinsically superior, given the range of criticisms to which it has been subject (Bernstein, 1985; Joas and Honneth, 1991). There are substantial grounds then for investigating whether Critical Theory could incorporate aspects of other representative interpretations of the current phase of social development. Habermas' (1984; 1987a) debate and critical adaptation of systems theory informed his renunciation of immanent critique, yet it equally demonstrated that any syntheses presuppose that the perspectives involved should be amenable to immanent critique. Even though the social-historical reflexivity that distinguished Critical Theory now encompasses its internal evolution, the decomposition of its original and subsequent theoretical programmes may be less remarkable when it is weighed against its methodological ambition. A theory that finds its justification in disclosing the potentials for transformation in the present development of society will almost inevitably contain an exacerbated sense of its limitations and an awareness of the uncertainties generated by its connections to some form of anticipated historical practice.

Postmodernism, Risk Society and Globalization

Of all recent theoretical perspectives on the present, postmodernism explicitly combines a number of the arguments about the difficulties of pursuing immanent critique. Even though it is an inadequate perspective for addressing social change, postmodernism articulated a set of considerations that broadly anticipate the current tensions between immanent critique's empirical analysis and normative principles. In the first instance, postmodernism translated Lévi-Strauss' (1966) structuralist critique of western thought's privileging of historical reasoning into a general scepticism towards the appeal of modernist culture to notions of progress and development. The fact that a postmodernist assertion of this claim can only be antinomic highlights how a rejection of normative and evaluative standards is disorienting. It is possible, of course, to discover disorienting trends in the fragmentation of meaning that postmodernist discourses regularly associate with consumer capitalism and media spectacle (Featherstone, 1991; Baudrillard, 1998). The postmodernist contention that the idea of progress has lost its legitimizing function acquires substantial form in the ecological arguments that suggest that modern progress is actually endangering. Horkheimer and Adorno (1972) already recognized in their critique of instrumental reason that such an ecological analysis places in question the exercise of an *immanent* logic. The self-referential practices that Lyotard (1984) attributes to the postmodern episteme can be plausibly sourced to this kind of dilemma. In particular, the postmodernist acceptance of dilemmas of this order means, according to Lyotard, that paradox becomes the mode of innovation and an interest in indeterminacy displaces the modernist aspiration of certainty.

Postmodernism equally gave expression to a new awareness of pluralism, despite many of pluralism's ramifications being independent of it. Postmodernism emphasizes how universalism reduces plurality to singularity; it often draws relativist conclusions from the rather trivial insight that an apparently internal position is external from another point of view or discourse. Postmodernism does without a dialectical conception of reason in embracing the view that cultural pluralism entails scepticism towards all generalizing claims. Postmodernism appears relevant to the situation characteristic of identity politics, where the interests of subordinate groups may not conform to the principles of universalization that are constitutive of general interests and the expression of cultural demands that may not fit the framework of liberal entitlements. Nancy Fraser (2003a: 18) considers that groups that are 'distributed throughout the entire class structure of capitalist society, occupy no distinctive position in the division of labour, and do not constitute an exploited class' currently advance such demands for cultural recognition. It is owing to the multiplicity of struggles that Fraser and Nicholson (1990) claim that the postmodernist 'antifoundational metaphilosophical perspectives' led to an exploring, however inadequately, of different modes of criticisms. Postmodern

> criticism floats free of any universalist theoretical ground. No longer
> anchored philosophically, the very shape or character of social criticism
> changes; it becomes more pragmatic, ad hoc, contextual, and local.
> (Fraser and Nicholson, 1990: 21)

The postmodernist concern with the instability of norms and knowledge claims
is usually regarded as inconsistent with the rational complexion of critique.
According to Wagner, this aspect of postmodernism potentially undermines the
aim of sociological analysis altogether: 'If postmodernity meant the questioning
of any possibility of providing a valid representation of the social world, then
a postmodern sociology would be a contradiction in terms' (Wagner, 2001b:
164). Undoubtedly, there can be no grounds for immanent critique if there is
no possibility of coherently representing even a part of the social reality criticized. A more substantial challenge is present in the contention that postmodernism introduces a radically different understanding of immanence. Immanent
critique has operated in relation to a hierarchical social structure and ordering
of values; postmodernism may imply that this type of domination determined
the discerning of the direction of emancipation and democratization. With its
idea of the dispersal of power throughout the social field, Foucault's analytics
of power suggest this reconsideration of immanence. Deleuze remarks that in
Foucault's analyses 'power is characterized by immanence of field without
transcendent unification, continuity of line without global centralization, and
continuity of parts without distinct totalization: it is a social space' (Deleuze,
1986: 27). Foucault's analyses exemplify a peculiar antinomy of a postmodernist understanding of immanence that is based on a disavowal of any notion of
transcendence. Foucault rejects any conception of an overarching historical
narrative whilst constructing a genealogy of modernity in which historical
movements for liberation undermine themselves (Foucault, 1972; 1978; 1979).
    Lyotard's (1984) claim that no language game is privileged over another in
'the postmodern condition' could similarly allude to an alternate understanding of social immanence. This idea of plurality can be articulated as an appreciation of differences within the present, rather than as an aspect of the
difference between the present and the future. Unlike the logical structure of
immanent critique, the dissolution of hierarchy would not belong to the future
actualizing of a potential subordinated in the present. Lyotard's sketch of the
postmodern condition can be considered an attempt to address the possible
end of immanent critique. He claims, firstly, that 'the critical model' originating
in Marx and the Frankfurt School 'lost its theoretical standing and was reduced
to the status of a "utopia" or "hope", a token protest raised in the name of man
or reason or creativity, or again of some social category' (Lyotard, 1984: 13).
Secondly, he contends that a dichotomizing approach to the 'social bond' was
a product of the dialectical reversal of critical positions into features of system
reproduction. A dichotomized image of society is 'haunted' by arbitrary distinctions and 'a principle of opposition' (Lyotard, 1984: 13). In Lyotard's (1984:
14) opinion, the 'partition solution' is 'out of step with the most vital modes of

postmodern knowledge'. The paradox is precisely that this knowledge is entirely immanent; critique is one position or 'language game' among others. Social practices are 'self-referential' because 'the striking feature of postmodern scientific knowledge is that the discourse on the rules that validate it is (explicitly) immanent to it' (Lyotard, 1984: 54).

Although Lyotard's assertion of an incredulity towards metanarratives points to the dilemma of the theoretical justification of immanent critique, it should be understood as a reflection on the politics of the problem of transformation, rather than as an epistemological statement. The impetus behind this postmodernist critique was originally political: the relation of theory to the immanent conditions of practice had served as a licence for political elites and their usurpation of power. In other words, it was primarily a reflection on how a theory of emancipation can become an ideology, as well as a consequence of the recognition of this change. Basically, this consideration had been worked out in the context of arguments over political practice within the group *Socialism or Barbarism* well before *The Postmodern Condition: A Report on Knowledge*. In part, Lyotard's volume reworked Castoriadis' (1987) analysis of social imaginaries' occluding of the formative instituting of society through a process of providing extra-social legitimation. The very social institution of society is disguised and denied in social imaginaries that offer metaphysical accounts of society and trace social institutions back to religious origins. Metanarratives of reason and progress can function in a not dissimilar way, by providing transcendent rather than immanent social reasons for social-historical processes. Since social processes are shaped in turn by their social imaginaries' horizon of meaning, the creation of social relations of heteronomy and inequality are, for the most part, rendered invisible. Drawing on this insight into the dual institution of society, it is possible to question whether critique has inevitably sought to validate itself by reference to the transcendental structure of theory. Despite its claims to immanence, critique has perhaps been neither properly historical nor social.

In a similar vein, Bauman's (1987) postmodernist questioning of the 'legislative' role of modernist thought concerns how theory has legitimized social structures by its very independence from actual conditions. If accepted, Bauman's argument would presumably warrant a change from immanent critique to the strictly interpretative position of internal criticism. Nonetheless, postmodernist criticism of theory may simply misrepresent the actual structure of immanent critique, since immanent critique is a process of articulating the consciousness of social struggles that exist independently of theory. It is more likely that theory endows these struggles with a utopian inflection. Similarly, as Habermas' concept of 'performative contradictions' details, postmodernist critiques are self-contradictory because they must entertain claims to reason, universality, morality or progress if they are to be either consistent or compelling (Habermas, 1990; Jay, 1992).

Yet, these refutations of postmodernism probably fail to engage with the most important dilemmas that it posed for immanent critique. In its most sophisticated forms, postmodernism is a questioning of logic and the intuition of an alternate modernizing of contemporary society. In these terms, its conceptions of immanence may have affinities with novel features of contemporary modernization, thereby assisting in illuminating the redeployment of the capitalist imaginary. This capitalist imaginary occludes in the manner Castoriadis ascribes to other social imaginaries, yet it is more flexible and adaptable than the earlier ideological legitimations of domination and hierarchy. In my opinion, the arguments of the social theories of the 'risk society' and globalization generally evidence a superior appreciation of the complexities of this redeployment. However, this does not make the contemporary challenge to immanent critique any less substantial. It may be owing to postmodernism that the redeployed capitalist imaginary is recognized to neither contradict nor actually supersede its earlier forms.

Beck's (1992) risk society thesis claims to resolve postmodernism's inadequate social-structural analysis of the contemporary period, yet it draws on similar experiences of rupture and contingency. On the one hand, Beck asserts that the continued unfolding of various processes of modernization is dissolving the institutional parameters and modes of understanding of its first industrial phase. On the other hand, in 'advanced modernity the social production of *wealth* is systematically accompanied by the social production of *risks*' (Beck, 1992: 19). Even so, Beck's theory is less ambiguous than postmodernism in its position on the normative and political grounds of social critique. In the first instance, the risk society thesis is a sociological elaboration of the implications of the ecological critique of late-capitalism. Beck finds that the logic of ecological problems exemplifies the characteristics of other trends in the contemporary period, from the restructuring of employment patterns to the dynamics of love and intimacy. The central idea of the 'reflexive modernizing of an already modern society' seems to presuppose, or even constitute, a social process of immanent criticism (Beck, 1992). However, Giddens' (1990; 1994b) parallel analysis demonstrates that even if this is the case then it may simply reflect the changed function of the typical attributes of critique. The unification of theory and practice ensuing from reflection need not have the radical transformative meaning it originally held for Critical Theory. Rather, reflexivity is a mundane feature of the post-traditional social order, where 'social practices are constantly examined and reformed in light of incoming information about those practices' (Giddens, 1990: 39). In Giddens' opinion, radical politics should be framed by a 'utopian realism' that appreciates the fallibility of critique, since the 'equation of knowledge with certitude has turned out to be misconceived' (Giddens, 1990: 39; see also Giddens, 1994a).

On the surface, Beck seems to adopt the standpoint of immanent critique in suggesting that ecological enlightenment is itself an outcome of immanent developments. He believes that he is applying standards that have arisen in the historical process and that these tendencies contain a significant potential. Indeed, he accentuates the difference between his idea of an increasing individualization arising from the further modernization of society and Horkheimer and Adorno's thesis of *the end of the individual* in the totally administered society. For all of that, there is a large discrepancy between these arguments concerning the prospects for democratization and much of the substantive content of Beck's diagnoses. The hazards and dangers of the risk society are defined as unintended, long-term, high consequence and imperceptible (Beck, 1992; 1994). Further, as a consequence, fear becomes the principal means for mobilizing social solidarity, whilst Giddens (1990; 1999) proposes that knowledge claims cannot dissolve the modern experience of fragility and uncertainty, because reflexive interrogation renews the dynamism of modernity and the contemporary 'runaway world'.

The risk society thesis radicalizes the notion of social construction to the point that any sense of the relationship between the origin of social processes and their outcome potentially breaks down. The homeostatic models of functionalist social theory are replaced by an appreciation of unpredictability; however, this conception of social organization may undermine the logical, if not the normative, basis of critique. Luhmann's (2005) analysis of risk points to the perverse consequences that can follow from heightened reflexivity concerning the implications of knowledge. Similarly, the problem of complexity influenced Habermas' (1976; 1987b) distancing of Critical Theory from immanent critique, whilst Offe (1996) argues that the risk society thesis primarily gives expression to the limiting of the political options of advanced welfare states. Even Beck (2000b: 218; 1994) admits that risk society analyses often point to 'what should *not* be done' rather than 'what *should* be done'.

Unlike the condition of industrial society, the risk society seems to involve paradoxes that undermine the identification of critique with either of the alternative projects of the 'transfiguration' or the 'fulfilment' of modernity (Benhabib, 1986). The idea of the reflexive modernization of the welfare state exemplifies this predicament. In part, the welfare state originates from demands for insurance against risks, especially those of workers and other groups peripheral to the labour market, and it involves a certain transfer of responsibility from the individual to the state. According to Beck (1994) and Giddens (1994a), despite its continuing to be critical to actualizing the values of modernity, the welfare state has depended on a model of compensation that is challenged by the displacement of the logic of distribution of industrial society, which framed the 'insurance principle' of the first modernity, and by the increasing individualization that is a consequence of its institutionalizing social rights. Indeed, for Giddens, the progressive aspects of welfare regimes often relied on a concentration of authority and rather limited individual knowledge, choice and lifestyle opportunities. The fact that Giddens has sought to 'rethink social democracy' from this standpoint probably explains some of the third way policy oscillations between states, markets and communities (Giddens 1998; 1994a; 1994b).

The emphasis on the self-endangering features of the risk society implies that the immanent processes of social development have negative, or at best indeterminate, consequences. If the logic of the distribution of *bads* replaces the logic of the distribution of *goods* then the conditions of democratic or emancipatory transformation are grounded in development itself precisely because they are threatened and risk being negated. This risk of negation is not because democratic change is impossible, but because change *per se* is perpetual and the key catalysts are the 'side-effect' and the very consciousness shaped by anxiety. These various trends create a new temporal order: the determination of the present by the future (Beck, 2000b). Owing to critique's participation in the projection of future scenarios, Giddens claims that a critical theory relevant to late-modernity is 'without guarantees' (Giddens, 1985; 1990). Risk scenarios involve both opportunities and threats; the difficulty of distinguishing between them can be traced back to the intimate connection between the methodology of inquiry and the substantive content of analysis. This connection is unlikely to be immanent critique's synthesis of method and analysis, but something else instead. Beck believes that his perspective is simultaneously realist and constructivist.

> [Risk] statements are neither purely factual claims nor exclusively value claims. Instead, they are either both at the same time or something in between, a 'mathematicized morality' as it were. (Beck, 2000b: 215)

The diagnostic value of the risk society thesis is substantial, although its reliance on the perverse logic of developments for justification may weaken the grounds of immanent critique. It is difficult to see how critique could avoid processes of distortion, since it is liable to encounter either the perception of risk that it has itself generated or the 'unawareness' that resists its illumination (Beck, 2000c). The fact that different schools of thinking about perceptions of emergencies and 'states of exception' involve quite different politics is telling (Agamben, 1998; 2005). These allude to how the antinomies of the risk society could become the basis of an authoritarian state. No doubt, this prognosis is inconsistent with the democratizing tendencies that Beck and Giddens associate with reflexive modernization, constituting its standpoint for critique. Significantly, Beck has always highlighted the nexus between global inequalities and the dangers of the risk society. It is therefore only by way of his unwarranted over-extension of the category of risk that the following contradictory trends could be considered under this one category. On the one hand, there is the risk that results from the expansion of citizenship rights and their effective implementation. These rights are embodied in welfare states, underpinning processes of individualization and detraditionalization. On the other hand, there is the risk associated with the opposite trend, that is, where the effects of globalization are mapped directly onto subjectivity without the mediation of citizenship, often through highly exploitative forms of employment (Beck, 2000d). The latter trend can be seen to precipitate shifts toward 'bare life' and struggles for existence (Agamben, 1998). Even if these two trends could be interconnected, they cannot be linked together in the way of the dialectical logic typical of earlier immanent critique. This discontinuity

and divergence partly explains why Beck counterpoises the normative potential of cosmopolitan globalization to the 'globalism' of a 'world market that
eliminates or supplants political action' (Beck, 2000a: 9).

There is no single universally accepted theory of globalization; nevertheless,
the associated discourses challenge some basic assumptions of immanent critique. Unless it is reduced to a single overarching tendency of trans-national
extension, like capitalism or westernization, globalization is not a uniform
developmental process and requires a conceptual break with notions of 'linear
modernization' (Beck, 2000a). Instead, globalization represents an unusual and
uneasy combination of progressive and regressive tendencies. Its logic is that of
the intersection of social processes having different origins and trajectories.
The result is a varying alignment of time and space, making it difficult for
immanent critique to identify the empirical conditions that give it orientation.
Given these tendencies towards, in Albrow's (1996) terms, 'multiplicity without
unity', the aspiration of critique probably needs to be redefined: critique would
be an intervention in processes that are subject to displacement. While there is
nothing new about the difficulties that social complexity poses for social
critique, globalization involves novel elements, with the institutionalization of
disembedding mechanisms and the exacerbating gradations of class and other
transnational capitalist asymmetrical interdependencies (Giddens, 1990;
Appadurai, 1996).

The more intensive interplay of the global and the local that is a typical
characteristic of globalization transforms the territorial basis of notions of
endogenous change and undermines the 'methodological nationalism' of most
social science (Beck, 2003). Critique may need to give greater consideration to
the implications of exogenous developments and how they are transformed
and reworked in local contexts; immanent critique has focused on endogenous
developments. Globalization results in an increasing discrepancy between the
originating intentions informing social actions and their ultimate consequences.
Even Habermas' (1998; 2001a) argument that social solidarity should follow
the processes of integration that have occurred through the extension of market relations and be translated into European democratic law does not fit the
idea of an immanent development that leads to the transcendence of present
conditions. It seeks instead the development of effective regulating institutions,
so that globalization appears in this case as the problem of an imbalance
between developmental trends, rather than a process that will give way or give
rise to another that supersedes it.

The connections between globalization and the risk society are equally evident in tendencies towards 'increasing social options' and the social disinte-
grating consequences of the increased mobility of capital compared to that of
labour (Sassen, 1988; Pieterse, 2004a; 2004b). The latter can simultaneously
extend and intensify exploitation, whilst paradoxically undermining the dialectic of class interdependency that had informed immanent critique. Neo-
liberal globalization extends the dialectic of interdependency in predominantly
anti-social forms, undermining the principles of equivalence and reciprocity

that frame notions of justice and the modern social imaginary of 'a moral order of mutual benefit' (Taylor, 2004). Overlapping theoretical diagnoses have highlighted how tendencies for social disintegration ensue from processes of systemic global integration. Bauman (2000) emphasizes how the temporal and spatial discordance of globalization involve more than the fact that its beneficiaries inhabit different zones from those excluded and disadvantaged by the same processes. In his opinion, globalization erodes the democratic space in which the subordinate can confront the dominant with the conditions of their disadvantage. The limited contact between them and its format produces an indifference on the part of those enhanced by globalization to the circumstances of those diminished by it. According to Touraine (2000), the 'desocializing' tendencies of neo-liberal globalization have resulted in a fragmenting of the culture that underpinned modern democracy. As a result, the mutually exclusive tendencies of the assertion of communal identities and economic individualism displace the modernizing project of the nation state and its universalistic commitments. Similarly, Habermas (1989a; 2001a) relates globalization to processes exacerbating the structural dilemmas of the welfare state, perceiving it to be creating a situation analogous to an interiorizing of the north and south polarity within single nation states. Touraine's (1995; 2000) conclusion that it is necessary to reconstitute the subject accurately reflects the difficulties that these diagnoses have in formulating an immanent potential for emancipation.

Immanent critique is based on an account of the volitional aspects of change and generative processes, typically either of the actions of subjects or the contradictory dynamics of systems. Although the contemporary global justice movement may be unable to constitute a different order, rudiments of a new democratic potential are present in the self-organizing principles of struggles against global capitalism and neo-imperialism. These struggles have substantially developed the critique of the linkages between the consumerist lifestyle of advanced nation states and global inequality. This critique is a significant challenge to the remobilization of the capitalist imaginary, because its legitimation has largely taken shape through the transformation of the conditions of consumption. Since Marx's (1971[1867]) diagnosis of capitalist commodity fetishism's disguising the asymmetries of production, consumption has been an object of critique. Postmodernist notions of consumption as the means of the production of subjectivity reflect the expansion of this aspect of dissimulation, potentially complicating critique's system of value.

From the standpoint of contemporary globalization, the difficulties consumption presents are of a different order. Consumption can be justifiably critiqued for its dependence on the exploitation of labour in the developing world, yet this critique would take the strictly external form of a normative critique of empirical conditions. It would not be the same as immanent critique's synthesis of normative principles and empirical developments, because consumption condenses several paradoxes of globalization. The interconnections that consumption involves are almost by definition constitutive of globalization, these being major means of individuals' participation in the world system. However, the contexts that are brought into relations of interdependence are highly disparate in terms of wealth, power and resources. This lack of proximity of conditions makes it difficult for critique to encompass the variant positions. The unity created through consumption is not based on reciprocity; hence it is unlikely that the direction of greater autonomy can be discerned in this process of integration.

At the same time, globalization is probably the interpretation of the present that is most amenable to immanent critique, since ideas of progress and development are explicitly endorsed in its practically most influential versions: from neo-liberal economic discourse through to the politics of the third way (Giddens, 1998; 2003). Given that these appeals to progress may simply replicate the standpoint of earlier modernization theory, it is worth recalling that certain strands of globalization theory emerged precisely in response to the discrediting of earlier social scientific theories of modernization and failures of many development models. This points to the notion of multiple modernities as the most credible position on global transformations, because it acknowledges that the uniformity that was taken to exist at the general level of modernity has been countered by the diversity of renderings and realizations of modernist projects. The perspective of multiple modernities could reinforce the position of immanent critique, particularly due to its interest in the tension between the value-horizon of programmes of social transformation and the dynamics of institutionalization. It can contribute to the lucidity of critique, disclosing the conflicting interpretations of cultural programmes of modernization and the contemporary 'repositioning of the major arenas of contestation' (Eisenstadt, 2000: 24). Still, multiple modernities introduces an understanding of modernity as a distinct civilization and applies a hermeneutic notion of world-constituting horizons that makes the exercise of critique itself the object of interpretation and the subject of social-historical analysis (Arnason, 2002; Eisenstadt, 2000; Wittrock, 2000). The litmus of the degree to which multiple modernities could be integrated with Critical Theory are the ties that it could have to the participant perspective of practice.

Contemporary representatives of Critical Theory broadly agree that the critique of globalization as an ideology should be grounded in the potential for cosmopolitan justice. The reasons for this are relatively straightforward: from a normative standpoint the value system of cosmopolitanism seems superior to most positions that would serve as a counter-contrast, nationally founded principles can provide a territorial basis for social exclusion. Even so, there is weak empirical basis for this commitment; the trans-national institutions that could give effect to human rights principles have limited implementation capacities. Similarly, the capitalist imaginary has constituted the dominant vision of globalization, shaping the version of cosmopolitanism endorsed by the relatively small category of the beneficiaries of *global citizenship* – corporate elites and professionals (Calhoun, 2003). A cosmopolitan solidarity would reject the neo-liberal definition of globalization, seeking to assert different principles of justice to the typical prescriptions of market efficiency and competitive advantage.

Since the alternatives to reorienting globalization in the direction of cosmo-politan justice are either relatively undesirable or unrealistic given the range of processes that cut-across national states, the differences between those identify-ing with Critical Theory concern its substantive content and means of realiza-tion. In general, they share with Habermas a cosmopolitan ideal that is 'more ambitious in theory and more difficult in practice' than Kant's vision of a global rule of law that would lead to a peaceful confederation of states (McCarthy, 2002). McCarthy observes that because 'individual liberties, democratic proce-dures, and redistributive mechanisms are interdependent aspects of cosmo-political justice,' in Habermas' view, 'no one can be adequately realized without the others' (McCarthy 2002: 258; see also Habermas, 2003).

Conclusion: New Synthesis and Capitalist Modernity

The developments in capitalist societies that have resulted from progressive struggles, including those which were somewhat inflected by the Frankfurt School's arguments, have produced certain changes in the distinction between traditional and Critical Theory. The standard versions of traditional theory still persist, with their commitment to an ahistorical conception of truth, their denial of their connection to the social context of their genesis, and their claims to be free of value-commitments (Calhoun, 1995). However, due to methodo-logical developments and social changes, traditional theory has itself under-gone various changes. In particular, traditional theory has itself become more reflexive and attuned to the implications of contingency. As a consequence, traditional theory has changed in a way that is consistent with the ideology of 'the new spirit of capitalism' and its forms of managerial organization and 'governance through change' (Boltanski and Chiapello, 2005; Boltanski, 2011; Browne, 2014a). The version of traditional theory that fed through to modern positivism was based on the separation of subjectivity and objectivity (Wagner, 2008). In its practical implications, positivism was consistent with the hierar-chical system of capitalist management and centralized authority. For this reason, there was an affinity between the critiques of capitalist management and critiques of epistemological positivism: managerial systems were criticized as dehumanizing, alienating and as promoting the dominance of objectivity over subjectivity (Marcuse, 1964). While the opposition to positivism, empha-sized the role of subjectivity in the constitution of knowledge (Habermas, 1978a). Similar implications followed, though sometimes unintentionally, from communicative accounts of knowledge. Communication theory's disclosure of the inherence of meaning in any representation and conception of objectivity have promoted social constructionist arguments challenging positivism.

In any event, the critical principle: that things could be otherwise came to influence the types of knowledge that play the role of 'traditional theory' today, that is, those theories that bestow some explanatory purpose and organization. The aim of these theories is less the satisfaction of claims to representation of an objective reality, rather it is the provision of justification and legitimacy, because claims to knowledge and expertise are recognized to be fallible and provisional. This reflexivity concerning the contingency of knowledge has led to the use of 'tests', particularly tests that anticipate potential future scenarios, such as the 'stress tests' on banks during the recent economic crisis or the 'psychological test' of performance. In one sense, the use of tests is simply a result of the growth in 'auditing culture' and 'reflexive monitoring', to use Giddens' term, in conjunction with a value system or 'economy of worth' that distributes reward and assesses contributions to the common good in terms of 'activity' or performance (see Boltanski and Chiapello, 2005; Boltanski and Thévenot, 2006; Giddens, 1990; 1991; Browne, 2014a; 2016). The methodology of 'tests' can serve the purpose of the critique of institutions as well as the reproduction of institutions and hierarchical authority (see Boltanski, 2011). In the latter consolidating of authority, critique is paradoxically applied to workers and citizens, especially to evaluate performance and to regulate them. Even more importantly, the test methodology is used to incorporate subjectivity and to thereby achieve a degree of complicity on the part of workers and citizens. Indeed, even highly progressive and democratizing initiatives, like citizens-juries and deliberative forums, may not be entirely immune to this manipulation.

It is through the application of these new practices, methodologies and 'regimes of justification' that the dichotomy of subjectivity and objectivity of traditional positivist theory is overcome, but without overturning the underlying system of managerial control. This is a more sophisticated form of incorporation than that which the Frankfurt School perceived with the integration of the working class into the capitalist order and the pacification of class conflict. It is possible to recognize some of the rationalization of techniques of integration in other areas, like the mass media, particularly through the power to shape public interest and opinion in advance. Critical Theory can, of course, expose the contradictions intrinsic to the discourses and justification of new capitalism. In fact, the discrepancy between claim and reality persists. Indeed, as noted at the outset, the notion of progress has even served social regression.

For the most part, the changes in the social order of late-capitalism that have been given prominence by the postmodernist, risk society and globalization perspectives have only recently been the subject of sustained sociological analysis by those identifying today with the tradition of Critical Social Theory (Dörre, et al., 2015; Cremin, 2015). Instead, the Critical Theory inspired discussions of these developments have tended to be conducted from the standpoint of normative political philosophy (Benhabib, 1997; Honneth 2004). In this respect, they have reinforced one implication of Habermas' original departure from the format of immanent critique; the distancing of normative reflection from the empirical analysis of processes of historical change. Habermas' (2000; 2001a) subsequent sociological analysis of the postnational constellation obliquely demonstrates the limitations of his previous reliance on a model limited to national societies. The reorientation associated with his communication paradigm has nonetheless resulted in initiatives that intimate at a new synthesis, one that reconciles positive liberty and social justice. This synthesis of positive liberty and social justice reflects a shift from emancipation to democracy as the leading motif of historical change in Critical Theory. From an intersubjective perspective, emancipation can only be realized through democracy. Even though Critical Theory still depends on giving expression to 'an historically effective reason', the democratic complexion of this synthesis privileges the participatory perspective of actors over attempts to ground social change in objective historical processes (Honneth, 2004: 237). The outlines of this new synthesis can only be sketched here with reference to a few key dimensions of Habermas' discourse theory and Honneth's account of the struggle for recognition.

Habermas locates positive liberty in the procedures of deliberative democracy and utilizes the normative standards of discourse in criticizing social injustice. Unlike the restrictions of political liberalism's notion of individual freedom, discourse theory asserts that citizenship rights extend intersubjective relations of mutual recognition, enabling processes of democratization as well as protecting individual liberties. Habermas aims to disclose the immanent potential of the constitution of a democratic state to found a project intended to elaborate and realize the system of rights that it contains (Habermas, 1996a; Benhabib, 2002). In his model, democratic legitimacy requires that the citizenship rights guaranteeing the private autonomy to enjoy subjective liberties are dependent on the public autonomy to participate in deliberative processes and law-making. Of course, it could be objected that in making the expression of communicative freedom the condition of social justice, discourse theory presupposes precisely what it intends to achieve, especially in its attempt to overcome the prescriptive features of the welfare state. Although Habermas assigns to social movements the role of revealing and countering the inconsistencies between legal equality and factual inequality, his reformulation of critique is based less on an analysis of the dynamics of transformation and more on an interpretation of the logic of discursively achieved agreement. He argues that mutual understanding is made possible by counterfactual idealized projections of rational consensus; these idealizations have an immanent-transcendent quality, exemplifying how the justification of validity claims may contradict the factual order of society, even though idealizations are factually necessary presuppositions of mutual understanding (Habermas, 1992a; 1996a; 2001b). This thesis shapes his new synthesis, with its claim that there is a logical or 'internal connection' between the rule of law and democracy (Habermas, 1996a). On the one hand, he claims that the 'facticity' and 'validity' dimensions of communication obtain an institutional equivalent in law. On the other hand, communicative idealizations ensure the progressive character and universalistic orientation of the argumentative redemption of validity claims.

Honneth's struggle for recognition version of Critical Theory restores immanent critique's intention of synthesizing normative and analytical perspectives, yet it is consistent with the change to the intersubjective paradigm of communication in seeking to make social justice an outcome of the expression of positive liberty. Its distinctive founding claim is that struggles against social injustice are not just the effect of material inequalities and driven by self-interest, but that they are motivated by experiences of disrespect. The moral content of these struggles derives from the intersubjective interdependence that characterizes social recognition. Honneth seeks to reveal an intrinsic connection between the injustices of pathological experiences of denied recognition and the transformative experience of moral learning. The 'surplus validity' generated in struggles for recognition enable existing interpretations of moral principles to be revised and enlarged (Honneth, 2003a; 2003b).

This approach is meant to overcome Habermas' inadequate explanation of an underlying motivation for transformation, but it equally commits Honneth to a broad social grounding of the synthesis of positive liberty and social justice. Relations of recognition are constitutive of three domains of social integration, so that injustices may pertain to the spheres of intimate and familial relations of love, the legal relations of citizenship rights, and to the socio-cultural evaluations of achievement and individuals' contributions to a community (Honneth, 1995a). Honneth argues that the critique of injustice requires a vision of the good life and that the purpose of transforming the injustices of denied recognition is the construction of an intact identity that enables individual self-realization (Honneth, 2003b; Markle, 2004). The ensuing conception of autonomy is more strongly demarcated from that of political liberalism than Habermas' discourse theory reformulation of positive liberty. It suggests, in Honneth's opinion, a *social* model of justice and democracy that reverses what he believes is the privileging of the political sphere in Habermas' conception of deliberative democracy and, in a different way, its appreciation of the diverse contexts of recognition is a corrective to Fraser's idea that social movements are the main instigators of claims for recognition in the public sphere (Honneth, 1998; 2003a).

The synthetic aspirations of Honneth's struggle for recognition and Habermas' discourse theory programmes of Critical Theory demonstrate that immanent critique has been circumscribed, but not discarded. The necessity for Critical Theory to constructively engage with social theories of the present remains, even though the logics of many influential perspectives are difficult to reconcile with Critical Theory's historical conception of reason. Postmodernism, the risk society and globalization can be viewed as providing limited insights into the renewed mobilization of the capitalist imaginary, mainly through depictions of certain paradoxical tendencies of contemporary transformations. Honneth's comments on the distortions of the capitalist recognition order's interpretation of achievement principle draws attention to some of its pathological dimensions and the experiential sources of 'immanent-transcendent' resistance (Honneth, 1995b; 2003a). Despite the introduction of new normative criteria being a defining feature of his theoretical project, Habermas' later discourse theory likewise preserves the idea of an immanent potential for democratization. In his opinion, the formal procedures of discursive deliberation and the universalistic principles of human rights enable the civil solidarity (that has been expressed at the national level in a liberal 'constitutional patriotism' and welfare state redistribution) to be extended in the direction of cosmopolitan justice and democracy (Habermas, 1998). It may be true that contemporary processes of social disintegration make this idea appear counterfactual; yet any process of democratization is likely to incorporate substantial elements of discursive deliberation.

5

POSITIVE LIBERTY AND SOCIAL JUSTICE

Introduction

There have been several significant attempts to recast the emancipatory intentions of Critical Theory in terms of a synthesis of positive liberty and social justice. Its variants include Habermas' conception of the discourse ethic and the mutual reinforcement of private autonomy and public autonomy in the exercise of communicative power, Fraser's notion of 'participatory parity' as a normative standard of justice that overarches the demands for redistribution and recognition, and Honneth's explications of the moral grammar of struggles for recognition and the institution of social freedom (Habermas, 1996a; Fraser, 2003a; Honneth, 2014). The debates over this 'dialectic of immanence and transcendence' have led to significant refinements (Fraser and Honneth, 2003). Like my contribution of 'democratic justice as intersubjective freedoms', these Critical Theory conceptions of immanent potentials for transcendence are continuous with Habermas' change to the paradigm of intersubjective communication (Browne, 2010). However, the recognition and redistribution perspectives rework and qualify Habermas' paradigm of understanding (Honneth, 1995a; Fraser, 1997; Fraser and Honneth, 2003).

Intersubjective perspectives equate emancipation with democracy or democratization. Autonomy is considered to be conditional on subjects' relations to one another and public discussion is a precondition of political legitimation. Critical Theory presumes that emancipation and democracy are interconnected but the Frankfurt School contended that liberal democracy's instituted form does not fully realize democracy. Democracy required the constitution of a different system of social relations and another type of subjectivity. Benhabib (1997) argues that Habermas' endorsement of liberal-democratic rights and institutions most distinguishes his discourse theory, and that of his successors, from the Frankfurt School. The greatest achievement of Habermas' discourse theory is probably that of both initiating a substantial reformulation of democracy and clarifying the processes by which democratization has been instantiated. Still, it delimits processes of transformation in proposing that radical democracy involves realizing the constitutional state's normative potential and defines col-lective self-determination in procedural terms. These aspects of discourse theory hardly appear adequate to satisfying Critical Theory's aspiration of transforma-tion. It is not surprising that Habermas has sought to explain the conditions for institutionalizing cosmopolitan law. By this means, he seeks to regulate processes of change that are already in train, including neo-liberal globalization's destruc-tive consequences (Habermas, 1998; 2001a; 2009; 2011).

Positive liberty has typically been contrasted with liberal political philoso-phy's notion of negative freedom. The negative freedom *from* interference has been juxtaposed to the positive freedom *to* do, or the power to actually enact freedom (Berlin, 1969; Taylor, 1985b). For the moment, positive liberty can be said to cover a range of positions that are concerned with the actuality and exercise of freedom. These focus on the conditions and capabilities of instanti-ating freedom, rather than defining freedom as a matter of non-interference and independence from the state. Even so, liberal notions of freedom normally involve more than just the specification of a negative liberty that is empty of content. This suggests that to sustain negative liberty it is necessary to establish conditions that go beyond it, including some basic level of social justice (Márkus, 1999). The most important contemporary liberal theories of justice, especially that of Rawls, appreciate this implication. This is one reason why Critical Theory has pursued a dialogue with liberal political philosophies (Rawls, 1971; Benhabib, 1997; Habermas, 1998).

It is possible to distinguish between those recent Critical Theory formula-tions of positive liberty and social justice that are primarily based on deriving this synthesis from liberal notions, on the one hand, and, on the other hand, those formulations that are framed more as critical responses to the limits of liberalism. Benhabib's three criteria for cosmopolitan democracy – egalitarian reciprocity, voluntary self-ascription, and freedom of exit and association – can be readily seen as extending liberal rights and principles. For Benhabib, these conditions enable the democratic iteration of liberalism (Benhabib, 2006). The contrast between liberal derivations and the critical supplements to liberalism versions of the synthesis of positive liberty and social justice equally reflect important differences in how these respective theoretical conceptions relate the spheres of the 'social' and the 'political', that is, the degree to which the politi-cal is taken to shape the social or whether the social is considered to constitute to a greater degree the political. In current discussions, the emphasis on politi-cal constitution is more aligned to the derivations from liberal principles, whereas the latter is more typical of interpretations of the limits of liberalism, such as that of Honneth (1995b; 2014).

The idea that social justice is conditional on the exercise of positive liberty has certain affinities with interpretations of justice in terms of capabilities, action and 'well-being' (Nussbaum and Sen, 2004). These consider that social justice is not just a matter of the objective distribution of material resources; it depends on the allocation of capabilities, like appropriate practical skills, knowledge, and 'cultural capital'. A sense of agency and a notion of actors' capacity are incorporated into these conceptions of justice, or injustice. There is an intersection between critiques of bureaucratic institutions and the perceptions of the limitations of objectivist and statistical conceptions of justice and inequality. These critical perspectives influenced notions of how the injustices of capitalist society could be transformed or ameliorated through the capacity of civil society for self-organization, or through the expansion of social capital (Putnam, 1993).

The intersubjective theories of justice are partly responses to changes in social struggles, with the class politics of labour no longer seeming to signify the prospects of general emancipation and the emergence of identity politics. The latter led to a greater sensitivity towards the suffering entailed by 'non-material' injustices and an appreciation of how the rectifying of these injustices requires the effective expression of an identity, such as those of ethnicity, gender, and sexuality (Calhoun, 1995; Fraser, 1995; 1997). The syntheses of positive liberty and social justice are more abstract or 'formal' than previous images of emancipation, because they are meant to encompass a greater diversity, or heterogeneity, of critiques of injustice. This diversity may explain the attempted derivation of some of these syntheses from liberalism, with its notions of private right, public opinion, and non-substantive egalitarianism. Fraser (2003a; 2003b) even describes the notion of *participatory parity* as an articulation of liberalism's core principles, despite participatory political projects regularly understood as challenging political liberalism (Pateman, 1970; Macpherson, 1977).

The Critical Theory conceptions of justice presuppose the abolition or transformation of capitalist society's material inequalities. This transformation is critical to how positive liberty is meant to be enabled by social justice, as well as, in turn, promoting social justice. Negative liberty is considered compatible with increasing inequality, although some formulations of negative liberty seek to delimit inequality. Importantly, the material inequalities that result from neo-liberal globalization have become major dimensions of social contestation. The depths of the current regressive redistributions of wealth in capitalist nation states could not have been predicted at the time of the initiating of post-material notions of justice. Post-material conceptions tended to be consolidated during the later phases of the social democratic era, to use Honneth and Hartmann's phrase, and its expansion of welfare state systems (Honneth and Hartmann, 2012).

My analysis suggests that the nexus between positive liberty and social justice constitutes a rubric for connecting the normative justification of critique with the potentials for social transformation. It represents a possibly internally compelling process of change and contains the potential for reconstructing the social bond in a manner consistent with the project of autonomy (Castoriadis, 1991; 1997a; 1997b). The Critical Theory conceptions of this synthesis clarify how to realize liberal democratic societies' promise of autonomy and justice. However, the elaborations of this synthesis are limited by their construction and execution. This assessment applies even to Honneth's conception of social freedom, which is an important corrective to recent Critical Theory's tendency to focus on law at the expense of broader social practices, to overemphasize procedures, and to subordinate historical processes (Honneth, 2014). Habermas' discourse theory is partly the source of these tendencies, as is the quite valid intention of providing normative justifications for rights in order to counteract regressive developments, such as those constitutive of half-positions (Benhabib, 2004). There are progressive, as well as defensive, dimensions to these normative justifications of citizenship and human rights, yet to the extent that such justifications derive from liberal visions of politics they risk evacuating the social.

I argue that the theories of Habermas and Honneth have difficulties explaining the dynamics of social processes, including those dynamics pertaining to the reproduction of social relations of domination. This is not just a matter of empirical deficiencies; rather these difficulties derive from weaknesses in their respective theoretical conceptualizations of society. Even though their syntheses of positive liberty and social justice establish normative grounds for critique and promote emancipation, the conditions of change are different from those implied by their conceptions. In short, the change necessary for realizing positive liberty and social justice involves a more conflictual dynamic and explicit confrontation with institutionalized sources of domination and injustice. This proposition is relevant to any attempt to address the structural contradictions of capitalist modernity.

Social Justice and Positive Liberty

The syntheses of positive liberty and social justice are meant to clarify the normative perspective of Critical Theory and the emancipatory quality of social transformation. Critical Theory considers that freedom is historically and socially conditioned. There is no finished form to freedom, although there are substantive social preconditions and impediments to freedom. Marx criticized the liberal institution of freedom as merely formal and determined by private property, especially because of the exclusion of the working class from political authority (Marx, 1977c; Marx and Engels, 1977). Marx may have underestimated the importance of liberal freedoms, but recent Critical Theory's trajectory has not just been towards liberalism but away from the Marxian dialectical methodology that emphasized social process. This movement reflects uncertainties about social development. In my opinion, Critical Theory's dialectical approach to social processes remains integral to its deployment of the distinction between the potential and the actual. In its practical enactment, the synthesis of positive liberty and social justice should constitute both a form of emancipation and a means of transformation.

The original Marxian conception of positive liberty and social justice presupposed some collective transformation, because it assumed that collective agency is required to enact change. Critical Theory subsequently argued that the regulation of labour and the welfare state limited the injustices of capitalist society and that citizenship rights have somewhat empowered individuals. It could be argued that Critical Theory's more sociologically informed approach means that the term 'positive liberty' is misleading. Positive liberty appears to be a category determined by its opposition to the liberal idea of negative liberty, hence the critical rejection of the latter renders the use of the former superfluous. Isaiah Berlin's specification of positive liberty was certainly intended to be critical of collectivist notions of freedom and assertions of the dangers of rendering freedom in collective terms were a cornerstone of Berlin's entire construction (Berlin, 1969). Berlin's arguments have naturally been disputed. Notably, Charles Taylor argues that positive liberty has, on the contrary,

> no necessary connection with the view that freedom consists purely and simply in the collective control over the common life, and that there is no freedom worth the name outside a context of collective control. (Taylor 1985b: 212)

Although Taylor rightly contests Berlin's equation of positive liberty with collective control, with its implication that positive liberty includes a potential for totalitarianism, the notion of positive liberty generally incorporates social, or collective, considerations that are less salient to negative liberty.

Positive liberty may be more consistent with the classical Republican conception of the intrinsic value of participation in governance than is the case with the modern liberal idea of negative liberty, but positive liberty is informed by the modernist view that there is no real freedom in an unfree society (Márkus, 1999; Pettit 1997). It is possible to interpret the idea of equal liberty in egalitarian liberal terms, yet a strict version of negative liberty appears insufficient for the problems of overcoming entrenched forms of domination and injustice. Negative liberty is primarily about demarcating the domain of private freedom from that of the public authority of the state. It is basically a political doctrine concerning the rights of the individual. Negative liberty does not specify how these private rights should be exercised. From the standpoint of Critical Theory, there is little point developing conceptions of positive liberty, or equivalents like communicative power (Habermas, 1996a) and social freedom (Honneth, 2014), unless they signify a freedom that instantiates or enables social justice. It is the *synthesis* of positive liberty and social justice that distinguishes the Critical Theory approach, although some notion of social justice may be implied in other conceptions of positive liberty. Positive liberty typically denotes the freedom to be self-determining or self-realizing, rather than simply the freedom from authority.

> The 'positive' sense of the word 'liberty' derives from the wish on the part of the individual to be his own master. I wish my life and decisions to depend on myself, not on external forces of whatever kind. I wish to be the instrument of my own, not of other men's, acts of will. I wish to be a subject, not an object; to be moved by reasons, by conscious purposes,

which are my own, not by causes which affect me, as it were, from outside. I wish to be somebody, not nobody; a doer – deciding, not being
decided for, self-directed and not acted upon by.... (Berlin, 1969: 131)

The self-control signified by positive liberty implies that this is a freedom that
creates the conditions of future freedom. This is a major part of the criteria of
social justice that derives from the notion of positive liberty. Positive liberty
should be apparent in the 'flourishing' of individuals. It should represent a rich
interpretation of autonomy: self-determination and self-realization, or authenticity (Taylor, 1991; Honneth, 2014). These aspects of positive liberty involve
considerations that deepen its distinction from negative liberty. First, in the
case of positive liberty, it is necessary to take into account other subjects and
to make their autonomy the condition of one's own freedom. The latter is
presupposed by communicative conceptions of freedom. It is why Hannah
Arendt's idea of power as acting in concert is an interpretation of positive
liberty (Arendt, 1973). Second, positive liberty depends on the existence of
substantive conditions that promote its actualization, which include material
resources, cultural understandings, and prior socialization. The reasons why is
clear from Taylor's remark that *positive* liberty is an 'exercise-concept',
whereas it is sufficient to treat *negative* liberty as an 'opportunity concept'
(Taylor, 1985b).

Berlin's statement about 'wishing to be a subject, not an object' points to an
aspect of positive liberty that is specific to its framing within Critical Theory.
Critical Theory's critique of social relations that have become like *second
nature*, that is, where objectivity dominates subjectivity, has a conception of
positive liberty as its normative-emancipatory standard. Positive liberty is not
just enabled by social institutions, it entails the power to shape and constitute
institutions. Positive liberty requires some measure of collective transformation
in order to facilitate genuine subjective agency in relation to institutions.

The liberal notion of negative liberty entails a conception of subjects' power
to shape institutions. However, this power is circumscribed. The whole point
of the concept of negative liberty is to delimit state power. The other side of
this standpoint is a restriction on participation in power. As a consequence,
notions of positive liberty developed from critiques of modern conceptions of
political representation and delegation. It has been recurrently claimed that
liberal democracy provides limited opportunities for self-determination. These
critiques generated arguments for direct or participatory democracy, on the one
hand, and, on the other hand, the contention that modern political freedoms
are thin or abstract led to assertions that real freedom can only exist if it is
realized in *social* practices and social relations. These social practices and social
relations interface with the political order but extend beyond it, because they
apply to every dimension of life circumstances, including work, the family, civil
society and everyday life. In many ways, similar conclusions were drawn from
the social critique of the limitations of legal freedoms in a capitalist society,
such as the claim that individuals have the freedom to live in poverty. The more

expansive position of *social* liberalism has, to be sure, sought to address material inequalities through the institution of citizenship and liberalism's visions of public opinion is supposed to enable participation (Marshall, 1991).

Generally, conceptions of positive liberty should contain a notion of subjects' 'self-determination' and a strong sense in which subjects' actions generate institutions or social structures. This amounts to extending to the domain of the *social*, or translating into a social form, the originally strictly political notion of democratic autonomy, that is, of subjects being the authors of the laws to which they are the subjects or addressees. Specifications of positive liberty emphasize the institution of conditions that enable self-determination, such as material resources, cultural expression, or socialization. The interpretations of injustice in terms of action and capabilities accept the significance of these conditions, but suggest that they do not by themselves enable subjects to have the power to shape institutions. Now, it is not only conservative and liberal thinkers that have highlighted the potential disempowering consequences of state programmes and how provisions intended to alleviate injustices and inequalities have served to undermine the agency that is required for autonomy. It is argued that state programmes have instituted more insidious modes of governance (Foucault, 1978; 1980; Austin-Broos 2009). These assessments actually strengthen the case for positive liberty's generative property and the need for a corresponding social ontological conception of subjects' capacities.

Discourse Theory and the Struggle for Recognition

Habermas and Honneth consider that liberalism suffers from a *social* deficit and that explicating the *intersubjective* formation of identity is constitutive of an alternative to liberalism's individualist suppositions. The intersubjective framework of communication implies that social justice derives from a *discursively* formed and organized collective will, rather than collective control in the sense that Berlin intended: the concentration of the powers of administration and coercion (Berlin, 1969; Browne, 2010). For Berlin, the articulation of collective control in administrative systems results in the subordination of individuals, because it addresses aspects of the subject that are considered incompatible with the exercise of freedom, or the possibility of action inconsistent with the collective will or the collective good (Berlin, 1969). Habermas and Honneth's communicative conceptions are intended to prohibit this potential subordination of individuals, and they found freedom in an irrevocable intersubjective mediation. Namely, participation in democratic discourse mediates the relationship between the individual and collective. Collective control is only legitimate if it has been constituted through public discourse. This is evident from Habermas' discourse principle that: 'Only those norms can claim to be valid that meet (or could meet) with the approval of all affected in their capacity as participants in a practical discourse' (Habermas, 1990: 67; 1996a: 107).

Critical Theory's conception of democracy includes more demanding considerations than those of liberal political philosophy. Namely, it seeks to establish an 'internal connection' between the normative universalism of the notion of the equal consideration of all and the democratic ideal of the full participation of citizens. Habermas distinguishes his position from Rawls' political liberalism on the basis of his conception of the intersubjective constitution of identity and the 'Kantian Republicanism' that ensues from it. Discourse theory supposes that nobody

> can be free at the expense of anybody else's freedom. Because persons are individuated only by way of socialization, the freedom of one individual cannot be tied to the freedom of everyone else in a purely negative way, through reciprocal restrictions. Rather, correct restrictions are the result of a process of self-legislation conducted jointly. (Habermas, 1998: 101)

Habermas wants to show that discursive justice is consistent with the norms of social interaction and the learning processes that enable individuals to comprehend how their actions contribute to the constitution of society. The participation of individuals in discourse gives expression to their capacities for self-determination, although there is a considerable disjunction between the discourse principle and subjects' actual practices in contemporary society.

Discourse theory emphasizes the requirement of the reciprocity of the public and private spheres. It presupposes that the autonomy of subjects in each sphere is dependent on the exercise of autonomy in the other sphere (Habermas, 1996a). The discourse principle of justice contains criteria that require the transformation of heteronomy in order for it to be effectively implemented and the democratic exercise of communicative power is the condition for enacting this change. In developing this construction, Habermas was particularly influenced by feminist struggles, which had disclosed how progressive legal and bureaucratic reforms intended to produce greater equality were undermined by their framing in terms of traditional assumptions about gender roles, for instance, the right to equal pay for comparable work may not result in the degree of anticipated change due to limited access to childcare (Habermas, 1996a). Discourse theory proposes that rights extend intersubjective relations of mutual recognition, thereby enabling processes of democratization as well as protecting individual liberties.

Honneth's theory of recognition centres on the dynamics of social interaction, rather than the formal pragmatics of communication. Honneth argues that expectations of mutual recognition shape the formation of identity. In particular, Mead's description of 'taking the standpoint of the other' points to the affirmation involved in the other's recognition of oneself as an autonomous subject (Mead, 1934; Honneth, 1995a). Like Habermas' discourse theory, the struggles for recognition framework opposes the tendency of liberal thought to detach individuals and their rights from the social context. However, litmus of the differences between these two communicative approaches is the degrees of continuity and discontinuity that they have with liberalism and its notions

of citizenship and democracy. There are good reasons nevertheless for accentuating the overlap between these variants of the intersubjective paradigm.
Habermas' early work contributed to the delineation of the recognition theory
framework and Honneth's conception of social struggles' moral grammar
appealed to Habermas' discourse ethic in adjudicating between liberating and
regressive claims for recognition (Honneth, 1999; Habermas, 1974; 1978a).

There are equally significant differences between Honneth's account of the
struggle for recognition and discourse theory. Honneth's conception is tailored
to a rather different set of experiences to that of Habermas' discourse theory,
which is guided by the rationality of mutual understanding. Habermas' model
starts from the reflective reconstruction of those norms actors presuppose
whenever they enter into processes of communicative action oriented towards
mutual understanding. By contrast, the Critical Theory that is guided by the
idea of struggles for recognition addresses the forms of social and individual
pathology that result from the denial of recognition and the experience of disrespect (Honneth, 1995a; 2007). For this reason, it readily takes into account
the historically consequential types of lack of recognition, including those
deriving from the practice of liberal democracy. In Honneth's opinion, the
intentions of Habermas' discourse theory changed over time and its aspiration
of underpinning radical critique diminished as it became more concerned with
the 'normative reinforcement of liberal-democracy', hence it is limited in its
questioning of this tradition (Honneth, 1999; 2014).

Honneth's model is intended to illuminate the threats that capitalist social
organization poses to a democratic culture. It questions liberal-democratic
institutional arrangements in light of Critical Theory's 'suspicion' of an accom-
panying 'social pathology of capitalist society as a whole', and in terms of the
consequently disregarded innovations in moral learning (Honneth, 1999: 249).
Habermas presumes that democratic deliberation extends the principles of the
constitutional state and that these constitutional norms can frame a radical
democratic project (Habermas, 1996a). On this view, liberal-democratic institutions are open, in principle, to demands for civil solidarity and to correcting
the pathologies of capitalist society. The implication of Honneth's struggle for
recognition perspective is that the constitutional framework of democratic
deliberation is, however necessary, unlikely to be sufficiently socially grounded
to remedy experiences of individual and social pathology. Honneth applies this
assessment to Habermas' notion of 'constitutional patriotism'; a notion that
Honneth does not reject. He seeks instead to clarify how 'constitutional patriotism' originates in more diffuse social practices and culturally ingrained normative convictions (Honneth, 2014).

In Honneth's (1991) opinion, Habermas' theory of communicative rationalization brackets the asymmetry of power between speakers and the intersubjective conflict that is intrinsic to communication under conditions of inequality.
The implication of this critique is that the problem of socially grounding a
democratic culture extends beyond achieving the acceptance of the procedures
of domination free communication in the legitimation of institutions, the

reproduction of culture, and the socialization of individuals. It is the problem of how to complement the normative justification of this achievement with an explication of the genesis of demands for freedom from domination in the first place. These demands do not only arise in realms of social interaction where communicative action oriented to mutual understanding can be pursued in an unimpeded manner. Instead, a phenomenology of communication suggests that denials of intersubjective reciprocity occur in all social contexts in which recognition is at stake. The struggle for recognition model takes its bearings from pre-political experiences of 'communicative relatedness', seeking to delineate how a sense of justice arises from the reciprocal relations of association between subjects (Honneth, 1993; 1998).

Similarly, Honneth argues that Habermas' juxtaposition of system integration and social integration limits the discerning of the moral consequences of the unequal distribution of power and the importance of the sphere of labour in the formation of identity (Honneth, 1991). Honneth's programme distinguished itself at the outset by its reconsideration of work as a sphere of moral experience and by the suggestion of innovative social learning through resistance to class domination. Honneth argued that Habermas' explanation of the injustices and subordination of late-capitalism could never offer a plausible account of the resistance, because individuals do not experience the injustices and heteronomy of capitalist social relations as distortions of the formal structure of communication (Honneth, 1994; 1995b). Rather, they experience injustice as disrespect towards their identities and violations of the moral order. The philosophical anthropology of recognition is the key to Honneth's explicating these practical struggles to alter social relations of domination.

The contemporary impetus behind his struggle for recognition framework is similar to the normative orientation that Habermas (1987a) described as that of new social movements. New social movements drew 'attention to the political significance of the experience of social or cultural disrespect' (Honneth, 2001: 44). The new social movements' conceptions of justice, like those of second-wave feminism and gay liberation, relate to claims to dignity and integrity. This does not mean that 'struggles for recognition' are solely concerned with the cultural articulation of identities. Honneth (2001) is critical of Taylor's (1994) essay on multiculturalism for creating this misleading impression. But it is true that new social movements contributed to a shift in the vocabulary of justice, specifically because the social conflicts that they mobilize around differ in their logic from those of the struggles over the distribution of material goods and its framing ideal of economic equality.

For Honneth, the shift in conceptions of justice to that of securing social and individual respect and dignity is the contemporary manner of expressing a general tendency of social struggles. The experiences of indignation and disrespect that motivate struggles for recognition imply that social conflicts have a *moral* quality. Honneth has sought to re-actualize the aspiration of Hegel's Jena writing on struggles for recognition. In his Jena writings (1802–1805; see

Hegel, 1979; 1986), Hegel wanted to explain: 'how the experience of recognition could bring about progress in ethical life'. This resulted in an attempt to disclose the dynamic relationship 'between the intersubjective acquisition of self-consciousness and the moral development of entire societies' (Honneth 2007: 132; 1995a; see also Deranty, 2009).

Hegel's idea that struggles originate from the rupturing of the ethical infrastructure of social relations differs from modern political philosophy's dominant view of conflicts as driven by struggles for self-preservation and the strategic pursuit of self-interest (Honneth, 1995a). By highlighting political conflict's ethical underpinning, this framework suggests that a democratic culture is distinguished by its incorporating the 'enlargement in moral sensibility associated with struggles for recognition' (Honneth, 2001: 44). Honneth originally sought to disclose an intrinsic connection between the injustices of pathological experiences of denied recognition and the transformative experience of moral learning that emerge from the normative objectives of struggles for recognition (Honneth, 2003a: 113). Struggles for recognition can revise existing interpretations of normative principles and generate a 'surplus validity' that shapes progressive change (Honneth, 2003a: 186; 1995a).

> At the time, Hegel was convinced that struggle among subjects for the mutual recognition of their identity generated inner-societal pressure toward the practical, political establishment of institutions that would guarantee freedom. It is individuals' claim to the intersubjective recognition of their identity that is built into social life from the very beginning as a moral tension, transcends the level of social progress institutionalized thus far, and so gradually leads – via the negative path of recurring stages of conflict – to a state of communicatively lived freedom. (Honneth, 1995a: 5)

Honneth's contention that the dynamic of the intersubjective recognition of identity involves struggles that generate progressive transformation is undoubtedly appealing. It draws a strong connection between the normative perspective of critique and the practices of subjects to alter circumstances of social subordination and to resist the suffering resulting from social injustice, especially insofar as social interaction is experienced as violating their expectations of recognition or respect. Yet, the centrality of identity to Honneth's conception of justice has led to questions over the limits of this approach and whether recognition theory constitutes a satisfactory response to the problematic of the translation between social action and social institutions. In the context of his debate with Fraser over Critical Theory's conception of justice, Honneth proposed that: the quality of social relations of recognition should be the reference point of a conception of justice' (2003a: 177). The content of this synthesis of positive liberty and social justice is meant to vary in accordance with different spheres of social relations. This important presumption is probably less than effectively conveyed in Honneth's statement:

> Thus, for modern societies, I proceed from the premise that the purpose of social equality is to enable the personal identity-formation of all members of society. (Honneth, 2003a: 177)

On the one hand, leaving aside whether it is actually a justified inference, Fraser (2003b) argues that Honneth reduces the moral problem of justice to the question of the development of an intact identity. On the other hand, this statement might be perceived as creating a tension, or even inconsistencies, between the strong accentuation of the experience of identity and the endorsement of the multifaceted character of social relations. This tension makes the exact status of Honneth's later arguments in *Freedom's Right* somewhat ambiguous (Honneth, 2014).

Freedom's Right can be read as extending and deepening the multifaceted conception of justice and morality, or as a far more substantial revision of the earlier recognition theory framework. In the latter case, it may be interpreted as marking a definite shift away from the grounding of positive liberty and social justice in the psychological formation of identity. Rather, it suggests a perspective that emphasizes external institutions. Honneth's recognition framework's explication of a plurality of social spheres is very much based on the types of individuals' 'self-relations' that are appropriate to each social domain. These self-relations of self-respect, self-confidence and self-realization are constituted through the interaction dynamics of intersubjective recognition. Self-relations represent different ways of enacting morality and agency; and therefore different components of autonomy. In Honneth's recognition theory model of society, the character of subjects' self-relations determines the assessment of the social sphere or institution to which they are related.

Honneth classifies the forms of recognition deriving from intimate and affective relationships as belonging to the sphere of 'love'. Recognition of this affective type will always have a particularistic quality, since its primary forms are the family and friendship. Yet, affective recognition is a precondition of individuals' basic *self-confidence*. In the sphere of 'love', the patterns of struggles are structured around the polarities of independence and attachment. Honneth argues that successful 'affectional attachment' 'is dependent on the mutual maintenance of a tension between symbiotic self-sacrifice and individual self-assertion' (Honneth, 1995a: 96). The particularly disturbing modes of denying this pattern of reciprocity, such as the degradation of the body through torture and rape, reveal why self-confidence is a precondition for engagement in all modes of intersubjective relations. In the second pattern of recognition, it is *self-respect* that constitutes the normative dimension of social integration through rights. Appeals for recognition in this case refer to the right of each individual to equal treatment under the law. Rights involve a general determination of the moral dignity of the person and, as Kant asserted, universal respect for the autonomy of individuals. Struggles relating to the moral demand for respect have expanded the categories of persons entitled to rights and the substantive content of rights, so that rights to education and material security have been recognized as preconditions of individual autonomy.

One can readily appreciate the connection that Honneth draws between the specific types of self-relation, such as to self-respect, and particular spheres of social relations, like the legally constituted sphere of citizenship in modernity. For this reason, violations of anticipated recognition constitute moral injuries and struggles rectifying injustices have resulted in progressive revisions in moral understandings and corresponding changes in social institutions. The third pattern of recognition develops the implications of the intersubjective relations of membership of a particular group or community. Solidarity concerns the esteem a person acquires from her unique participation in a cultural form of life. Here it is the distinctive traits and qualities of a person that are valued, rather than the universal category of autonomy, as is the case in the pattern of rights. Honneth argues that in modern societies the hierarchically stratified category of honour, which was associated with corporatist forms of social order, gives way to a more pluralistic view of 'esteem'. Modern esteem values, or recognizes, individuals' *self-realization*, especially in its contributions to the common good and intersubjectively shared cultural values.

Like the struggles of the three patterns of interaction – love, rights and solidarity – Dewey's conception of 'reflexive cooperation' highlights the *social* origins of democracy and how the normative ideal of democracy can be an immanent principle of a culture committed to justice in the distribution of material rewards and the rights of citizenship (Honneth, 1998). It is this vision of 'democratic ethical life' that Honneth later elaborates upon in *Freedom's Right* (Honneth, 2014). It nevertheless marks a departure, in my opinion, from some aspects of the original framework of his recognition theory. Its point of reference is not Hegel's early Jena writings, but Hegel's later *Philosophy of Right*, which has been predominantly read as a conservative text in light of its depiction of the rationality of existing reality and the morality of established institutions (Hegel, 1967[1820]). The most significant shift is the degree to which institutions are considered to structure the contexts of interaction and this consideration substantially undermines the sense of contestation, agency, and autonomy implied by struggles for recognition. The following commentary on the debate between Honneth and Fraser over recognition and redistribution clarifies some of the issues and difficulties that precipitated this shift in theoretical approach. This debate has been characterized by commentators as one between recognition theory's grounding of justice in identity and Fraser's defining justice as a matter of status in the notion of parity of participation (Zurn, 2003; Kompridis, 2007).

Recognition and Redistribution: Complementary or Competing Conceptions

Fraser's initial critique of the recognition paradigm and defence of the complementary normative position of redistribution was not so much directed at the specifics of Honneth's proposals. Rather, Fraser's critique was based on an interpretation of the paradigm of recognition as a product of a 'cultural turn' in social thought and the rise of identity politics, such as in relation to debates over multiculturalism and shifts in feminist discourses. In this respect, Taylor's sketch of the politics of recognition may be more representative of the positions Fraser wanted to contest with her intervention, though in reality Fraser's criticism was directed at broad tendencies (Taylor, 1994; Fraser, 1997). In her opinion, recognition perspectives seek 'cultural or symbolic change' and this differs from rectifying injustice through redistribution, such as is involved in the redistribution of income, the reorganization of the division of labour, and the democratic regulation of capitalist markets.

The simultaneous espousal and critique of recognition led Fraser to develop her own conception of justice in terms of *participatory parity*. Fraser describes parity of participation as giving expression to the value of equal autonomy and moral worth (Fraser, 2003b: 228). It involves the according of full status to partners in interaction and the ability to interact with others as a peer. These norms and values are not really at issue in the debate between Fraser and Honneth. Rather, what is at issue, according to Honneth, is whether the direct move Fraser's approach makes from 'individual autonomy to the idea of social participation' is sufficient or whether Honneth's 'move from individual autonomy first to the goal of the most intact possible identity-formation, in order to then bring in principles of mutual recognition as that goal's necessary presupposition' is more satisfactory (Honneth, 2003a: 176).

For Fraser, what is important is the existence of 'real' or effective conditions that enable equivalent possibilities for participation. Social justice compels the abolition of those institutionalized 'obstacles' to parity of participation. It is not difficult to perceive how this conception of justice is informed by those claims to civil rights and equal liberty that have been advanced by the women's movement and ethnic and racial minorities. Although these movements are explicit about their demands for recognition, Fraser argues that parity of participation has been pursued in relation to class inequalities and by the labour movement; hence her proposal is intended to illuminate how the welfare state contributes to autonomy. Participatory parity requires the satisfaction of two conditions:

> First, the distribution of material resources must be such as to ensure participants' independence and 'voice'. This I shall call the *objective* condition of participatory parity. It precludes forms and levels of economic dependence and inequality that impede parity of participation. [...] In contrast, the second condition requires that institutionalized patterns of cultural value express equal respect for all participants and ensure equal opportunity for achieving social esteem. This I shall call the *intersubjective* condition of participatory parity. It precludes institutionalized norms that systematically depreciate some categories of people and the qualities associated with them. (Fraser, 2003a: 36)

Fraser simultaneously elaborates and delimits the notion of recognition, making in the process useful, though disputed, distinctions, like that between the justice orientations connected to the affirmation and transformation of identity (Fraser, 1997). Many of Fraser's criticisms of Honneth's theory are consistent with those made by others, such as that concerning difficulties in adjudicating between justified and unwarranted demands for justice based on claims for recognition. Fraser's main contention is that Honneth's recognition model positions the psychology of identity as an arbiter of justice. Like other critics, Fraser makes the valid point that the ethic of self-realization appears much more significant in Honneth's recognition approach to justice (Fraser, 2003a; 2003b; Kompridis, 2004). Fraser is wrong to consider that Honneth's framework's deficiencies reflect a conceptual 'monism' but right to allude to the problems that ensue from the over-extension of the category of recognition (Fraser, 2003a; 2003b).

Unlike Honneth, Fraser does not develop a philosophical anthropology of recognition; her conception of recognition is basically political and moral. In Fraser's opinion, the demands that subordinated groups make for recognition should be viewed as a matter of 'social status', that is, a subordinate status reflects the institutionalized restraints on equal participation (Fraser, 2003a). It is necessary to rectify the injustices of misrecognition because it accords subordinated groups and individuals a lower status or standing, such as through cultural representations of gender that limit women's careers or that meant that homosexual couples do not possess the same rights as heterosexual couples. On Fraser's view, it is the 'institutionalized cultural values' that struggles for recognition should seek to change (Fraser, 2003a). Participatory parity then serves as a standard for assessing injustice, since it discloses the unequal standing of groups and the negative evaluation of their practices.

> Whereas class stratification corresponds to maldistribution, status hierarchy corresponds to misrecognition. Morally speaking, however, the effect in both cases is the same: some members of society are prevented from participating on a par with others in social interaction. Thus, both orders of subordination violate a single overarching principle of justice, the principle of participatory parity. (Fraser, 2003b: 218)

Fraser distinguishes this notion of justice from Honneth's linking justice to subjects' self-realization and his depiction of experiences of denigration that motivates social struggles. 'On the status model, misrecognition is neither a psychical deformation nor an impediment to ethical self-realization' (Fraser 2003a, 29). Fraser emphasizes the institutionalized character of social injustice and public discourse, because the subjective experience of suffering is not a suitable standard of justice. Indignation, she argues, does not necessarily coincide with injustice. The determination of justice should be based on the public evaluation of claims presented by movements, especially given demands for justice's contentious character and owing to subjective experience not being incorrigible (Fraser, 2003a; 2003b). This points to the basic difference in their respective framings of recognition. Honneth argues, with considerable justification, that social subordination and the denial of recognition undermine subjective self-relations, such as self-confidence, self-respect and self-esteem, and thereby curtail those capacities necessary for the public expression of demands for justice. This is partly why historically enduring injustice often remain veiled and why, as Fraser appreciates, the translation of a subordinate groups' experience of injustice and suffering into the categories of the dominant public idiom can result in the distortion of experience and even the self-negation that Bourdieu described as symbolic violence (Bourdieu, 1991a; Fraser, 1997; 2003a; Honneth, 2007).

Fraser does not accept Honneth's claim that because recognition is integral to the formation of identity it entails that justice should be defined in terms of a conception of the 'good life', that is, as an ethical notion of subjects' self-realization. Fraser's status model, Honneth argues, retracts some of 'the point of recognition' (Honneth, 2003b). He claims that the recognition theory's clarification of the origins or sources of morality contributes to explanations of not just the normative-political principle or procedures of social justice but also discloses the bases of subjects' commitment to social justice and motivations for enacting justice (Honneth, 1995a; 2003a; 2003b).

Fraser's view that the politics of recognition was overtaking that of distribution was not entirely unwarranted. Her response was that this movement went potentially too far. It was necessary to retrieve the politics of redistribution, rather than accepting it belonged to the past history of progressive political movements. However, Fraser's well-intentioned correction of the occlusion of material inequalities was rather regressive and inadequate with respect to the symbolic and interpretative character of production and exchange. Underpinning Fraser's position was the rather under-complex formulation of the distinction between material (redistribution) and cultural (recognition). Fraser's reliance on this dualism has been a recurrent criticism of her proposal (see Young, 2008).

Honneth proposes that material distribution is an expression of recognition, even though capitalist production and class divisions make distribution a rather distorted mode of recognition. Honneth may be right, but his conception is limited with respect to the complexity of distribution's symbolic and material processes. The social institution of an economy involves a more expansive horizon of meaning (see Browne, 2014a; 2016). Fraser's claim that Honneth's recognition interpretation of distribution is circular is probably valid:

> Honneth goes from the true premise that markets are always culturally embedded to the false conclusion that their behaviour is wholly governed by the dynamics of recognition. (Fraser, 2003b: 216)

Even so, the recognition approach enables a critique of markets and a conception of markets as a normative order, rather than an arrangement of self-interested actors or a system that is coordinated through unintended consequences. These intentions are important and potentially consequential, irrespective of their deficient realization. Fraser rightly highlights the weaknesses of the 'achievement principle' that Honneth draws on to explain 'redistribution as recognition'. Fraser argues that the injustices of the global capitalist system and its 'maldistribution' have less to do with the application (or misapplication) of the achievement principle, such as in struggles over the comparative worth of labour, and more to do with 'systematic imperatives and governance structures' (Fraser, 2003b: 215).

There are alternatives at stake in the contrast between the politics of redistribution and recognition, but there are, Fraser argues, 'false antitheses'. This is simply due to the fact that either denied recognition or a lack of material resources translates into the other. Groups with limited material resources are impeded in asserting their identities, while cultural deprecation then manifests itself in material situations, such as employment in secondary labour markets. Fraser's argument was not that redistribution and recognition are disconnected, but rather that it is a mistake to either reduce one to the other or to pursue one on the assumption that it necessarily translates into the other. Fraser seeks to show how the demands for autonomy find expression in the claims of social movements for justice and attempts to institute democratic justice. That is, 'the parity standard can only be properly applied dialogically, through democratic processes of public debate' and as 'the principle idiom of public reason' it can adjudicate conflicting claims to justice, whether they be those associated with recognition or redistribution (Fraser, 2003b: 230).

Fraser describes 'participatory parity' as expressing the liberal values of 'equal autonomy and moral worth of human beings' (Fraser, 2003b: 224). Honneth does not disagree with Fraser over the rectifying of inequalities that would ensue from instituting participatory parity (Honneth, 2003b: 259). He argues that participatory parity is more of a *means* than an end. The notion of justice in Critical Theory should be directed to the achievement of an anticipated good life and individual self-realization. In other words, Honneth considers that the conditions of a synthesis of positive liberty and social justice are simultaneously more demanding and more fulfilling, since it derives from the notions of the good life and self-realization. Fraser's view of redistribution as an end in itself mainly contributes to positive liberty in the sense developed in liberal welfare states, that is, of underpinning basic conditions of citizenship. This position is, to be sure, not insignificant in the context of increasing material inequalities in capitalist nation states. In order to better take into account the dilemmas of globalization, Fraser introduced the additional justice criteria of representation, which concerns the question of 'who' is able to make claims to justice. In short,

> people can be impeded from full participation by decision rules that deny them equal voice in public deliberations and democratic decision-making; in that case they suffer from political injustice or misrepresentation. (Fraser, 2009: 60)

The most interesting aspect of Fraser's distinction between recognition, redistribution and representation is its potential for clarifying the divergences and contradictions between them. Fraser has a stronger sense of these tensions than Honneth, something that is unsurprising given his position on 'redistribution as recognition'. Fraser is developing this approach to the antinomies of justice, as she considers that it is necessary to address the 'abnormal' injustices of globalization (Fraser, 2009). In her opinion, this requires a practically efficacious conception of a transnational public sphere (Fraser, 2009; Fraser et. al., 2014). Fraser's interpretation of globalization's consequences has affinities with that presented in the preceding chapters. In my opinion, Fraser does not detail the conversion between the subjectivity of actors and the objectivity of institutions to the same extent as my analysis. For similar reasons, Fraser does not have as developed a notion of positive liberty as constitutive. Honneth counter-poses to Fraser's objections a more elaborated image of emancipation, that is, a richer image of self-realization and self-fulfilment. He likewise highlights two components of normative progress in liberal democratic societies, that is, those of growing individualization and increasing inclusion, with formerly excluded categories of persons being included as formally equal. Fraser's recent proposal of emancipation as a long-term movement of modern society, which receives expression in the public sphere and civil society, represents an alternative explanation of normative progress. These domains of society interface with the market economy and the state, but are organized on a different basis and enable public discourses applying the principles of participatory parity (Fraser, 2011; 2013a).

Conclusion

Habermas' discourse theory and Honneth's notion of struggles for recognition each contain conceptions of democratic culture that, to varying degrees, reinforce and contest the model of political liberalism. Both of these elaborations of Critical Theory seek to forge connections between positive liberty and social justice. One stresses the demands for justice informing social struggles; the other accentuates the communicative freedom to participate in democratic will-formation and, from this then, the translation into law of the rational agreements that are arrived at through deliberative discourses. The struggle for recognition framework and Habermas' civil solidarity model of discourse theory can be viewed as complementary, as well as contrasting. Habermas accepts that struggles for recognition have played an important part in redefining the relationship of public and private autonomy. As we have seen, the intersection of this dual autonomy in discourse theory is the key to his affirmation of social and cultural rights. Still, from Habermas' perspective, civil solidarity is the end point of struggles for recognition. This theoretical, as well as practical-political, conclusion possesses considerable justification, although it is obviously limiting and restricting. It subordinates the meaning of struggles to the realization of abstract formal procedures and, despite the inspiration of feminist politics on the mutuality of public and private autonomy, it does not envisage social struggles infusing substantially new meaning into the already institutionalized normative principles of the democratic constitutional state.

Nevertheless, this is a quite legitimate inference to the extent that Honneth's version of struggles for recognition appeals to discourse theory's formal ethic in order to delineate the progressive direction of historical change.

A more significant difference emerges from Honneth's elucidation of the claims to recognition associated with different spheres of interaction and the moral grammar of love, rights and solidarity. These practices of reciprocal recognition could lead to a 'habitualizing' of democracy, but on the condition that they obtain a corresponding *social* embodiment in the structuring of social relations. The pre-political character of these democratic practices distinguishes the struggle for recognition model from the ethical politics of republican approaches and the ideal of a social embodiment of democracy addresses the problem of complexity in a way that need not privilege the procedures of deliberation and legal mediation. Rather, in *Freedom's Right* Honneth wants to develop a theory of justice and notions of freedom that can encompass public deliberation and law, but which are based more on an appreciation of how freedoms are founded on a 'web' of diffuse 'routine and often only weakly institutionalized practices and customs' (Honneth, 2014: 67). Honneth's debate with Fraser over recognition and redistribution clarified some of the potential, though disputed, limitations of the original recognition theory synthesis of positive liberty and social justice. Although it does not satisfy the conditions of this synthesis, the normative standard of participatory parity that Fraser proposed is a readily applicable notion of social justice. It is consistent with liberal interpretations of social autonomy in terms of inclusion, active citizenship, and public deliberation.

Despite the validity of many criticisms of Honneth's theory of recognition, it is important that these criticisms do not generate misplaced effects or lead to the wrong conclusions. One of the strengths of Honneth's theory of recognition is its connection to pre-theoretical experience and convergence with individuals' own sense of suffering and claims for justice. The difficulties that it has in adjudicating claims for justice on the basis of denied recognition should be viewed a result of this connection and subsidiary to disclosing the sources of critique that are present in subjects' experience. By highlighting subordinate groups' experiences of disrespect and the invalidating of their identities, it captures motivations for struggling for change and moral self-understandings. In no sense does this diminish the complications of assessing the ensuing demands for justice. Honneth has focused on struggles' moral grammars and less the explication of the politicizing dimensions of these conflicts (see Deranty and Renault, 2007). Politicization is relevant to comprehending the actual character of antagonisms and the objectives of struggles.

Honneth shows that the experience of recognition and its antonyms can be described in phenomenological, anthropological and moral terms. This is because recognition is an integral feature of personal development and social integration. Honneth argues that demands for recognition are not simply instrumental and matters of individual self-interest, since recognition is always intersubjective. This conception differs from the notion of struggles for recognition in Bourdieu's work, which puts a greater emphasis on the advancement in a field, the accumulation of capital, and how the exercise of symbolic power involves processes of recognition and misrecognition (Bourdieu, 1990). Honneth, by contrast, underlines how there is a shared and general interest in recognition. In other words, he explicates the moral component of recognition and how it establishes a 'we' perspective, rather than the outlook of 'I' perspectives and their combination (Honneth, 2012). Recognition's intersubjective format entails a conception of autonomy that is social; individual autonomy is contingent on mutual recognition and the autonomy of others (Browne, 2010). Like Mead and Habermas, Honneth believes that recognition underpins identity and that it enables the development of a moral consciousness that applies norms in a universalistic manner.

The significant features of Honneth's theory of recognition that have been outlined – its connections to experiences and motivations, its contention that struggles have a moral character, and its disclosure of potentials for immanent-transcendence – are not really contested at the level of their intentions by Fraser. Indeed, to some extent, these three intentions are consistent with Fraser's own use of the category of recognition. Even Honneth's notion of autonomy is not disputed in its own right, rather Fraser critiques its potentially precluding those alternative conceptions of autonomy that subjects may constitute through participation in public discourses and because it appears to derive from a privileging of a moral-psychological standpoint on identity. The same line of reasoning informs Fraser's objections to Honneth's defining justice in terms of self-realization and the 'good life'. Fraser's alluding to the problem of institutionalization does seem to have resonated. Honneth's subsequent emphasis on institutions in the concept of social freedom is an undoubtedly important development in terms of the problems that Fraser was posing under different categories. The diminution that results from this conception is even more consequential for Critical Theory. Honneth's framing of institutionalization qualifies and somewhat undermines aspects of the three significant features of the theory of recognition that have just been highlighted, particularly the interpretation of potentials for immanent-transcendence, the elucidation of social conflict, and the salience of motivation. The last had originally differentiated Honneth's Critical Theory perspective from that of Habermas' version of the paradigm of communication.

6

SOCIAL FREEDOM AND SOCIAL AUTONOMY

Introduction

Honneth's (2014) conception of social freedom is largely consistent with his positions in the debate with Fraser. There are, however, several noteworthy theoretical modifications, such as the lesser orientation towards conflict and agency. These changes are sufficient to constitute an important divergence from Honneth's earlier recognition perspective. This is despite his later explication of the 'We' perspective of various spheres of social freedom, principally those of the market economy, the democratic polity, and the private sphere, being an application of the intersubjective approach of recognition theory. In principle, the changes in Honneth's theoretical approach should be viewed positively. Notably, the account of social freedom is more substantive than the earlier theory of recognition; it specifies in greater detail the historical development of social spheres. The caveat is that this historical account is extremely partial, precisely because Honneth provides a 'normative reconstruction' (Honneth, 2014). What this means is that Honneth's social-historical reconstruction of freedom is stylized and incomplete. A 'normative reconstruction' involves attenuated explanatory claims.

These preliminary considerations may give some insight into the paradox that a more substantive or institutional approach usually places greater, rather than lesser, weight on the types of factors that were prominent in Honneth's earlier work, especially conflict and social divisions. In this instance, the reverse appears to be the case. The relative subordinating of conflict and divisions is not just a matter of presentation or emphasis, it is a consequence of weaknesses in the construction of Honneth's later theory and its perspective on society. My analysis emphasizes five deficiencies. First, Honneth's theory is deficient with respect to the dialectic of control inherent in contesting heteronomous social relations. Second, Honneth is equivocal with respect to the collective realization of social freedom. The need to rectify this weakness is a reason for retaining the reference to positive liberty. Third, Honneth's conception privileges, to use Castoriadis' terminology, instituted society in relation to instituting society; this is partly why it has difficulties integrating dialectics of control into its approach. Fourth, Honneth's retrieval of Critical Theory's historical perspective is significant, but it lacks a proper interpretation of periods or phases of modernization, hence it is surprisingly limited with respect to complex social dynamics. Fifth, Honneth may be right that social freedom develops incrementally but weaknesses ensue from his teleological perspective. Honneth cannot explain the reversals in social freedom that he details.

Revisions are necessary to rectify these five interconnected deficiencies and to achieve a stronger theory of social freedom. Before suggesting sources for a constructive revision, my analysis justifies these claims in the context of exploring the substantial intentions of Honneth's conception of social freedom. The notion of dialectic of control is deployed to revise Honneth's conception and, with reference to relevant social theory perspectives, to convert social freedom into a notion of social autonomy that is consistent with the synthesis of positive liberty and social justice.

Normative Reconstruction and Pathological Freedom

Honneth's later proposal is less transformative in its implications than his 'struggle for recognition' model. The relative subordination of 'transcendence' is very much related to his intention of demonstrating the actuality or objective institution of freedom. If this approach is successful then it would certainly disclose immanent potentials for social justice, rather than establishing the possibility of transcendence through the depiction of some abstract normative ideal or the assertion of a 'context-transcending' justification of emancipation, such as Habermas attributes to discourse as a regulative ideal of communication (Habermas, 1996a). Honneth seeks to show how the institution of freedom in modernity forms the basis for progressive social change. Unlike what might have been expected from his theory of struggles for recognition, *Freedom's Right* does not explore the tensions and conflicts of the instituted order in depth. These conflicts and associated injustices are naturally acknowledged and Honneth proposes a critical diagnostic framework. Moreover, he regularly employs a kind of defensive strategy; that is, he notes how his normative reconstruction may appear implausible given the existing social reality of capitalist societies, such as in the case of the mass media (Honneth, 2014).

There are more than contingent reasons why conflicts, tensions, and dialectics of control are not central to this analysis. These difficulties derive from those approaches to the social order of modern societies that inform Honneth's later framework, specifically Hegel's *Philosophy of Right* and Talcott Parsons' model of social integration (Hegel, 1967[1820]; Parsons, 1951). One of the other reasons why conflict is relatively less prominent is how collective actors are conceived to extend the moral grammar of social freedom, but not really to creatively transform it. The oppositional and antagonistic characteristics of conflict are marginal to Honneth's analysis. This is not by chance, as it reflects the general conception of society that underlies his interpretation of freedom. Honneth is equivocal about the notion of freedom as the self-realization of a collective. This possibly limits his exploration of conflicts, certainly compared to perspectives like those of multiple modernities and social imaginaries, which highlight the modern movements that pursue this sense of freedom (Calhoun, 1995; Eisenstadt, 1999a; 1999b; Taylor, 2004).

If these observations pinpoint weaknesses in Honneth's later theoretical position then they also allude to some of its strengths. Of particular significance, Honneth develops a notion of social freedom that is close to equivalent to the synthesis of positive liberty and social justice. This is no small achievement. *Freedom's Right* seeks to show how justice can derive from the enactment of freedom and how justice, in turn, enables freedom. For this reason alone, Honneth provides additional justifications for pursuing the ambitions of Critical Theory today. Yet, it may be the case that whilst this theoretical perspective offers a justification for critique and an index for determining injustice, it functions less as an exercise of critique in itself and more as a normative conception that can be mobilized in support of more strongly critical perspectives. Honneth's theoretical framework contains the nucleus of a critical diagnosis of the present. It is based on the conceptualizations of the 'misdevelopments' and 'pathologies' of freedom, as well as the contrast between them:

> The difference between such misdevelopments and the pathologies we have already discussed consists in the fact that, in the first case, we were dealing with deviations that were not engendered or promoted by the corresponding system of action: The pathologies of legal and moral freedom represent social embodiments of misinterpretations for which the rules of action themselves are at least partly responsible; after all, the normative practices in both these spheres are incomplete on their own and require supplementation by lifeworld relations, without, however this being made apparent in the performance of these practices. (Honneth, 2014: 128)

Pathologies ensue, in effect, from the presumption that freedom is real when the social foundations necessary for enacting or realizing freedom do not exist. In other words, it is to confuse the 'possibility' of freedom with its reality or actuality. No doubt this critical diagnosis has contemporary relevance, even though it is meant to have a more general application, because it implies that some of the justifications for limiting and denying freedom have been demolished. The critical diagnosis' salience to current circumstances is equally evident in its affinities with Honneth's analysis of the paradoxes of 'organized self-realization' (Honneth, 2012). Honneth argues that the current phase of capitalist modernization generates expectations of autonomy and self-realization that it structurally undermines. The impossibility of meeting these expectations is damaging to subjectivity. Honneth points to work on the prevalence of depression and the

cases of suicide linked to reforms in work organization as evidence of paradoxes' pathological implications (Honneth, 2012).

Honneth's diagnosis of the pathological effects of confusing the mere possibility of freedom with its actuality constitutes a strong critique of many alternate conceptions of freedom, especially those of negative liberty and, to my
mind, the broad range of theories based on the notion of individual choice.
Indeed, it could be argued that these theories make an equivalent mistake to
the confusion of individuals concerning the conditions of freedom. Honneth
does not explain in detail why it is the case that institutions can exist to enable
freedom but do not function in this manner. In a similar vein, it would not be
too difficult to flesh out this critical diagnosis, such as in terms of the injustices
of class and gender. This would enhance the complexity of Honneth's analysis
and give greater insight into the dynamics of contestation. It may be possible
to explicate the connections between this diagnosis and the circumstances of
half-positions, where one is unable to confidently expect that existing rights
will be upheld.

The fact that Honneth offers a normative reconstruction, rather than a more
complete explanation, is a major cause of these limitations. Normative reconstruction justifies a critique of misdevelopments and pathologies that is based
on revealing the distortion of accepted principles. The ensuing problem is that
Honneth's attempt to demonstrate the direction of historical progress obscures
complications and subordinates counter-considerations, such as the conditions
of the resistance to reform and the discontinuity involved in actualizing an
enlarged sense of freedom. Honneth's reconstruction of the market is a case
where the normative reconstruction's selectivity is detrimental (Honneth,
2014). This assessment holds in spite of the fact that Honneth's diagnoses of
the pathologies of the market are perspicacious and valid.

It is worthwhile underlining those dimensions of Honneth's approach in
Freedom's Right that are particularly important to Critical Theory. In my opinion, Critical Theory should adhere to many of the intentions underlying this
work, irrespective of whether Honneth's own framework actually satisfies its
aspirations. I have already identified considerable problems with the execution
of these intentions and how these deficiencies have a deeper source in the construction of Honneth's theoretical framework. Nevertheless, Honneth's conception importantly reconnects normative political philosophy and substantive
social analysis. He describes his intention as that of deriving normative propositions from the analysis of historically unfolding social processes and structures of interaction. It is no criticism to claim that were Honneth to do
otherwise then some of the justification of his theses about freedom and justice
would be diminished. This approach is very much a restitution of the Hegelian
orientation of Critical Theory. Honneth is rightly critical of the manner in
which discourse theory became increasingly disconnected from history.

Honneth could not be more explicit about his disagreement with the focus
of Critical Theory discussions on law and the procedures of justification.
'Nothing has been more fatal to the formulation of a concept of social justice',

he states, 'than the recent tendency to dissolve all social relations into legal relationships in order to make it all the easier to regulate these relationships through formal rules' (Honneth, 2014: 67). Honneth seeks, instead, to clarify the more diffuse and general conditions of social practices and social relations. In this way, he reconstructs how freedom is consolidated through discourse procedures and democratic law. Important consequences flow from commencing from social practices and examining law in light of them, rather than approaching social justice from the other way around.

> This one-sided approach has caused us to lose sight of the fact that the conditions of justice are not only given in the form of positive rights, but also in the shape of appropriate attitudes, modes of comportment and behavioural routines. Most of our individual freedoms, which have become the epitome of a contemporary conception of social justice, we owe not to legal entitlements granted by the state, but to the existence of a web – one which cannot be so easily disentangled – of routine and often only weakly institutionalized practices and customs that give us social confirmation or allow us to express ourselves. (Honneth, 2014: 67)

The problem of the approach that Honneth is rejecting is not just that conceptualizing justice in terms of legal relations involves some abstraction from the more diffuse and indeterminate quality of regular practices. Rather, it is that in following this tendency Critical Theory risks becoming a highly specialized discourse, or even only a critical perspective within a specialized discourse. In this respect, *Freedom's Right* is consistent with the expansive approach of earlier Critical Theory. It continues Critical Theory's distinctive practice philosophical interest in the social translation and institution of philosophical conceptions, especially freedom and rationality. This does not mean that Honneth's approach to practices is entirely satisfactory. His framework prioritizes individuals' performance of internalized role obligations over the practical character of action. This prioritizing reflects the somewhat problematic predominance of instituted structures relative to the instituting social practices in his conception of society. The subordinating of instituting social practices is a major reason why Honneth delimits potential social transformation and it is a source of the deficiencies in his explanation of the structuration of institutions, such as with respect to the dynamics of contestation and power.

The Institution of Social Freedom

The main lines of Honneth's arguments in *Freedom's Right* are not difficult to identify; they are developed with rigour and elegance. Freedom, he argues, is the singular value of modernity that is universally accepted. More specifically, it is the value of individual freedom that is universally approved, since there is some resistance to collective conceptions of freedom, such as we have seen from the discussion of Berlin's critique of positive liberty. Drawing on the framework of Hegel's *Philosophy of Right*, Honneth argues that freedom has been interpreted in terms of three primary forms in modernity: negative freedom, reflexive freedom, and social freedom, with various internal differentiations (Hegel, 1967[1820]; Honneth, 2014). In short, freedom is realized in more than one manner. The limits of particular versions of freedom necessitate more expansive conceptions and institutionalizations. In other words, the restrictive interpretation of freedom as negative liberty is insufficient, though its sense of the right of individuals to independence and to withdraw to a space of their own that is free of interference persists in modernity. These dimensions of the concept of negative liberty should be preserved in the more elaborate and complex conceptions of reflexive freedom and social freedom (Honneth, 2014). Reflexive freedom derives from the internally directed agency of subjectivity; 'individuals are free if their actions are solely guided by their own intentions' and are the 'product of a reflexive act' (Honneth, 2014: 29).

The two variants of reflexive freedom – autonomy or self-determination and authenticity or self-realization – differ from negative freedom in their specifying positive attributes of subjectivity. In the case of authenticity, it is the reflexive acts of self-discovery, the realization of inner desires, and the expression of the self in external forms. Whereas Kant's notion of autonomy involves the freedom of 'self-legislation' and the 'rational self-restriction' of a subjectivity that applies the 'criterion of potential universality' and acts in accordance with the norm of universal respect (Honneth, 2014: 34; 32). Despite the significance of self-determination and self-realization, Honneth argues that the specification of subjective attributes is a necessary but not sufficient condition for the comprehension and facilitation of actual freedom. This evaluation expands on the conclusions that Hegel reached through

> logical operation: On the one hand, the purely negative concept of freedom lacks subjectivity, which must somehow be capable of being understood as free; on the other hand, the resulting concept of inner, reflexive freedom lacks objectivity, because external reality is still only regarded as a heteronomous sphere. (Honneth, 2014: 47)

The fact that each version of reflexive freedom was 'weakened' or compromised over time reinforces the need to conceive of freedom in a way that takes into account objective conditions.

Honneth argues that the notion of freedom has not been adequately developed with respect to the requirements of the theory of justice. In his opinion, this reflects the deficiencies of conceptions of freedom in terms of a theory of society and the analysis of the social grounds of freedom. The implication of this position leads Honneth to develop the notion of social freedom. Social freedom differs from negative liberty and reflexive freedom in its social institutionalization, or, what Hegel termed in the *Philosophy of Right*, 'objectivity' (Hegel, 1967[1820]). That is, Hegel considered that real freedom requires objective social conditions; it is not just a subjective state or capability. In particular, freedom is social because it is enabled by mutual recognition. This means that other subjects condition each individual's freedom. The other, Hegel contended, complements and completes one's freedom. This equally entails that the other's freedom is a condition of one's own and that freedom is, in actual fact, founded on social circumstances of interdependence. Social freedom is animated by the 'we' standpoint that develops out of the intersubjective relations of mutual recognition, rather than the 'I' perspective that forms the starting point of the liberal notion of negative liberty, as well as most conceptions of reflexive freedom. Social freedom, by contrast, involves the mutual realization by subjects of their aims. Honneth argues that social freedom constitutes a normative ideal that is present in different spheres of modern liberal democratic societies. Since he claims that different dimensions of social freedom result in progressive change through the institutionalization of conditions necessary for their realization, there is a qualified 'historical teleological' approach underpinning his normative reconstruction (Honneth, 2014).

Honneth's argument is that the intersubjective freedom of social freedom is an extension of reflexive freedom, because reflexive freedom requires not just internal reflexivity but external conditions for its actualization. In this model, intersubjectivity continues to be constitutive of individual identity and therefore reflexivity; however, Honneth places greater emphasis on the *institutional* implications of the intersubjective character of the social bond. These 'we' relations are consolidated into institutions that have an actuality or objectivity. The distinctive feature of Hegel's conception is that social institutions are part of freedom, rather than, as in most other conceptions, objective social relations that are external to freedom and set against it (Honneth, 2014). Institutions are social freedom's 'medium' and 'condition'; intrinsic elements of freedom rather than separate entities that are related to agency in order to meet expectations of justice, as institutions are in the notions of negative freedom and reflexive freedom.

> Only the third, social idea of freedom takes account of additional social conditions, linking the realization of freedom to the condition that other, accommodating subjects confirm my aims. By emphasizing the intersubjective structure of freedom, we can glimpse the necessity of mediating institutions that inform subjects in advance about the interdependence of their aims. Hegel's idea that individual freedom must be 'objective' thus merely means that appropriate institutions, viz. institutions of mutual recognition, are needed to promote the actual realization of individuals' freedom. (Honneth, 2014: 65)

Honneth's critical derivation of the notion of social freedom is probably as important as his 'normative reconstruction' of its historically instituted forms. In my opinion, it is possible to endorse this derivation whilst dissenting from aspects of his actual depiction of social freedom. Significantly, this means that a different interpretation of the historical institution of social freedom is possible on the basis of Honneth's critical differentiation of social freedom from negative freedom and reflexive freedom. Unlike the latter two, social freedom is intended to be equivalent to the synthesis of positive liberty and social justice. Social freedom should constitute a genuine synthesis of freedom and justice, rather than just a combination of these two dimensions, where they continue to exist independently of each other. The somewhat difficult notion of 'ethical life' that Honneth takes from Hegel is meant to represent this synthesis of freedom and justice, as well as those institutional conditions that contribute to the persistence of social freedom. Social freedom's basic social ontological difference is conveyed by Honneth's comment that

> neither of these two models of reflexive freedom interpret the social conditions that enable the exercise of freedom as elements of freedom itself. (Honneth, 2014: 40)

In this sense, Honneth consolidates Hegel's approach to the 'reality' of freedom without relying on the metaphysical assumptions of Hegel's theory. Despite its importance, this intention means that Honneth carries over into his framework some of the disputed implications of Hegel's approach, such as that it interprets institutions in a manner that blunts criticism of them.

The social character of freedom owes initially to the intersubjective structure of mutual recognition. The key to Hegel's conception is 'contained in his formulation of being "with oneself in the other"' (Honneth, 2014: 42). For Hegel, the other completes one's freedom and this means that reciprocal recognition is central to freedom. It is manifested in the mutual appreciation of how the fulfilment of desires and aims is dependent on the actions of each other and the acknowledgement of the implication of this relationship of interdependency. Honneth argues that the perception of the other as necessary to the formulation and realization of one's aims is constitutive of a change from the standpoint of reflexive freedom to that of intersubjective freedom. Communication is naturally required for the mutual understanding of each other's intention and desires.

Hegel claimed that the freedom deriving from intersubjective recognition was not just shaped by an experience of mutuality, but that it also entails 'complementary norms' and practices that can be formulated and justified in universal terms. This is a particularly demanding standard. The Kantian tradition, by contrast, has a more limited conception of the basis of reflexive freedom's universalism. It founds the universalism of moral autonomy on individuals' reflection on intentions or the application of procedures. These are somewhat separate from actual practices. Hegel emphasizes instead how reflexivity and procedures are contingent on the social context that makes them possible and that has to infuse them for them to be effective. Hegel's notion of freedom involves a reversal of the tendency to treat legitimating procedures as the first condition of freedom and social justice as a secondary requirement.

> For Hegel, in order for a modern social order to be 'just', it cannot merely embody the outcome of a fictional social contract or a process of democratic will-formation, for those proposals ascribe to subjects a kind of freedom they can only enjoy by participating in institutions that are already just. (Honneth, 2014: 57)

There are many interconnected elements to the 'reality' of freedom. Hegel's conception of the institutional supplementing and support of freedom expands and transforms the notion of freedom from an intersubjective conception into a properly 'social' one. In Hegel's view, 'reciprocal comprehensibility' is ensured by 'institutions of recognition, that is, by bundles of behavioural norms that "objectively" integrate individuals' aims' (Honneth, 2014: 45). Institutions make available the conditions and goods that are necessary for actualizing freedom. Honneth argues that there is another equally, if not more important, reason why theories of recognition give precedence to institutions; institutions should socialize individuals into an intersubjective understanding of freedom.

Hegel's conception of freedom implies some sense of reconciliation between subjectivity and objectivity. The transposition of subjectivity and objectivity that this entails draws attention to a substantial tension present in Honneth's conception of social freedom. In general, Honneth and Hegel consistently underline the priority of the objective reality of existing institutions in relation to the development of subjective capabilities. Honneth, however, accepts that genuine reconciliation presupposes that subjectivity is capable of shaping institutions. This presupposition arguably alters the comparative precedence of institutions.

> Hegel, after all, not only searches within social reality for the conditions that enable the realization of autonomous aims, he also aims to thaw the frozen 'material' of reality just enough so that it once again conveys objectively the structure of reflexive freedom itself. (Honneth, 2014: 47)

This aspect of Hegel's perspective on freedom is similar to what I described earlier as Critical Theory's distinctive intention of disclosing the constitutive and generative characteristics of positive liberty.

It should be apparent that disclosing the generative properties of freedom is in tension with some aspects of Honneth's later theoretical framework. Given this reservation, it is worth noting that Honneth argues against Arnold Gehlen's claim that the Marxian vision of freedom implies the Fichtean idea that subjects are free only to the extent that they constitute all objectivity (Gehlen, 1983). In Honneth's opinion, Gehlen failed to take into account the implications of an intersubjective standpoint. Intersubjectivity means that the subject is constituted by what it has not entirely created itself and that the other is partly constitutive of one's identity and freedom. Gehlen represents a more extreme version of the view that social freedom is bound to institutions. In his view, according to Honneth, subjects have to 'hand themselves over to institutions', because they lack the capacity to independently formulate goals and have 'too little internal motivations' (Honneth, 2014). Gehlen's position entails a dominance of objectivity over subjectivity that contrasts with Hegel's belief that institutions enable subjects to realize their aims by acting in concert. Yet, the social objectivity of institutions is necessary for their enabling of freedom.

> For Hegel, institutions belong to the concept of freedom because the intersubjective structure of freedom must be relieved of the necessary task of coordinating subjects. (Honneth, 2014: 53)

There are many similar assertions about institutions in social theory. Habermas claims that the systemic 'steering media' of money and power relieve communicative action of its role in the coordination of action, and Boltanski suggests that institutions stabilize meaning and that this semantic security reduces uncertainty (Habermas, 1987a; Boltanski, 2011). In Honneth's case, he wants to depict institutions in a way that captures their relative independence from the subjectivity of individuals without compromising their enabling, or embodiment of, social freedom. Whilst it is not surprising that he advances a quite normative approach to this dilemma, it results in difficulties with respect to power, conflict and inequality. Honneth refers to Parsons' notion of 'relational institutions' and Hegel's idea of 'ethical spheres' to explicate the intersubjective complementing and completing that is institutionalized, and not just at the level of interpersonal interaction. At this 'second level', interaction occurs on the basis of 'normative status' and the expectations attached to corresponding roles. Institutionalized normative obligations are important to coordinating complex systems of action, because subjects can only formulate and execute intentions if they expect the consideration of others (Honneth, 2014: 125). These assumptions form the basis of Honneth's reconstruction of different spheres of freedom in modernity.

The major strength of this approach to institutions is that the normative considerations that inform a notion of social justice are already present in it. Similarly, one of its major weaknesses is that it may imply the existence of a higher level of justice than is actually the case and considers that injustices are primarily a distortion of institutions' principles of integration and coordination. In my opinion, Honneth's exposition of the institutional spheres of freedom in modernity reveal both of these strengths and weakness. Besides the related criticisms of the difficulties Parsons' functionalism had with respect to power and conflict, Parsons' perspective on the integration of society was faulted for its exaggerated sense of the homogeneity of values and the depths of individuals' internalization of these values and commitment to roles (Wrong, 1961; Giddens, 1979). The fact that Honneth's framework is open to similar objections is apparent from his description of its overall conception of society:

> The social order prevailing in the society we are to reconstruct could be understood as an institutionalized structure of systems of action in which culturally acknowledged values are realized in their respective

functional manner. All central subsystems, to use a term of Talcott Parsons, must embody specific elements of the overarching ideas and values that ensure the legitimacy of the social order as a whole. To normatively reconstruct such an order would thus mean to analyse whether and how culturally accepted values are in fact realized in various different spheres of action, and which norms of behaviour ideally prevail. (Honneth, 2014: 64)

The implication of this conception of systems of action is that normative role obligations coincide with social freedom to the extent that they enable individuals to realize their aims and intentions. Honneth contends that this is a kind of freedom that involves the 'unfolding of personality', but based upon the complementary response of others. For this reason, he considers that the corresponding conception of justice is opportunities to participate in institutions of recognition (Honneth, 2014: 61). Clearly, not every institution satisfies the criteria of justice and it is necessary to distinguish between institutions. To this end, he argues that Hegel adopted the standpoint of the long-term historical development of freedom. Hegel considered that the transmission of freedom through socialization is a substantial reason for freedom's dependence on institutions. 'In Hegel's doctrine of freedom, therefore, institutions only appear as lasting embodiments of intersubjective freedom' (Honneth, 2014: 53). Hegel's view is that the right of freedom is engrained as a practical habit. This presupposes an encompassing culture that reinforces it; although diverse institutions embody freedom in different ways, for instance, an institution like the family may be oriented to individual needs in a way that differs from the political public sphere's promoting self-determination (Honneth, 2014: 131). Hegel sought to detail these practices and their conditions with the notion of 'ethical life'.

It should be clear that social freedom and ethical life are effectively one and the same. In general, ethical life concerns the broad living conditions that enable the realization of justice and morality. Ethical life has a sense of practical objectivity or social institutionalization that differs from more abstract philosophical conceptions of morality and justice, which may or may not be applied in actual practices, like Kant's categorical imperative. Ethical life reflects the dependence of subjects on the social conditions that they inhabit, but its broad character makes it difficult to define. It is, nevertheless, central to Hegel's reversal of other perspectives on freedom. Honneth underlines that the distinctive character of Hegel's theory of justice consists in its being a theory of ethical relations. In simple terms, this could be described as the ways of living based on the practices that ensue from the values and institutions of society. Honneth defines ethical life as a 'layered order of institutions'. In his opinion, the various institutions that contribute to freedom do share one thing in common despite their different orientations and propensities. That is, because ethical life is founded on mutual recognition, social freedom is manifested in particular forms of communicative relatedness. Institutions incorporate this normative expectation to the extent that they engage in discourses that consider the circumstances of all. If nothing else, Honneth has attempted to specify the social reality that is close in modern liberal democratic societies to the discourse ethic.

Spheres of Democratic Ethical Life

Honneth provides what is admittedly an 'idealizing' historical reconstruction of social freedom in three spheres of ethical life: personal relationships, market economy, and democratic will-formation. Social freedom in then clarified in relation to more specific dimensions of each sphere. In short, the dimensions of friendship, intimacy and families in the case of personal relations; consumer markets and the labour market in the sphere of the market economy; and the public sphere and democratic constitutional state. Interpreting each of these spheres as institutionalizing intersubjective or social freedom is, to be sure, open to considerable disputation, although it is Honneth's interpretation of the market as a sphere of 'we' relationships that is the most contentious. It is not difficult to identify factual conditions that contradict social freedom in the spheres of personal relationships and democratic will-formation. But the explicit normative claim that the democratic polity makes to institute freedom and the degree to which individuals' agency is constitutive of personal relations mean that social freedom can be readily understood as potential organizing principles of these two spheres. Indeed, Habermas' conceptions of the communicative rationalization of the lifeworld and communicative power represent interpretations of intersubjective freedom in these two spheres (Habermas, 1984; 1987a; 1996a).

Similarly, Honneth's explication of the patterns of 'love, rights and solidarity' contains a rudimentary sketch of intersubjective freedom in these domains. It is more difficult to imagine that social freedom is a basic organizing principle of the market. Honneth's position assumes that there is a positive moral content to the market and that existing institutions of markets are a distortion of it. In developing an equivalent standpoint in the *Philosophy of Right*, Hegel drew on the early political economists' depiction of the moral implications of exchange and the supposedly mutually beneficial character of contractual relations and the market (Hegel, 1967[1820]). This appears a less tenable position after the intervening two centuries of capitalism. Honneth's own critical diagnoses of the 'hollowing out' of progressive developments in capitalist societies constitute grounds for reservations about the positing of social freedom in the sphere of the market.

Honneth regularly depicts the market as the primary cause of the rendering of recently acquired social freedoms insubstantial, such as through increases in mutual autonomy in intimate relations being distorted and undermined by market representations of emotional gratification as dependent on consumption. Honneth's entire conception of democratic ethical life is based on the supposition that each of the spheres underpins and reinforces the social freedom that exists in the other spheres; hence the effects of 'misdevelopments' and 'pathologies' are not limited to one sphere. The corollary of the mutual reinforcement is that the misconceptualization of one sphere has serious implications for the account of social freedom as a whole. It is not clear that the notion of 'misdevelopment' adequately captures the contradictory purposes of different spheres, but the fact that it might not is probably most evident and consequential in the case of the market. Honneth appears to consider that there is no alternative to the market and does not contemplate more radical conceptions of the institution of an economy, such as those of Castoriadis and Boltanski. The latter argue that it is not from the intrinsic normative orientation of the market but from instituting practices that the normative order of social freedom would be constituted (Castoriadis, 1991; 1997a; Boltanski, 2011).

Honneth endorses the argument that at the level of personal relations there has been a process of democratization. The general tendency is towards greater autonomy and justice, but features of capitalist modernization threaten these increases in social freedom. Social freedom is evident in the institution of normative expectations of egalitarian reciprocity. It is not surprising that Honneth's intersubjective conception works well in the sphere of personal relations. In the case of friendship, social freedom derives from replacing the strategic calculation of self-interest with the mutual interest of friends in each other's well being. It consists primarily in mutual articulation and dialogue over major existential or life decisions. Similarly, the idea of intimacy as a dimension of social freedom can be traced to Hegel's idea of love and its implication that each person is a condition of the freedom of the other. Yet, it is only really relatively recent transformations that enable intimacy to truly become a domain oriented by equality and reciprocity. Honneth describes the sexual revolution as being in 'hindsight' about the deinstitutionalization of the nuclear family. What differentiates intimacy from friendship's grounding in speech, discussion and advice about life decisions, is its physical and sexual character.

This interpretation of intimacy gives an insight into how social freedom is anchored in practical interaction. Subjective rights can only engender the features of intimate relations that have been highlighted, but they cannot produce the complementary reciprocity that is constitutive of social freedom in personal relations. Given this background, family relations have a similar trajectory. Recent decades have seen the 'cultural normalization of the anti-authoritarian movement' that took hold in the 1960s; one of its consequences has been an 'epochal transformation in child-rearing practices' (Honneth, 2014: 162). The consolidating of social freedom in the family is captured in the phrase that Honneth takes from a book's sub-title: from 'patriarchy to partnership' (Honneth, 2014; Mitterauer and Sieder, 1982). Social freedom denotes the moves towards equality in the relationship between partners and the modern family's strong emphasis on communication. For all of that, Honneth's reconstruction of personal life does not adequately convey the fraught and antinomic qualities of intersubjective relations of dependence and autonomy; certainly compared to comparable accounts, like Barbara Misztal's on vulnerability (Misztal, 2011; see also Browne, 2013). Likewise, Honneth's limited consideration of gender is indicative of oversights concerning the dialectic of control and his view of the increasing friendship 'across class lines' seems to confuse the normative potential of freedom with actuality, given the persistence of impediments like education and employment.

One of the intriguing things about Honneth's interpretation of the market is the extent to which it is 'idealizing' and counter-intuitive, especially as the extension of markets is considered to reinforce values antithetical to social freedom in the contemporary period. Honneth's interpretation is, nevertheless, of broad significance, because it addresses genuine problems modern societies confront. These include the institution of justice in the realm of economic relations and the practical implementation of democratic principles in this sphere. At issue is whether social freedom constitutes an alternative to the current order of the market and is contingent on a rupture with it, or whether social freedom is present, if not fully realized, in the current order of market relations and is a normative condition of the successful functioning of markets. It seems to me that Honneth previously argued more along the former lines but now tends towards the latter. It is the presumption of social freedom, he claims, that provides the market with normative legitimacy, since just 'like the other social spheres' the market relies 'on the moral consent of the participants' (Honneth, 2014: 184). The intersubjective norms of social freedom, like the reciprocal relations involved in the completion of one's freedom by the other, are widely misunderstood conditions of participation in the market.

Honneth's basic contention is that if we understand the market as an arena of social integration then it is possible to appreciate its moral content and immanent potential for institutionalizing justice. He endorses Durkheim's and Hegel's respective view that the market activity of contractual exchange rests on antecedent moral foundations and that subjects have to recognize each other 'morally and ethically as members of a cooperative community' to engage in market transactions (Honneth, 2014: 182). This means that the market is always embedded in social relations of solidarity. A number of implications follow from this conception of the market as founded on norms of reciprocal recognition. It implies that the representation of the market in strictly instrumental terms is a mistake. Similarly, the notion of the market as an autonomous system is equally false and veils this institution's historical constitution. The capitalist economic system could only become a dominant institution historically on the basis of 'massive intervention by the state'; including enacting legal frameworks that enable market exchange (Honneth, 2014: 179; see also Castel, 2003). Further, as a normative order of recognition, the market functions as an institution that all participants can consider justified, such as in its allocation of goods, operating according to supply and demand, and as a sphere of social freedom in which the partners in exchange are able to contribute to the fulfilment of each other's material needs.

Honneth argues that Durkheim and Hegel subscribed to a normative functionalist standpoint in considering social solidarity to be the basis of the market's 'harmonious integration' and market participants' obligation to treat each other fairly. The problem is that this leads to Honneth's theory's incorporating some of functionalism's weaknesses, such as in treating conflict and domination as secondary to social integration, and basing his reconstruction on individuals' internalization of presumed role obligations. Honneth's historical reconstruction of the two dimensions of the consumption market and labour market presupposes some measures of demonstrating the degree of social freedom's institutionalization. The institutional mechanisms that Honneth most concentrates on are 'discursive procedures' and 'bastions of equal opportunity'. Not surprisingly, he claims that there have been normative advances where such mechanisms have been established;

> while normative misdevelopments will emerge wherever such institutionalizations, in spite of public pressure, remain absent over time or are rescinded. (Honneth, 2014: 197)

Honneth's sketch of consumption and labour markets establishes clear historical lines of normative progress. Social freedom has been consolidated through various processes of institutional regulation. These subject market relations to principles of cooperation and mutual obligation.

The chief problem with Honneth's historical reconstruction is that it seeks to show how resistance and reform were based on the intention of realizing the 'normative promise' of the market rather than opposition to it. The dynamics of struggles, such as the mentioned actions of bread riots and strikes, involved a higher level of contestation and regularly diverged from the notion of the market as a realm of mutuality (see Jütten, 2015). Honneth rather implies that social freedom in the market was originally inhibited by the lack of discursive mechanisms for representing the interest of all participants. No doubt the establishment of discursive mechanisms contributed to the social freedom that has been achieved, but Honneth's conception has difficulties explaining the historical reversals of social freedom in the sphere of the market. It effectively describes the contemporary 'hollowing out', yet Honneth's approach differs from the former Critical Theory intention of exposing the ideology of the market as a source of injustice and how principles of socialization are in contradiction with the system of capitalist production. The 'socialization from below' that Honneth details, such as in attempts to 'co-determine' the conditions of the exchange of labour power, is presented as primarily drawing its justification from demands that the market fulfil its principle of cooperation (Honneth, 2014: 231).

The third sphere of social freedom is that of the 'we' of democratic will-formation. Honneth's explication of the democratic public sphere, the constitutional state, and political culture expands on his criticism of liberal conceptions of the political order. He argued that Habermas' discourse theory made justice contingent on the outcome of the political articulation of demands. Drawing on Dewey, he proposed that democracy depends on prior experiences of social cooperation. Honneth now seeks to delineate the institutional 'embodiment of social freedom' in the mutual and complementary relations of a democratic public sphere, where 'citizens form generally acceptable beliefs through deliberative discussion, beliefs that form the principles to be obeyed by the legislation in accordance with the rule of law (Honneth, 2014: 254). Similarly, after Dewey, he conceives of the constitutional state as a kind of 'reflexive agency' of social relations of communication, rather than as a political order that is constituted by its separation from the social. This reconstruction's key difference from that of the other two spheres is that a more critical perspective results from evaluating the public sphere and the constitutional state from the standpoint of social freedom. Honneth consistently highlights the discrepancy between the purported ideals of political freedom and the actual social reality that is constituted by conditions external to these ideals, including class inequalities, nationalist identification, and mass media disinformation.

Honneth contests the claim that the political sphere defines the form and meaning of freedom and rejects the related conceptions of public deliberation as a kind of 'supreme court' of legislation. He argues that these conceptions misrepresent the practices of democratic deliberation and the *social* character of the norms of interaction. In Honneth's opinion, state legislation can influence these norms but it cannot generate them of its own accord. The strength of this position derives from its explication of substantive social conditions, rather than the formal requirements of democratic deliberation. It enables Honneth to detail the historical limitations to the development of the democratic sphere of social freedom and to provide a nuanced interpretation of, what Marx critically termed, the abstraction of political freedom (Marx, 1977c). Honneth argues that the communication paradigm 'grasps the relationship between the state and the public in a way that is neither plebiscitary nor representative' (Honneth, 2014: 304–5). The state should seek to enable the social freedom of public opinion and will formation that it then seeks to implement. 'In this conception of the state, all our normative attention is turned away from state organs and directed toward the conditions of non-coercive self-legislation among citizens', and thus towards the public sphere (Honneth, 2014: 305).

The idea that social freedom is based on the affirmation of the freedom of others is undoubtedly important to understanding the struggles to expand the groups that are able to participate in the political sphere and to the achievement of equal liberty. The exclusion of subordinate classes and women from the public sphere until the twentieth century meant that it did not satisfy the conditions of social freedom. In short, the public sphere's normative principles, such as those of the incorporation of all opinions and open deliberation, existed somewhat independently of the actuality of this institution. Honneth points to how a proletarian quasi-public sphere developed during the same period by way of the emergence of working class associations that sought to address the labour and living conditions of members of that class. Although these proletarian forums may not have attained the same level of rational debate as that of the bourgeois public sphere, the topics of their discussions were certainly of equal, if not greater, importance from the standpoint of social freedom. Honneth's reconstruction of the historical institution of social freedom in the constitutional state makes the same point. Even after the formal institution of political rights, the operations of the modern state were conditioned for a considerable period by class and gender perspectives that resisted equal liberty.

Honneth perceives the nascent social freedom of the democratic 'we' as historically enabling and enabled by the 'constitutionalization' of rights. The establishment of political rights of participation did not immediately attain the substantive grounding in social practices that is necessary for social freedom. Rather, this discrepancy is indicative of how 'the idea of unforced will-formation among equal citizens was realized in social struggles, but not in reality' (Honneth, 2014: 261). Similarly, the features that drove the public sphere's historical development contributed to the discrepancy between its ideal and actuality. The 'transformation of the political space of communication' and the 'evolution of media technologies' facilitated greater inclusion in the public sphere whilst contributing to the distorting of the objectives of democracy. Media technologies, like the creation of mass circulation newspapers, expanded the scale of the public sphere to that of the nation. Yet, the public sphere's national scale gave rise to a historically significant tension between its universalistic ideal and particular expression. Nationalism has been associated, Honneth argues, with 'a deep-seated misunderstanding about the type of political unity within which members of society, through processes of mutual recognition, begin to form a many-voiced "We" of public will-formation' (Honneth, 2014: 265).

Where membership of the nation has been defined in an 'essentialist manner', such as in ethnic definitions of a people, the outcome has been forms of exclusion that are inconsistent with democracy. Nationalism may constitute a distorted manifestation of the ideal of the democratic 'we' of social freedom but it is indicative of the experience of social bonds that the notion of constitutional patriotism requires in order to be practically effective. In Honneth's opinion, this consideration is important, because transnational economic and political developments have come to outstrip the national state. The consequences are similar to those of the structural contradiction between globalization and democracy. Honneth emphasizes the contrast between how the consolidation of social freedom increases expectations of democratic legitimation and the 'threadbare' character of the actual legitimacy of modern democratic institutions (Honneth, 2014). He rightly notes that the pronounced contemporary disillusionment with the democratic state is qualitatively different from the apathy that was described by the Frankfurt School, Dewey and Arendt (Arendt, 1958; Dewey, 1984). At the same time, social freedom is necessary to overcome the democratic deficits that now appear at the transnational, as well as the national, level.

One can entirely agree with this critical diagnosis and the general intentions behind it, while recognizing that it requires a stronger sense of the democratic form of collective self-determination to transform the reification of political institutions, the reflexive manipulation of the public sphere by the mass media, and the power of global capital to influence political contexts while evading effective control and regulation. In a similar vein, Honneth argues that Dewey's notion of intelligence clarifies the processes by which social freedom entails a democratizing of the political order and it may be possible to expand on the potential implication of the sense of collective reflexivity that is implied by this vision of the state as emanating from social relations of interaction. On this view, the state is democratic to the extent that its actions derive from open and inclusive public deliberations that satisfy the criteria of sufficient information and equal participation. The latter presupposes the limiting of social inequality and material conditions sufficient for the participation of all. Dewey argued that the more universal is participation in public deliberation the greater is the social intelligence that is applied to the problems of the collective (Dewey, 1984; 1993). It could be argued that Honneth does not fully pursue the radical democratic implications of Dewey's pragmatism, however, his reconstruction of social freedom is consistent with the pragmatist position of 'continuous democratization' (Browne, 2009b), that is, the recognition of the limitations of the existing institution of democracy stimulates practices intended to further democratization. Democracy is a means as well as an end of transformation; it is practically grounded in the mutuality of social interaction and individuals' dispositions towards open dialogue, cooperation and reflexivity.

The Dialectic of Control and Social Autonomy

Honneth's normative reconstruction of social freedom is a substantial demonstration of how progressive change has been institutionalized. Its disclosures of how social freedom has enabled the extending of social justice is significant. Honneth is right to claim that the alternative modern conceptions of negative freedom and reflexive freedom have a less internal connection to social justice and rely on supplementary considerations, especially through positing the enacting of legislation that is initially external to social practices. In part, social justice is intrinsic to social freedom because of the intersubjective character of this type of freedom. Social freedom presumes that the freedom of an individual is conditional on the freedom of others and gives institutional expression to communicative relations of mutual recognition. These intentions of Honneth's conception of social freedom are of enduring relevance to the programme of Critical Theory, irrespective of evident deficiencies in its formulation and application. The flaws in execution of these intentions reveal more substantial problems in the conceptual framing of social freedom and the basic elements of the corresponding theory of society, including those central elements of social relations, agency and institutions.

   Honneth's position is inadequate with respect to the dynamics of the structuration of the institution of social freedom; that is, the constraints and conflicts of the extant production and reproduction of the spheres of ethical life. No doubt this inadequacy is partly due to the limitations of the methodology of normative reconstruction. It permits Honneth to acknowledge the salience of relations of power and domination, but it subordinates the analysis of them.

This is apparent, for example, in the relatively limited consideration given to gender in the reconstruction of personal relations and his underestimation of the current barriers to cross-class friendship. The structuration of social freedom involves the intermingling of normative orientations and modes of power, including power in the standard sense of domination and power as a capacity to enact social freedom. One of the underlying difficulties is the priority of instituted society in relation to instituting society, or instituting practices. In principle, at least, there is no intrinsic problem with presuming the priority of the existing society compared to the present contexts of social action. Even Castoriadis accepts that autonomous individuals can only make and transform a society that has fabricated them and that permits social practices to make a meaningful difference in both institutions and themselves (Castoriadis, 1991). The problem is rather the manner in which Honneth develops the precedence of institutions.

Honneth's image of social integration draws upon Parsons' normative functionalist approach to society. In such a model individuals are considered to act in a manner consistent with the normative roles presented to them. While this is illuminating, it tends to obscure the tensions manifested in actual action and it produces a misleading image of the dynamics of contestation. For example, it means that while Honneth considers that the changes to female gender roles in the family are important to the contemporary extension of social freedom, he does not really clarify the more ambiguous dynamics of enacting this change and the contestation that ensues from resistance, both overt and covert, to such change. Honneth is aware of these considerations and acknowledges that there are discrepancies between the normative role obligations and actual practices (Honneth, 2014). Even so, there are alternative contemporary approaches, such as that of Boltanski, which have sought to disclose how social action manifests the tensions between existing institutions and the practices that serve their reproduction or transformation (Boltanski and Thévenot 2006; Boltanski, 2011; see Browne, 2014a).

Honneth's framing of the priority of the instituted reality is one reason why his theory of social freedom is inadequate with respect to the structuration of institutions, that is, the processes of their production and reproduction (see Giddens, 1979; 1984). This limitation has significant implications for Honneth's claim to represent the 'reality' or actuality of freedom as social freedom. In a theory of structuration, the tensions, contingencies and conflicts of the processes of the genesis and reproduction of institutions are considered to involve a combination of normative rules, material resources, and modalities of power. In fact, this limitation is not just due to the fact that a normative reconstruction is not a complete account of structuration; Honneth follows Hegel in prioritizing existing institutions on the basis that they enable social progress and that social freedom is contained in these institutions. This approach risks complacency about existing institutions. In this instance, the prioritizing of existing institutions was partly motivated by the intention of consolidating critique. Honneth rightly seeks to overcome the tendency of some versions of critique to point to the discordance between an abstract normative principle of justice and the substantive social reality. Instead, he seeks to show how existing social reality contains normative potentials for progress and that justice can be based on 'socially valid criteria' (Honneth, 2014: 63). For this reason, change is presented as the realization of the normative principles of institutions. Although this approach is consistent with Critical Theory's intention of finding within the development of society those tendencies that if fulfilled would result in emancipatory or democratizing transformation, the noted deficiencies with respect to the complexity of structuration processes have some deleterious consequences. Honneth's normative reconstruction does not have the dialectical sense of progressive change that is present in his earlier notion of struggles for recognition, where social conflict was taken to drive the expansion of moral grammars (Honneth, 1995a).

Honneth's theory of social freedom's problems in addressing domination and conflict are connected to the prioritizing of existing institutions relative to instituting practices. A more complex account of the structuration of institutions is necessary in order to reveal how the existing normative representations of justice are ideological and open to conflicting interpretations. Habermas' contention that communicative action always involves taking a position on validity claims appears to acknowledge a higher degree of disputation than Honneth's normative reconstruction (Habermas, 1984). Honneth contends that ethical life depends on the mutual reinforcement of the social freedom institutionalized in the different spheres and that the tensions and conflicts between spheres are a source of pathological developments. The latter is especially the case when the sphere is organized in a manner inconsistent with the intersubjective principles of social freedom, so that, for example, the dominant logic of consumerism does not just distort the social freedom of the market, but also the interpersonal communication of needs in the sphere of intimate relations (Honneth, 2014). This critical diagnosis appears entirely justified but Honneth's theory of social freedom does not present a developed explanation of why the market operates in this manner and how power is incorporated into the mechanisms of the reproduction of the market. In this sense, the assumption that pathologies are due to distortions of the principle of social freedom appears insufficient in terms of the complexity of the social processes. These analytical weaknesses can be seen in the account of spheres.

The problems of Honneth's conception imply that a sociologically adequate notion of social freedom should be founded on the explication of the dialectics of control involved in the institutionalization of intersubjective freedom and processes of structuration. To paraphrase Giddens (1979; 1984), the structuration of social freedom is a medium and outcome of dialectics of control; social freedom's practical enactment is a more dynamic and contested process than is implied by Honneth's notion of institution. One of the reasons why this is the case is that Honneth's framework rightly depicts the existing institution of social freedom as the enabling condition of future freedom, but in a way that limits the latitude of autonomy available to current action. The notion of 'roles' that he adapts from Parsons' theory reinforces this tendency and thereby undermines this framework's capacity to grasp the contestation characteristic of dialectics of control. The notion of dialectics of control is consistent with the intersubjective perspective of Honneth's conception of social freedom. It was Hegel's conception of struggles for recognition that initiated the modern appreciation of the intersubjective character of dialectics of control (Hegel, 1986[1804–5]). The following statement by Giddens conveys how the dialectic of control is integral to social processes of structuration and it draws attention to how this notion discloses aspects of agency that less dialectical perspectives obscure:

> For it is my argument that the dialectic of control is built into the very nature of agency, or more correctly put, the relations of autonomy and dependence which agents reproduce in the context of the enactment of definite practices. An agent who does not participate in the dialectic of control, in a minimal fashion, ceases to be an agent. As I have emphasised before, all power relations, or relations of autonomy and dependence, are reciprocal; however wide the asymmetrical distribution of resources involved, all power relations manifest autonomy and dependence 'in both directions'. (Giddens, 1979: 149)

It would seem that Honneth's relative occlusion of conflict results, paradoxically, from attempting to provide a basis for the Critical Theory methodology of immanent critique in the demonstration of historical processes of progressive change. Although this intention possesses considerable validity, it is compromised in this instance by the failure to adequately explain the processes that generate the 'hollowing out' of the social freedom in different spheres. Honneth rather explores the consequences of the erosion of social freedom, rather than the dynamics of the processes of structuration. For example, he could have more effectively linked the 'hollowing out' to the contradictions of the extant social relations of interdependency and the conditions of the disempowering of agents' resistance. The notion of the dialectic of control offers a means of explaining the practical enactment of opposition to the progressive unfolding of social freedom and the converse challenges by individuals and groups to the constraints on the realization of social freedom. The dialectic of control is closer to Honneth's earlier conception of struggles for recognition. It is these recognition struggles' orientation to change and transformation that demarcates them from the depiction of social freedom, rather than the assumption that social integration is founded on a moral consensus (Honneth, 1995a).

Honneth's concepts of misdevelopment and pathology do illuminate limitations and distortions of social freedom. Yet, compared to the notion of the dialectic of control, they are too readily suggestive of social processes that amount to a deviation from a normal pattern. The dialectic of control instead sustains a focus on the tensions and conflicts of confrontations with injustice. It can similarly account for the complicated outcomes of remedial measures and unstable institutional compromises that emerge in order to manage conflicts, such as the neo-corporatism that Honneth describes as a 'misdevelopment' (Honneth, 2014). The dialectic of control makes it possible to elucidate how the positive intersubjective relations of democratic cooperation can emerge from the negative interaction of opposed perspectives. Habermas' conception of the non-coercive force of the mutual understanding that derives from rational arguments represents a somewhat formal example of such a process and Karagiannis and Wagner's notion of *synagonism* could be interpreted as specifying a more dynamic process of interaction (Habermas, 1984; Karagiannis and Wagner, 2005). Similarly, Honneth's interpretation of how struggles for recognition can generate revisions in moral perspectives exemplifies the positive ways in which the dialectic of control can contribute to social autonomy (Honneth, 1995a). These formulations are indicative of the different manners in which dialectics of control can be reconfigured. For these reasons, the notion of the dialectic of control arguably enables a greater appreciation of the constraints upon the fulfilment of social freedom and it is more open with respect to the potentials of its actualization.

Honneth is nevertheless right to emphasize the different forms of the 'hollowing out' of social freedom, especially the erosion of social rights and the declining material circumstances that have resulted from the expansion of market capitalism. It is certainly the case that there is a substantial difference between the pathological effects of the hollowing out of the institution of social freedom and the injustices of the conditions prior to the achievement of this institution, such as with respect to the rights of political participation or the recent enhancement of the dialogical complexion of friendship. Honneth's failure to explain the structuration processes that generate the hollowing out of social freedom is likewise related to the absence of a conception of overarching phases or periods of capitalist modernization, such as Wagner's notion of 'organized modernity' or even Habermas' conception of late-capitalism (Wagner, 1994; Habermas, 1976). It can be presumed that an overarching conception of a phase of modernization would contain a more complex interpretation of the dynamics between the spheres of social freedom. Honneth's position is the normatively appealing one of the mutual reinforcement of social freedom in the spheres of democratic ethical life. A conception of the structuration of social freedom would clarify the variations in the dynamic between the spheres and the tensions between them. Honneth's assessments of the social constraints that have limited women's and subordinate classes' political expression in the democratic public sphere and the effects of altered labour markets on realizing social freedom gesture towards such a perspective.

The notion of dialectics of control enables a better understanding of the constraints upon social freedom and the mechanisms of contestation that underpin the reversals involved in 'misdevelopments' and 'pathologies'. In particular, the earlier analysis in this work of dialectics of control drew attention to how the conflicts around persisting injustices are transformed and receive a more mediated expression during later periods of capitalist modernization, such as owing to the effects of globalization on the preceding displacement of class conflict in welfare states. It is likewise the case that the notion of dialectic of control could illuminate how the processes of hollowing out are conditioned by a variety of sources of resistance to progressive change, for instance, the perspective of multiple modernities has emphasized how 'fundamentalist religious movements' mobilized in response to feminist struggles for women's autonomy and equal liberty (Eisenstadt, 1999a).

If there is no intrinsic barrier to Honneth's framework's specifying how alternate and emergent forms of resistance limit social freedom then the relevant question would be why many of the complications associated with dialectics of control are overlooked. One explanation is that Honneth's proposal concerning the development of social freedom is teleological; this is a means by which he connects prior historical process to future progressive change. The teleological standpoint downplays the contingencies of enacting social freedom. It means that social freedom appears somewhat limited in its capacity to creatively challenge its existing institutions. The latter is evident in how Honneth notes that Dewey (1984; 1993) and Arendt (1958; 1973) suggest that democratic communication makes possible creative innovations but emphasizes how the radical democratic possibilities that these two standpoints opened up were constrained by historical circumstances (Honneth, 2014). This assessment is by no means wrong and it is even consistent with the estimations Dewey and Arendt made at the time; the problem is, rather, that of Honneth's limited consideration of alternatives and his relative closure of the prospects of social freedom to generate innovative change. There are parallels here with the prioritizing of instituted society relative to instituting practices. Despite this limitation in relation to social creativity, a major strength of Honneth's perspective is its consistent focus on the injustices resulting from the impediments to the realization of social freedom.

The different limitations of Honneth's elaboration of social freedom that have been noted – the weaknesses with respect to structuration, the relative neglect of dialectics of control, and the lack of a conception of phases of modernity – are sources of the risk that his reconstruction overestimates the degree to which social freedoms have been achieved and received institutional consolidation. Honneth is critical of the normative self-understanding of liberal-democratic societies for its tendency to overestimate the level and universality of achieved freedom. The difficulty is that these theoretical weaknesses detract from this criticism and they reveal a potential tension between the conception of social freedom and its practical expression. Honneth's historical account of the overturning of the constraints on social freedom regularly highlights the role of collective agency, such as in the form of the action of the labour movement or the movement for consumer cooperatives. Even so, collective agency is conceived more as a means to achieving social freedom and less as an instance of it.

The notion of positive liberty is based on a stronger sense of collective agency than Honneth's conception of social freedom. How to conceive of a collective form of social freedom that meets the demands of democratic legitimacy is a complex problem. It is a problem that is open to considerable disputation, as the work of Boltanski and Thévenot (2006) on justification has revealed. Honneth is aware of how social freedom is generated through the collective agency of challenging heteronomy and institutionalized restraints. His reservations about the fraudulent unification of individuals in an undifferentiated collective is legitimate and highlights the importance of democratic modes of acting together in the enacting, as well as the achieving, of social freedom. It is not clear how a Critical Theory of capitalist societies could do without some conception of collective self-determination and this may be one reason for retaining the reference to the notion of positive liberty, especially given the existing limitations of Honneth's conception of social freedom.

Given the critical deployment of positions derived from the theoretical perspectives of Giddens, Castoriadis and Boltanski, it is worth clarifying the ensuing constructive contributions that they make to conceptualizing social autonomy. Each of these theorists incorporate some sense of a dialectic of control in their respective interpretations of autonomy and their understandings of effective agency are consistent with considerations that inform the notion of positive liberty, even though they may dispute the veracity of this category (see Castoriadis, 1997c). The notion of dialectics of control not only highlights the salience of power to contexts of social interaction, but it discloses some of the contingencies of enacting social freedom, such as the unintended consequences of regressive reactions to the enhancing of the autonomy of formerly subordinated groups and the contradictory imperatives of institutions. Institutions can simultaneously enable and constrain social freedom; hence it is necessary to explicate processes of structuration. That is, the ways in which social action draws upon and is limited by institutionalized rules and resources.

The theoretical conceptualization of this process has been the distinctive concern of Giddens' theory of structuration. His work illuminates various aspects of the practices of social freedom. In particular, the notion of the dialectic of control in the theory of structuration is meant to clarify the relative balance in the relationship of autonomy and dependency, as well as the contrast between recursive and transformative practices. From this perspective, the contingencies of enacting social freedom include how social relations organize or 'bind' time and space. These considerations could supplement Honneth's contention that social freedom requires substantive conditions for its actualization, so that the current expansion of inequality in capitalist societies undermines social freedom. From the structuration theory perspective, these inequalities are not only articulated in the organization of time and space relations, such as in the distinction between the mobile social elite and the immobile majority, but they are constituted and reproduced by the changing temporal and spatial relations. In other words, Giddens' theory alludes to the broader social ontological conditions of practices and why it is necessary to take into account how they are incorporated into social freedom (Stones, 2005; Browne 2017).

Without using the term, Boltanski outlines elements of the notion of the dialectic of control in delineating the connection between his pragmatic sociology of critique and that of the promotion of emancipation (Boltanski, 2011). In particular, he proposes that investigating the nexus between domination and social classes could be based on 'the analysis of the relationship to rules' and 'on consideration of capacities for action' (Boltanski, 2011: 151). The variation between actors with respect to these properties has significant implications for the interactions between them, including the interaction of collective actors like social classes. Boltanski emphasizes, as well, the ability of dominant groups to circumvent the rules that supposedly organize social relations and the converse: the subjection of subordinates to rules that constrain their agency or capacities for action. The fact that he considers that these relations are moral and involve normative justifications is indicative of how explicating these elements of the dialectic of control can clarify the forms and processes of enacting social freedom.

In terms of the dialectic of control, the most salient difference between Boltanski's approach and Honneth's interpretation of social freedom is its greater concern with the contingencies and uncertainties of social practices. For Boltanski, these facets of social practices contribute to the prevalence of disputation; and disputes, as well as the potential for disputes, reinforces them. Disputation is closely connected to critique and, to the extent that conflict does not become violent, it involves justifications. Like Honneth's conception of struggles for recognition, disputes can have, on this view, a constructive or creative quality, such as through generating moral innovations and disclosing the sense of justice that is applied. Similarly, disputes are stimulated by experiences of injustice and indignation. In the pragmatic framework that Boltanski outlined with Thévenot (2006), the moral grammars of disputes are more variable than is the case in Honneth's theory. Further, their work seem to suggest that a greater amount of hermeneutic testing of reciprocal understandings is necessary for the mutuality that is associated with social freedom. Boltanski and Thévenot propose that the practical enactment of different regimes of justification involves the invocation of some image of common humanity and a principle for determining worth or value in accordance with it, such as to hierarchical positions or to extending networks. These regimes of justification can serve to clarify or resolve disagreements. In Boltanski's opinion, institutions serve to reduce uncertainty through the provision of semantic security, yet this construction of reality is potentially fragile. It is threatened by the fact that institutions fail to meet their own conceptions and the 'reality' that institutions consolidate can be undermined by the wider horizon of meaning of the 'world' that goes beyond it (Boltanski, 2011).

It is not necessary to explore here the entire range of contrasts between the work of Boltanski and Honneth (see Browne, 2014a; 2014b; Boltanski, Honneth and Celikates, 2014). Boltanski's pragmatism implies that social freedom depends on subjects' possession of a range of competences in order to deal with contestation and uncertainty; it suggests that Honneth's interpretation of social freedom overlooks some of the contestation over the institutionally defined reality. Like Giddens' theory of structuration, there is a greater concern with explicating how rules and resources are incorporated into social practices. The dialectic of control is evident in Boltanski's view that institutions are sources of symbolic violence, as well as semantic security. This position could imply that Honneth's conception too readily embraces an institutional resolution of the practical dilemmas of social freedom and that it overlooks the extent to which institutions struggle against the 'unmasking' of their contradictions (Boltanski, 2011). Boltanski's perspective is more concerned with the intrinsic limitations of institutions and his pragmatism is relevant to disclosing the 'pathologies' of freedom, which Honneth contends reveal themselves in the performance of practices. For example, Boltanski and Chiapello (2005) detail how the dialectic of control was implicated in the metamorphosis of initiatives intended to enhance autonomy and establish a more just organization. The result was that the freedom-enhancing reforms inspired by the artistic critique of capitalism were undermined by the rendering of them compatible with the logic of the market. In this way, Boltanski and Chiapello's conclusions are simultaneously consistent with Honneth's notion of the pathological implications of capitalist modernization's paradoxes and critical of Honneth's general framing of social freedom, since they demonstrate how complications and discrepancies reveal themselves in the process of instantiation.

In the case of Castoriadis' interpretation of the imaginary institution of society, the dialectic of control is present in the relationship that is established between the instituted society and instituting society (Castoriadis, 1987). One of the conditions of heteronomy is how instituted society conceals its dependence on instituting society; hence autonomy requires explicit, deliberative and reflexive instituting practices. In Castoriadis' opinion, the project of autonomy depends on an overall reorientation of society. It is a mistake, in his view, to equate this with the transformation of intersubjective relations, even though this project encompasses these relations and is given expression in the commitment to mutual autonomy (Castoriadis, 1991). Like Honneth, Castoriadis argues that individual autonomy presupposes the autonomy of other individuals. At the same time, he emphasizes that an autonomous individual has to will the autonomy of other individuals and this implies that a higher level of agonism is involved in the actualization of social freedom. The agonism is not only at the level of the relationship between individuals but even more so in terms of the intrapsychic conflicts of the individual. In fact, the dialectic of control is critical to the socialization of the individual and the relative disempowering, to use an inapposite term, of the individual psyche. This makes the individual an instituted fabrication of society and it requires collective creativity to facilitate an autonomous society, which enables the instituted order and its imaginary signification to be placed in question by individuals.

Given that Castoriadis and Boltanski each point to how the dialectic of control is present in the relationship of social action to the wider interpretative horizon of meaning that a society institutionalizes, the capacity to create and transform meanings may be a facet of social freedom that warrants more detailed consideration. In fact, one of the major contributions of the pragmatism of Dewey and Mead to the explication of social freedom is the linking of democracy to the creation of meaning (Browne, 2009a; 2009b). Similarly, Castoriadis argues that the meanings of the social imaginary are manifested in how the different spheres of society are organized and the relationships between them. Although this contention may not represent a significant discord, it implies a greater antinomy than Honneth suggests between the imaginary of the project of autonomy and that of the capitalist institution. On Castoriadis' view, capitalism is not really open to the project of autonomy on the basis of its actual, though unacknowledged, dependence on social cooperation. Rather, it is the struggles associated with the dialectic of control that have brought the project of autonomy to bear on capitalist social relations. This antinomy explains why reforms have been countered, such as through hierarchical management and the attempted veiling of heteronomy through the image of the network. Indeed, while Honneth points to similar developments and immanent contradictions, the vision of social freedom that he presents is one in which institutions live up to their normative ideal. The risk contained in this vision, for Castoriadis, is that it may be contiguous with instituted society's closure of meaning and it may conceal the torsion involved in the struggles against heteronomy. Castoriadis once described the distinctive attribute of the western creation of reflexivity and autonomy as 'self-questioning on the individual and collective levels':

> To place oneself at a distance from oneself, to produce this strange dehiscence within the being of the collectivity as well as in that of subjectivity, to say to oneself, 'I am me, but what I think is perhaps false,' these are creations of Greece and of Europe. It is a local accident. I am neither willing nor able to insert it into any theology or teleology of human history. (Castoriadis, 1997a: 103)

Conclusion

If we were to take up Castoriadis' contentions then the implications of incorporating a greater sense of the dialectic of control would be a move from the notion of social freedom to that of social autonomy, since autonomy presupposes a broad background social imaginary and a stronger sense of altering the relation of instituting practices to instituted society. Similarly, I have argued that the notion of positive liberty should be retained at this point of time, because it conveys the sense of collective agency that is required for social autonomy or social freedom. Honneth's notion of social freedom arguably represents the closest approximation to the synthesis of positive liberty and social justice of the Critical Theory notions considered. In saying this it is important to note that it is heavily dependent on the principles of Habermas' discourse theory and that social freedom broadly implies the standard of parity of participation, though not all the specific details and emphases of Fraser's formulation. Honneth's approach overcomes some of the flaws of the recent discussions of social justice that have been influenced by liberalism and it pursues the distinctive Critical Theory method of linking normative political philosophy and social theory. Honneth rightly criticizes the abstract, procedural and legalistic format of prevailing discussions in normative political philosophy. Since I share the intentions of Honneth's conception of social freedom, my criticisms mainly relate to their execution and the limitations of his social theory framework, which undermine some of the objectives of his approach.

The limitations of Honneth's theory do not detract from the significance of his derivation of social freedom and the importance of its deepening the intersubjective paradigm's interpretation of democracy. The key deficiencies of Honneth's theory that have been identified can be readily turned into positive features of a notion of social autonomy: the priority of instituted society can be reversed in favour of the constitutive praxis of autonomous instituting, the incorporating of the notion of the dialectic of control enables the actual objective conditions and the dynamics of transformation to be properly taken into account, especially as the overturning of heteronomous social relations involves some version of collective agency and would encounter resistance, accentuating the contingency of social autonomy permits the explicating of the creative genesis of new understandings of justice and the conditions of realizing it, and by clarifying these processes of structuration it is possible to explain the contemporary hollowing out of social freedom. These elements of a theory of social autonomy have been elaborated upon, to varying degrees, by theorists like Castoriadis, Giddens and Boltanski that seek to rework the intuitions of the philosophy of praxis. The Critical Theory synthesis of positive liberty and social justice is ultimately conditional on its practical enactment and these practices confront the antinomy of having to contest the social injustices that preclude positive liberty.

CONCLUSION

In this work, I have sought to develop the social theory framework of Critical Theory. Critical Theory is shaped by its historical orientation and a recognition of its grounding in the social context. The challenges that these considerations pose have been met through revised conceptions of Critical Theory's key categories and a complementary explanatory approach that discloses the contradictions that underlie the conflicts of capitalist society. The notion of the dialectic of control was deployed in order to delineate the relationships that social actors seeking to realize autonomy have to these structural contradictions and the dynamics of conflicts to instantiate a just social order. I have focused on three contradictions: the conflict between globalization and democracy, the paradox of compelled but thwarted participation, and the current dynamic of system integration and social disintegration. This analysis contributes to the explanation and critique of the injustices, irrationalities and oppression of capitalist society. It is consistent with the Critical Theory methodology of specifying tendencies developing within present society that would lead to substantial emancipatory and democratizing transformations were they fully realized. In this way, Critical Theory's immanent critique of the contradiction between the norms and ideals of autonomy and justice present in contemporary society and the actuality of its organization and institutionalized social relations has been consolidated. At the same time, changes in the ideological complexion of capitalist society have been detailed and the disorienting effects these changes have had on strands of social theory were explicated.

My analysis of capitalist modernization makes use of some of the classical dimensions of the social theory standpoint of Critical Theory. Marx's labour theory of value provided something of a guide for this analysis, but it was treated not simply as a proposition of political economy. Rather, its implications as a statement about the translations and conversions between the subjectivity of social actors and the objectivity of social institutions were developed. This enabled the illuminating of different orders of structural contradiction and the experiences of heteronomy and injustice ensuing from individuals' alienated relations to their own actions and forms of social disintegration. My analysis reconfigures Habermas' preceding reworking of value theory in the thesis of the 'internal colonisation of the lifeworld' (Habermas, 1987a). Like Habermas' theory, it proposed an enlarged sense of the conversions and interchanges between subjects and institutions, lifeworld and system. By taking into account the political and cultural dimensions of social reproduction, this proposal intersects with another Critical Theory *problematique* deriving from classical social theory, that is, the *problematique*

associated with Weber's notion of rationalization as a process of institutionalization and the limits that it imposes upon any radical transformation of
modern society. Critical Theory accepts this Weberian *problematique* but contests the reification that ensues from capitalist rationalization. I argued that the
processes of globalization transfigure some dimensions of reification and that
this is apparent in developments, like the second order abstractions associated
with the instruments of global finance, the inverted cosmopolitanism of the
half-positions of exclusionary integration, and the lack of effective agency on
the part of institutions meant to represent the general interest.

Besides proposing several refinements to the concept of reification, I com-
menced a reinterpretation of the notion of institution. Drawing on strands of
contemporary social theory, this reinterpretation rectifies deficiencies in
Honneth's formulation of social freedom and it underpins a questioning of the
representation of the economy as a self-determining and coherent system. The
revised notion of institution is based on a synthesis of relevant perspectives,
especially those of Castoriadis, Boltanski and Giddens. Its aim is a social theory
approach that centres on the practical constitution of society and the critique
of constraints upon autonomy. It highlights the relationship of instituted forms
to instituting practices, the dynamics of social reproduction, and how institutions combine cultural meanings and material structures. This approach is
especially relevant to Critical Theory's distinctive synthesis of normative and
empirical analysis. Honneth is right to emphasize how Critical Theory discloses the normative potential of substantive social developments (Honneth,
2014). This results in a distinctive social theory approach to justice. I explored
how the synthesis of positive liberty and social justice, which is implied by
notions of deliberative democracy, participatory parity and social freedom,
represents a potential for transforming and superseding the injustices and irrationalities of capitalist modernity.

Given its historical orientation and connection to transformative social
practices, there is always an element of indeterminacy to Critical Theory.
Critical Theory is interested in the potentials for altering in the present the
heteronomous social relations inherited from the past and establishing the
conditions for the autonomous constitution of society (Calhoun, 1995). The
synthesis of positive liberty and social justice is open to different modes of
democratic expression and this reflects the dialogical relation between Critical
Theory and the practices of progressive social and political movements. Of
the various estimations of the potentials of social and political movements
that have been outlined, the idea of self-organization is probably the most
novel feature of social movements' current theory and practice. For the most
part, it is an iteration of attempts to instantiate participatory democratic alternatives to hierarchical and bureaucratic organization. Yet the emancipatory
potential of the theory and practice of self-organization could be queried on
the grounds that overlapping notions, like that of *autopoiesis*, have been
appropriated, in a distorted form to be sure, by the managerial discourses of

flexible and network capitalism. Boltanski and Chiapello (2005) argue that these originally critical categories became significant components of new capitalism's regime of justification.

Two contrasting modes of self-organization have been refered to in this work: that of strands of the alter-globalization movement and the 'unplanned coordination' of the 2005 French riots. The former derives from an explicit conception of autonomy, an ideological opposition to the political forms of delegation, a valourizing of processes of public communication, and a belief in how participation gives rise to creative inventions in social practices and political understandings. The 'unplanned coordination' of the 2005 French riots, by contrast, was not a product of ideology but of shared prior experiences of latent contestation, circumstances of exclusion and marginality, and disillusionment with the movements meant to represent grievances. The rioters' actions, like burning cars and engaging the police in street battles, represented a kind of voiceless communication by those excluded from the dominant public sphere and an enacting of creative disrespect (see Browne and Mar, 2010). Creative disrespect refers to actions that mobilize the significations of a stigmatized identity in order to challenge its imposed and humiliating definition. The riots enacting of creative disrespect served to achieve a sense, albeit quite limited, of agency. One of the contrasts between these exemplars of self-organization is that of scale. The self-organizing strands of alter-globalization are part of a transnational movement. Their practices may be contextually enacted but their intention is to initiate changes that are cosmopolitan or civilizational in scale. Although transnational processes, especially those of historical patterns of migration and shifts in manufacturing, constitute a significant part of the background, the actual practices of the 2005 French riots were directed at the immediate context of discontent, whether it be the state's agency of the police, the physical environment of the *banlieues*, and the embodied subjectivity of the rioters themselves as internally excluded.

Despite the manifold differences between these two instances of self-organization, I argue that both contest dimensions of reification, particularly those exacerbated by processes of globalization. Similarly, the practices of alter-globalization and the 2005 French riots challenge, though in the different ways noted, established political processes and the parameters of the definition of the political. There is, however, to be precise, only a tenuous connection between the politics of creative disrespect, exemplified by the 2005 French riots, and the elements of democratic creativity that are present in strands of alter-globalization. It could be argued that the connection is located in the motivating experience of indignation and in the contestations' mobilizing forms of counter-power in self-organizing. Even if these claimed connections are correct, they are probably shared with a range of movements. Nevertheless, creative disrespect can be a catalyst for democratic creativity. The creative disrespect of the self-immolation that provoked the Tunisian protests leading to the Arab Spring and the subsequent inspiration it gave to anti-austerity protests may be indicative of this catalytic potential. The transference of meanings and practices that is made possible by a transnational public sphere reinforces the significance of this catalytic potential. Naturally, these remarks on two instances of self-organization gesture towards a critical theory of creative democracy that has so far received only limited theoretical elaboration (Browne, 2009a; 2009b; 2014c; Browne and Susen, 2014).

The notion of the dialectic of control is not just relevant to understanding resistances to heteronomy, injustice and reification. It contributes to the explanation of the oppositions and counter-movements to creative democratic processes of 'democratizing democracy'. The need to take into consideration the factual dynamic of struggles opposing progressive change influences the criticisms that were advanced of Honneth's conception of social freedom and the vision of social autonomy deriving from the synthesis of positive liberty and social justice. Similarly, the social theory framework that has been developed in this work is not just concerned with explicit conflicts; rather, it enables the discerning of everyday experiences of injustice and heteronomy that remain below the threshold of public deliberation or collective protest. The conceptual revisions that have been proposed, like that of alienation as compelled but thwarted participation, are meant to clarify these pre-theoretical experiences and the participants' perspective of social actors.

The proposed social theory framework and analysis has implications for the potential lines of the future development of Critical Theory. The concerns of normative political philosophy have been a prominent feature of recent discussions in Critical Theory and this represents a continuation of Habermas' discourse theory programme. Some of the limitations of this approach from the standpoint of social theory have been underlined and attention was drawn to the deficiencies of conceptualizing social freedom or social autonomy solely from the perspective of normative political philosophy. Democratic discourses are, nevertheless, fundamental conditions of legitimation and justification. Communicative rationalization, in the sense of the expectation of discursive justification and the organizing of social relations on the basis of communication, has been a major means of democratization in the current period. These considerations imply that Critical Theory should endeavour to expand on the radical democratic potential of the demands for justification and that are strongly ingrained in modern subject's lifeworld. The expansion of 'the right to justification', to use Rainer Forst's term, goes together with the decline of authoritarian social structures (Forst, 2014). The latter is a significant change from the perspective of Critical Theory, given the Frankfurt School's investigations into authoritarianism. Similarly, discourse theory continues to provide critique with normative underpinnings. The works of Benhabib and Forst demonstrate how discourse theory contributes to debates over justice, both those concerning its overall meaning and specific substantive applications, such as in relation to policies on refugees (Benhabib, 2004; Forst, 2014).

The radicalizing of the discourse theory principle of justification can be pursued in a somewhat different, though potentially complementary, manner. The pragmatic sociology of value, morality, and critique that Boltanski and Thévenot (2006) initiated explores diverse modes of justification in a less formal way than Habermas' discourse theory. It is by no means a complete social theory, but it clarifies the practical enacting of a sense of justice and the competences of subjects to resolve conflicts (Boltanski and Browne, 2014). Boltanski and Thévenot (2006) sketch a matrix of critical practices that derives from different political-philosophical visions of the just polity or regimes of justification. For these reasons, their approach to justification provides insights into the contestation of dialectics of control and the processes of combining positive liberty and social justice (see Blokker and Brighenti, 2011). Boltanski and Thevénot's insertion of communicative practices into fields of tensions is instructive with respect to radicalizing expectations of justification, but their mediation of political philosophy and empirical social science is not the same as that of Critical Theory. Critical Theory is oriented by the aspiration of the realization of a 'historically effective reason'. This informs its evaluation of constructions of value, whereas Boltanski and Thevénot treat political philosophies as if they were alternate grammars and seek to disclose the underlying rules conditioning their enactment in conflicts and disputes. Despite the divergences that the now considerable discussion of the contrasts with Critical Theory have highlighted, French pragmatism offers substantive and methodological insights into the broad social practices of critique and justification (see Celikates, 2006; Susen and Turner, 2014; Browne, 2014a; 2014b).

My approach to the relationship of social contradictions and social conflicts implies that Critical Theory is likely to continue to become increasingly global in its orientation. In large measure, this has become the precondition of understanding the trajectories of modernity (Wagner, 2012). The failure to develop the standpoint of global modernity would lead, as Domingues (2012) remarks, to misunderstanding the historical context and the dynamics of modernization. In a similar vein, the tension between the normative ideal of globalization and its actuality has generated considerable work on cosmopolitanism and related themes, like transnational citizenship, international law, and the transnational public sphere (Benhabib, 2006; Fine, 2007; Habermas, 2008; Delanty, 2009; Fraser et al., 2014). The present analysis implies that the discourses of cosmopolitanism are likely to undergo modifications as a result of reassessments of this disjunction between facts and norms. In particular, the contradictory tendencies of globalization are difficult to reconcile. On the one hand, the dominant tendencies of globalizing processes undermine much of the normative appeal of cosmopolitanism. This is evident in transnational institutions' promotion of austerity programmes in response to the economic crisis of capitalism. On the other hand, it remains the case that some version of cosmopolitanism is the only viable approach to many transnational processes, especially the ecological crisis and migration. Cosmopolitanism could represent an unprecedented form of collective self-determination.

The dilemma of cosmopolitanism being promoted by the same processes that undermine it has resulted in recourse either to the category of hope and a kind of limited utopianism with respect to the facets of liberal democracy, such as to public deliberation, law, or human rights (Browne, 2005). It will probably take struggles to expand social freedom to demonstrate whether cosmopolitanism has a mobilizing power equivalent to that of other modern-ist ideologies and to effectively disclose the potential of cosmopolitanism for social innovation.

During the initial phase of the Frankfurt School, Critical Theory engaged in revisions of Marxist political economy and even Habermas' elaboration of the change to the paradigm of understanding in *The Theory of Communicative Action* was intended to serve as a reconstruction (Habermas, 1984; 1987a). *The Theory of Communicative Action* contains an almost irresolvable tension between its critique of the basic suppositions of traditional political economy and its social theory diagnosis of the origins of late-capitalist social patholo-gies. It argued that pathologies are the result of displacements of the political economic contradictions of capitalist reproduction and the institutional media-tion of class relations (Habermas, 1987a). It would be fair to claim that Habermas' theory precluded a creative exploration of this tension. His com-munication theory replacement of the Marxian paradigm of production gave Critical Theory a normative justification that was independent of political economy. Honneth's theory of recognition subsequently enabled a certain retrieval of Critical Theory's engagement with some key categories of political economy, especially generating important work on labour (Smith and Deranty, 2012). However, the overall implication of Honneth's theory of recognition is broadly the same as that of Habermas' theory, even if Fraser's view that recog-nition theory went even further because of its conceptual monism is misleading (Fraser, 2003a; 2003b). The paradigm change in Critical Theory rectifies Marxist political economy's restrictive and reductive approach to culture and politics. Similarly, the fact that Critical Theory's normative justification is inde-pendent of political economy is a positive development. Nevertheless, there are some genuine dilemmas that Critical Theory confronts concerning political economy in a broad sense and they are certainly relevant to the future elabora-tions of Critical Theory.

These dilemmas concerning political economy are not really new, although the context of contemporary capitalism has clarified some of them. The core dilemma goes back to the contradiction that Castoriadis sketched between Marx's original intention of formulating a critique of political economy and Marx's later commitment to elaborating a political economy (Castoriadis, 1987). In other words, it amounts to a shift from opposing political economy and its suppositions to embracing, however dialectically and critically, political economy. In my opinion, Castoriadis is right to claim that the critique of the notion of an economy as a coherent system is integral to the furthering of the project of autonomy. This deconstruction could draw on a range of sources, such as the work of economic anthropology on 'economic' meanings and prac-tices, and Bourdieu and his interlocutors' extensions of it in relation to the social recognition and misrecognition of value, as well as Adorno's critique of the logic of identity underlying economic reason and the attempts to refine Castoriadis' elucidation of the capitalist imaginary, like Johann Arnason's uncoupling of the imaginary signification of unlimited accumulation from that of rational mastery (Arnason, 2005b; 2015a; 2015b). The critique of the notion of an economy is conditional on the reconceptualization of institutions and the elucidation of the permutations in the capitalist imaginary (see Browne, 2016). The critique of the capitalist imaginary should be undertaken in dialogue with the perspective of global modernity. The latter perspective is important because it underlines the historical approach of Critical Theory and the long-term perspective of its social theory framework. At the same time, the implications of the contemporary resurgence of capitalism have been so substantial that Critical Theory needs to develop its own political economic explanation of these developments.

The future lines of the development of Critical Theory are contingent on its engagement with the social-historical context and the vicissitudes of the project of autonomy. In its strongest formulation, the veracity of Critical Theory is contingent on practices of social transformation and the reorganizing of social relations according to radically democratic principles of justice. However, the distinctive synthetic orientation of Critical Theory partly resulted from the recognition that the historical rationalization of bourgeois society simultaneously diverged from Marx's expectations and that Marx's theory incorporated elements of the imaginary of capitalist rationality that it was intended to contest. Critical Theory continues to confront the questions flowing from the failure to transcend the contradictions of capitalist social relations and the historical supersession of the original context of the elaboration of the Frankfurt School's conception of Critical Theory. In part, it was the need to address these complications that led Habermas to prioritize the renewal of the normative foundations of critique and to emphasize how the democratizing potential of intersubjective communication is present in social interaction and the legitimation of modern institutions, particularly the public sphere, the constitutional state and law. Like Honneth's theory of recognition, this work continues the intersubjective paradigm of understanding whilst explicating the dynamics of conflict and struggle that were subordinated by the Frankfurt School's model of organized capitalism and discourse theory.

Finally, Critical Theory remains a project animated by a series of distinctive intentions. Critical Theory endeavours to disclose the sources of oppression and injustice that are concealed or misunderstood, while presupposing that its critique derives its justification from subjects' pretheoretical interest in general social emancipation. It considers that the reproduction of the social relations of capitalist society is inherently contradictory and that the rationalization of institutions modifies how these contradictions are manifested, as reflected in diagnoses of subjectivity's erosion, distorted understandings, disrespected identities, and compounding material inequalities. Critical Theory seeks to transform the heteronomous relationships of social institutions to the practices of their instituting. It delineates those practices immanent within the development of society that anticipate its emancipatory reorganization. It is an open question whether democratic discourse and mutual recognition will eventuate in a substantial alteration in capitalist social relations, but they represent facets of social reproduction that hold open the possibility of dialogue and deliberation over democratizing transformation. The contestations associated with dialectics of control similarly represent continuing modes of resistance to social injustice and somewhat inchoate renderings of the modernist aspiration of social autonomy.

BIBLIOGRAPHY

Adorno, T. (1973a) *The Jargon of Authenticity*. Evanston, IL: Northwestern University Press.

Adorno, T. (1973b) *Negative Dialectics*. London: Routledge.

Adorno, T. (1978) 'Subject and Object', in A. Arato and E. Gebhardt (eds) *The Essential Frankfurt School Reader*. Oxford: Blackwell. pp. 497–511.

Adorno, T. (1981) *Prisms*. Cambridge, MA: MIT Press.

Adorno, T. (1982) *Against Epistemology: A Metacritique: Studies in Husserl and The Phenomenological Antinomies*. Oxford: Blackwell.

Adorno, T. (1985) *Philosophy of Modern Music*. New York: Continuum.

Adorno, T. (1989) 'Society', in S. Bronner and D. Kellner (eds) *Critical Theory and Society: A Reader*. New York: Routledge. pp. 267–75.

Adorno, T. (1991) *The Culture Industry: Selected Essays On Mass Culture*, J.M. Bernstein (ed.) London: Routledge.

Adorno, T. (1994) 'Messages in a Bottle', in S. Žižek (ed.) *Mapping Ideology*. London: Verso. pp. 34–45.

Agamben, G. (1998) *Homo Sacer: Sovereign Power and Bare Life*. Stanford: Stanford University Press.

Agamben, G. (2005) *States of Exception*. Chicago: The University of Chicago Press.

Albrow, M. (1996) *The Global Age*. Cambridge: Polity.

Althusser, L. (1969) *For Marx*. London: Allen Lane.

Althusser, L. (1971) *Lenin and Philosophy and Other Essays*. London: New Left Books.

Amato, M. and Fantacci, L. (2012) *The End of Finance*. Cambridge: Polity Press.

Anderson B. (1983) *Imagined Communities*. London: Verso.

Anderson, J. and Honneth, A. (2005) 'Autonomy, Vulnerability, Recognition and Justice', in J. Christman and J. Anderson (eds) *Autonomy and the Challenges to Liberalism: New Essays*. Cambridge: Cambridge University Press. pp. 127–49.

Antonio, R. (1981) 'Immanent critique as the core of Critical Theory: Its origins and development in Hegel, Marx and Contemporary Thought', *British Journal of Sociology* 32: 330–45.

Appadurai, A. (1996) *Modernity at Large*. Minneapolis: The University of Minnesota.

Arato, A. and Gebhardt, E. (eds) (1978) *The Essential Frankfurt School Reader*. Oxford: Blackwell.

Arato, A. and Breines, P. (1979) *The Young Lukács and The Origins of Western Marxism*. New York: Seabury Press.

Arendt, H. (1958) *The Human Condition*. Chicago: University of Chicago Press.

Arendt, H. (1973) *On Revolution*. Harmondsworth: Penguin.

Arendt, H. (1979) *The Origins of Totalitarianism*. New York: Harcourt Brace.

Arendt, H. (1992) *Eichmann in Jerusalem*. London: Penguin.

Arnason, J.P. (1979) 'Review of J. Habermas, Zur Rekonstruktion des Historischen Materialismus', *Telos* 39: 201–18.

Arnason, J.P. (1980) 'Reflections on The Crisis of Marxism', *Thesis Eleven* 1: 29–42.

Arnason, J.P. (1982) 'Universal Pragmatics and Historical Materialism', *Acta Sociologica* 25: 219–33.

Arnason, J.P. (1984) 'Contemporary Approaches to Marx, Reconstruction and Deconstruction', *Thesis Eleven* 9: 52–73.

Arnason, J.P. (1989) 'The Imaginary Constitution of Modernity', *Revue Européenne des Sciences Sociales* 27 (86): 323–37.

Arnason, J.P. (1991a) 'Praxis and action – mainstream theories and Marxian correctives', *Thesis Eleven* 29: 63–81.

Arnason, J.P. (1991b) 'Modernity as project and as field of tensions', in A. Honneth and H. Joas (eds) *Communicative Action*. Cambridge: Polity Press. pp. 181–213.

Arnason, J.P. (1993) *The Future That Failed*. London: Routledge.

Arnason, J.P. (1994) 'Reason, Imagination, Interpretation', in G. Robinson and J. Rundell (eds) *Rethinking Imagination*. London: Routledge, pp. 156–70.

Arnason, J.P. (1998) *Social Theory and Japanese Experience*. London: Kegan Paul.

Arnason, J.P. (2002) 'The Multiplication of Modernity', in E. Ben-Rafael (ed.) *Identity, Culture and Globalization*. Leiden: Brill. pp. 130–54.

Arnason, J.P. (2005a) *Civilizations in Dispute*. Leiden: Brill.

Arnason, J.P. (2005b) 'The varieties of accumulation: Civilizational perspectives on capitalism', in C. Joerges, B. Stråth and P. Wagner (eds) *The Economy as a Polity – The Political Constitution of Contemporary Capitalism*. London: UCL Press. pp. 17–36.

Arnason, J.P. (2015a) 'Theorizing Capitalism: Classical Foundations and Contemporary Innovations', *European Journal of Social Theory* 18 (4): 351–67.

Arnason, J.P. (2015b) 'The Imaginary Dimension of Modernity', *Social Imaginaries* 1 (1): 135–50.

Asad, T. (1991) 'Afterword: From the history of colonial anthropology to the anthropology of western hegemony', in G.W. Stocking, Jr. (ed.) *Colonial Situations*. Wisconsin: The University of Wisconsin Press. pp. 314–24.

Austin-Broos, D. (2009) *Arrernte Present, Arrernte Past: Invasion, Violence, and Imagination in Indigenous Central Australia*. Chicago: University of Chicago Press.

Balibar, É. (2004) *We, the People of Europe? Reflections on Transnational Citizenship*. Princeton: Princeton University Press.

Balibar, É. (2007) 'Uprising in the *Banlieues*', *Constellations* 14 (1): 47–71.

Banting, K. (2000) 'Looking in three directions: Migration and the European welfare state in comparative perspective', in M. Bommes and A. Geddes (eds) *Immigration and Welfare: Challenging the Borders of the Welfare State*. London: Routledge. pp. 12–33.

Barber, B. (2001) *Jihad versus McWorld*. New York: Ballantine Books.

Baudrillard, J. (1975) *The Mirror of Production*. St. Louis: Telos Press.

Baudrillard, J. (1981) *For A Critique of the Political Economy of the Sign*. St. Louis: Telos Press.

Baudrillard, J. (1983) *Simulations*. New York: Semiotext(e).

Baudrillard, J. (1998) *The Consumer Society: Myths and Structures*. London: Sage.

Bauman, Z. (1987) *Legislators and Interpreters*. Cambridge: Polity Press.

Bauman, Z. (1998) *Globalization: The Human Consequences*. New York: Columbia University Press.

Bauman, Z. (2000) *Liquid Modernity*. Cambridge: Polity Press.

Bauman, Z. (2004) *Wasted Lives: Modernity and its Outcasts*. Cambridge: Polity Press.

Bauman, Z. (2007) *Consuming Life*. Cambridge: Polity Press.

Bauman, Z. (2011) *Collateral Damage*. Cambridge: Polity Press.

Bauman, Z. (2012) 'Fuels, sparks and fires: On taking to the streets', *Thesis Eleven* 109 (1): 11–16.

Beck, U. (1992) *Risk Society: Towards Another Modernity*. London: Sage.

Beck, U. (1994) 'The Reinvention of Politics: Towards a Theory of Reflexive Modernization', in U. Beck, A. Giddens and S. Lash (eds) *Reflexive Modernization: Politics, Tradition and Aesthetics in the Modern Social Order*. Cambridge: Polity Press. pp. 1–55.

Beck, U. (1999) *World Risk Society*. Cambridge: Polity Press.

Beck, U. (2000a) *What is Globalization*. Cambridge: Polity Press.

Beck, U. (2000b) *Democracy Without Enemies*. Cambridge: Polity Press.

Beck, U. (2000c) *The Brave New World of Work*. Cambridge: Polity Press.

Beck, U. (2000d) 'The risk society revisited', in B. Adam, U. Beck, et al. (eds) *The Risk Society and Beyond: Critical Issues for Social Theory*. London: Sage. pp. 211–29.

Beck, U. (2003) 'Toward a new critical theory with a cosmopolitan intent', *Constellations* 10 (4): 453–68.

Beck, U. (2005) *Power in the Global Age*. Cambridge: Polity Press.

Beck, U. (2006) *Cosmopolitan Vision*. Cambridge: Polity Press.

Beck, U. and Beck-Gernsheim, E. (2002) *Individualization*. London: Sage.

Beilharz, P. (2008) 'Australian settlements', *Thesis Eleven* 95: 58–67.

Benhabib, S. (1986) *Critique, Norm, and Utopia: A Study of the Foundations of Critical Theory*. New York: Columbia University Press.

Benhabib, S. (1996a) 'The democratic moment and the problem of difference', in S. Benhabib (ed.) *Democracy and Difference: Contesting the Boundaries of the Political*. Princeton: Princeton University Press. pp. 3–18.

Benhabib. S. (1996b) 'Toward a deliberative model of democratic legitimacy', in S. Benhabib (ed.) *Democracy and Difference: Contesting the Boundaries of the Political*. Princeton: Princeton University Press. pp. 67–94.

Benhabib, S. (1997) 'On reconciliation and respect, justice and the good life – Response to Herta Nagl-Docekal and Rainer Forst', *Philosophy and Social Criticism* 23 (5): 97–114.

Benhabib, S. (1998) 'Democracy and Identity', *Philosophy and Social Criticism* 24 (2/3): 85–100.

Benhabib, S. (2002) *The Claims of Culture.* Princeton: Princeton University Press.

Benhabib, S. (2004) *The Rights of Others.* Cambridge: Cambridge University Press.

Benhabib, S. (2006) *Another Cosmopolitanism.* Cambridge: Cambridge University Press.

Benjamin, W. (1970a) *Illuminations. Essays and Reflections.* Bungay: Fontana.

Benjamin, W. (1970b) 'Theses on the Philosophy of History', in W. Benjamin, *Illuminations. Essays and Reflections.* Bungay: Fontana, pp. 255–66.

Benjamin, W. (1978a) *Reflections: Essays, Aphorisms, Autobiographical Writings.* New York: Schocken Books.

Benjamin, W. (1978b[1955]) Critique of Violence, in W. Benjamin, *Reflections: Essays, Aphorisms, Autobiographical Writings.* New York: Schocken Books. pp. 277–300.

Berlin, I. (1969) *Four Essays on Liberty.* Oxford: Oxford University Press.

Bernstein, R.J. (ed.) (1985) *Habermas and Modernity.* Cambridge, MA: MIT Press.

Bernstein, R.J. (1998) 'The retrieval of the democratic ethos', in M. Rosenfeld and A. Arato (eds) *Habermas on Law and Democracy: Critical Exchanges.* Berkeley, CA: University of California Press. pp. 287–305.

Bhambra, G. (2007) *Rethinking Modernity.* London: Palgrave Macmillan.

Biehl, J., Good, B. and Kleinman, A. (2007) *Subjectivity.* Berkeley, CA: University of California Press.

Bishop, C. (2012) *Artificial Hells.* London: Verso.

Bloch, E. (1986) *The Philosophy of Hope.* Oxford: Blackwell.

Blokker, P. (2014) 'The European crisis and a political critique of capitalism', *European Journal of Social Theory* 17 (3): 258–74.

Blokker, P. and Brighenti, A. (2011) 'Politics between justification and defiance', *European Journal of Social Theory* 14 (3): 283–300.

Blum, J.A. (2000) 'Degradation without deskilling: Twenty-five years in the San Francisco shipyards', in M. Burawoy et al. (eds) *Global Ethnography – Forces, Connections, and Imaginations in A Postmodern World.* Berkeley, CA: University of California Press. pp. 106–36.

Bohman, J. (1994) 'Complexity, pluralism, and the constitutional state: On Habermas's Faktizität und Geltung', *Law and Society Review* 28: 897–930.

Bohman, J. (1999) 'Habermas, Marxism and social theory: The case for pluralism in critical social science', in P. Dews (ed.) *Habermas: A Critical Reader.* Oxford: Blackwell. pp. 53–86.

Boltanski, L. (2011) *On Critique.* Cambridge: Polity Press.

Boltanski, L. (2012) *Love and Justice as Competences.* Cambridge: Polity Press.

Boltanski, L. and Browne, C. (2014) 'Experience is a mixture of violence and justification – Luc Boltanski in discussion with Craig Browne', *Thesis Eleven* 124 (1): 7–19.

Boltanski, L. and Chiapello, E. (2005) *The New Spirit of Capitalism*. London: Verso.

Boltanski, L. and Thévenot, L. (2006) *On Justification*. Princeton: Princeton University Press.

Boltanski, L., Honneth, A. and Celikates, R. (2014) 'Sociology of Critique or Critical Theory? Luc Boltanski and Axel Honneth in Conversation with Robin Celikates', in S. Susen and B. Turner (eds) *The Spirit of Luc Boltanski*. London: Anthem Press. pp. 561–89.

Bosniak, L. (2006) *The Citizen and the Alien*. Princeton: Princeton University Press.

Bourdieu, P. (1977) *Outline of a Theory of Practice*. Cambridge: Cambridge University Press.

Bourdieu, P. (1984) *Distinction: A Social Critique of the Judgement of Taste*. Cambridge, MA: Harvard University Press.

Bourdieu, P. (1990) *The Logic of Practice*. Cambridge: Polity Press.

Bourdieu, P. (1991a) *Language and Symbolic Power*. Cambridge: Polity Press.

Bourdieu, P. (1991b) *The Political Ontology of Martin Heidegger*. Stanford: Stanford University Press.

Bourdieu, P. (1998a) *Practical Reason: on the Theory of Action*. Cambridge: Polity Press.

Bourdieu, P. (1998b) *Acts of Resistance*. New York: The New Press.

Bourdieu, P (1999) 'The abdication of the state', in P. Bourdieu et al., *The Weight of the World*. Cambridge: Polity Press. pp. 181–8.

Bourdieu, P. (2000) *Pascalian Meditations*. Cambridge: Polity Press.

Bourdieu, P. (2001) *Firing Back*. New York: The New Press.

Bourdieu, P. and Passeron, C. (1977) *Reproduction in Education, Society and Culture*. London: Sage.

Brecher, J., Costello, T. and Smith, B. (2002) *Globalization from Below: The Power of Solidarity*, 2nd edition. Cambridge, MA: South End Press.

Bringel, B. (2015) 'Social movements and contemporary modernity: internationalism and patterns of global contestation', in B. Bringel and J.M. Domingues (eds) *Global Modernity and Social Contestation*. London: Sage. pp. 122–38.

Bringel, B. and Domingues, J.M. (eds) (2015) *Global Modernity and Social Contestation*. London: Sage.

Browne, C (2002) 'A New Nexus of Social Change?', in B.E. Hanna, E.J. Woodley, E.L. Buys and J.A. Summerville (eds) *Social Change in the 21st Century. Conference Proceedings*, Brisbane.

Browne, C. (2005) 'Castoriadis on the capitalist imaginary', *Modern Greek Studies (Australia and New Zealand)* 13: 282–98.

Browne, C. (2006) 'Democratic paradigms and the horizons of democratisation', *Contretemps: An Online Journal of Philosophy* 6 (1): 43–58.

Browne, C. (2009a) 'Democracy, Religion and Revolution', *Thesis Eleven* 99 (1): 27–47.

Browne, C. (2009b) 'Pragmatism and Radical Democracy', *Critical Horizons* 10 (1): 54–75.

Browne, C. (2010) 'Democratic justice as intersubjective freedoms', *Thesis Eleven* 101: 53–62.

Browne, C. (2013) 'Review of Barbara A. Misztal *The Challenges of Vulnerability*', *International Sociology* 28 (5): 518–22.

Browne, C. (2014a) 'The Institution of Critique and the critique of institutions', *Thesis Eleven* 124 (1): 20–52.

Browne, C (2014b) 'Experience is a mixture of violence and justification – Luc Boltanski in discussion with Craig Browne', *Thesis Eleven* 124 (1): 7–19.

Browne, C. (2014c) 'Between Creative Democracy and Democratic Creativity', in V. Karalis (ed.) *Castoriadis and Radical Democracy*. Leiden: Brill. pp. 196–217.

Browne, C. (2015) 'Half-positions and social contestation: On the dynamics of exclusionary integration', in B. Bringel, J.M. Domingues (eds) *Global Modernity and Social Contestations*. London: Sage. pp. 185–202.

Browne, C. (2016) 'Critiques of Identity and the Permutations of the Capitalist Imaginary', *Social Imaginaries* 2 (1): 95–118.

Browne, C. (2017) 'From the Philosophy of Praxis to the Sociology of Practice', in M. Jonas and B. Littig (eds) *Praxeological Political Analysis*. Routledge: London.

Browne, C. and Boltanski, L. (2014) '"Whatever Works": Political Philosophy and Sociology: Luc Boltanski in conversation with Craig Browne", in S. Susen and B. Turner (eds) *Luc Boltanksi: Critical Perspectives*. London: Anthem Press. pp. 549–60.

Browne, C. and Mar, P. (2010) 'Enacting half-positions: Creative disrespect in the 2005 French riots', in C. Browne and J. McGill (eds) *Violence in France and Australia: Disorder in the Post-Colonial Welfare State*. Sydney: The University of Sydney Press. pp. 202–24.

Browne, C. and Susen, S. (2014) 'Austerity and its antitheses: Practical negations of capitalist legitimacy', *South Atlantic Quarterly* 113 (2): 117–30.

Butler, J. (1997) *The Psychic Life of Power: Theories of Subjection*. Stanford: Stanford University Press.

Calhoun, C. (1995) *Critical Social Theory: Culture, History and the Challenge of Difference*. Cambridge, MA: Blackwell.

Calhoun, C. (2003) 'The class consciousness of frequent travellers: Towards a critique of actually existing cosmopolitanism', in D. Archibugi (ed.) *Debating Cosmopolitics*. London: Verso. pp. 86–116.

Calhoun, C. (2007) *Nations Matter: Culture, History and the Cosmopolitan Dream*. London: Routledge.

Calhoun, C. (2011) 'Series introduction: From the current crisis to possible futures', in C. Calhoun and G. Derluguian (eds) *Business as Usual – The Roots of the Global Financial Meltdown*. New York: New York University Press. pp. 9–42.

Calhoun, C. (2013) 'Occupy Wall Street in Perspective', *British Journal of Sociology* 64 (1): 26–38.

Castel, R. (2003) *From Manual Workers to Wage Labourers: Transformation of the Social Question*. New Brunswick, NJ: Transaction Publishers.

Castel, R. (2006) 'La discrimination négative, Le *deficit* de citoyenneté des jeunes de banlieue', *Annales* 61 (4): 777–808.

Castells, M. (1983) *The City and the Grassroots*. Melbourne: Edward Arnold.

Castells, M. (1996) *The Rise of the Network Society*. Oxford: Blackwell.

Castells, M. (2011) 'The crisis of global capitalism: Toward a new economic culture?', in C. Calhoun and G. Derluguian (eds) *Business as Usual: The Roots of the Global Financial Meltdown*. New York: New York University Press. pp. 185–210.

Castells, M. (2012) *Networks of Outrage and Hope: Social Movements in the Internet Age*. Cambridge: Polity Press.

Castoriadis, C. (1974a) *Modern Capitalism and Revolution*. London: Solidarity.

Castoriadis, C. (1974b) *Redefining Revolution*. London: Solidarity.

Castoriadis, C. (1984) *Crossroads in the Labyrinth*. Brighton: Harvester Press.

Castoriadis, C. (1987) *The Imaginary Institution of Society*. Cambridge: Polity Press.

Castoriadis, C. (1988) *Cornelius Castoriadis, Political and Social Writings*. Minneapolis: University of Minnesota Press.

Castoriadis, C. (1990) 'Does the idea of revolution still make sense?', *Thesis Eleven*, 26: 123–38.

Castoriadis, C. (1991) *Philosophy, Politics, Autonomy*. D.A. Curtis (ed.). Oxford: Oxford University Press.

Castoriadis, C. (1997a) *World in Fragments: Writings on Politics, Society, Psychoanalysis, and the Imagination*, D.A. Curtis (ed.). Stanford: Stanford University Press.

Castoriadis, C. (1997b) *The Castoriadis Reader*, D. A. Curtis (ed.) Cambridge, MA: Blackwell.

Castoriadis, C. (1997c) 'Democracy as Procedure and Democracy as Regime', *Constellations* 4(1): 1–18.

Castoriadis, C. (2007) *Figures of the Thinkable*. Stanford: Stanford University Press.

Castoriadis, C. (2014) 'On the work of Max Weber', in V. Karalis (ed.) *Cornelius Castoriadis and Radical Democracy*. Leiden: Brill. pp. 32–58.

Celikates, R. (2006) 'From Critical Social Theory to a social theory of critique: On the critique of ideology after the pragmatic turn', *Constellations* 13(1): 21–40.

Chatterjee, P. (1983) *Nationalist Thought and the Colonial World*. Minneapolis: University of Minnesota Press.

Chatterjee, P. (2004) *The Politics of the Governed: Reflections on Political Society in Most of the World*. New York: Columbia University Press.

Chatterjee, P. (2008) 'Democracy and economic transformation in India', *Economic and Political Weekly* April 19: 53–62.

Cohen, I. (1989) *Structuration Theory: Anthony Giddens and the Constitution of Social Life*. London, Macmillan.

Cohn-Bendit, G. and Cohn-Bendit, D. (1969) *Obsolete Communism: The Left Alternative*. Harmondsworth: Penguin Books.

Comaroff, J.L. and Comaroff, J. (2006) 'Law and disorder in the postcolony: An introduction', in J. Comaroff and J.L. Comaroff (eds) *Law and Disorder in the Postcolony*. Chicago, IL: University of Chicago Press. pp. 1–56.

Cowlishaw, G. (2004) *Blackfellas, Whitefellas and the Hidden Injuries of Race*. London: Blackwell.

Cox, R. (1997) 'Democracy in hard times: Economic globalization and the limits to liberal democracy', in A. McGrew (ed.) *The Transformation of Democracy?* Cambridge: Polity Press. pp.49–72.

Crapanzano, V. (2003) 'Reflections on hope as a category of social and psychological analysis', *Cultural Anthropology* 18 (1): 3–32.

Cremin, C. (2015) *Totalled: Salvaging the Future from the Wreckage of Capitalism*. London: Pluto Press.

Crouch, C. (2005) *Post-Democracy*. Cambridge: Polity Press.

Crouch, C. (2009) 'Privatized Keynesianism: an unacknowledged policy regime', *British Journal of Politics and International Relations* 11 (3): 382–99.

Debord, G. (1995) *Society of the Spectacle*. New York: Zone Books.

Dejours, C. (2012) 'From the psychopathology to the psychodynamics of work', in N.H. Smith, and J.P. Deranty (eds) *New Philosophies of Labour: Work and the Social Bond*. Leiden: Brill. pp. 209–50.

Delanty, G. (2009) *The Cosmopolitan Imagination – The Renewal of Critical Social Theory*. Cambridge: Cambridge University Press.

Deleuze, G. (1986) *Foucault*. Minneapolis: University of Minnesota Press.

della Porta, D., Massimiliano, A., Lorenzo, M. and Herbert, R. (2006) *Globalization From Below: Transnational Activists and Protest Networks*. Minneapolis: University of Minnesota Press.

Deranty, J.P. (2008) 'Work and the precarisation of existence', *European Journal of Social Theory*, 11 (4): 443–63.

Deranty, J.-P. (2009a) 'What is Work? Key Insights from the Psychodynamics of Work', *Thesis Eleven* 98: 69–87.

Deranty, J.-P. (2009b) *Beyond Communication. A Critical Study of Axel Honneth's Social Philosophy*. Leiden: Brill.

Deranty, J.-P. and Renault, E. (2007) 'Politicizing Honneth's ethics of recognition', *Thesis Eleven* 88: 92–111.

Dewey, J. (1984) 'The Public and its Problems', in J.A. Boydston (ed.) *John Dewey: The Later Works, 1925–1953, Volume 2: 1925–1927*. Carbondale and Edwardsville: Southern Illinois University Press. pp. 235–372.

Dewey, J. (1993) *The Political Writings*, D. Morris and I. Shapiro (eds). Indianapolis: Hackett Publishing.

Domingues, J.M. (1995) *Sociological Theory and Collective Subjectivity*. London: Macmillan.

Domingues, J.M. (2006) *Modernity Reconstructed*. Cardiff: University of Wales Press.

Domingues, J.M. (2012) *Global Modernity, Development and Contemporary Civilization*. London: Routledge.

Domingues, J.M. (2015) 'Vicissitudes in Critical Theory', in B. Bringel and J.M. Domingues (eds) *Global Modernity and Social Contestation*. London: Sage. pp. 86–101.

Doogan, K. (2009) *New Capitalism: The Transformation of Work*. Cambridge: Polity Press.

Dörre, K., Lessnich, S. and Rosa, H. (2015) *Sociology, Capitalism, Critique*. London: Verso.

Dubiel, H. (1985) *Theory and Politics: Studies in the Development of Critical Theory*. Cambridge, MA: MIT Press.

Duménil, G. and Lévy, D. (2004) *Capitalism Resurgent: Roots of the Neoliberal Revolution*. Cambridge, MA: Harvard University Press.

Duménil, G. and Lévy, D. (2011) *The Crisis of Neoliberalism*. Cambridge, MA: Harvard University Press.

Durkheim, E. (1957) *Professional Ethics and Civic Morals*. London: Routledge and Kegan Paul.

Durkheim, E. (1984) *The Division of Labour in Society*. Basingstoke: Macmillan.

Eisenstadt, S.N. (1992) 'A reappraisal of theories of social change and modernization', in H. Haferkamp and N. Smelser (eds) *Social Change and Modernity*. Berkeley, CA: University of California Press. pp. 412–29.

Eisenstadt, S.N. (1999a) *Fundamentalism, Sectarianism, and Revolution*. Cambridge: Cambridge University Press.

Eisenstadt, S.N. (1999b) 'Multiple modernities in the age of globalization', *Canadian Journal of Sociology* 24 (2): 283–95.

Eisenstadt, S.N. (2000) 'Multiple modernities', *Daedalus* 129 (1): 1–29.

Eisenstadt, S.N. (2007) 'The reconstruction of collective identities and inter-civilizational relations in the age of globalization', *Canadian Journal of Sociology* 32 (1): 113–26.

Elias, N. (1978) *The Civilizing Process*. Oxford: Blackwell.

Eschle, C. (2001) 'Globalizing civil society? Social movements and the challenge of global politics from below', in P. Hamel, H. Lustiger-Thaler, J. Nederveen Pieterse and S. Roseneil (eds) *Globalization and Social Movements*. Basingstoke: Palgrave. pp. 61–85.

Fanon, F. (1967) *The Wretched of the Earth*. Harmondsworth: Penguin.

Fanon, F. (1986) *Black Skin, White Masks*. London: Pluto Press.

Fassin, D. (2007) *When Bodies Remember*. Berkeley, CA: University of California Press.

Faux, J. and Mishel, L. (2001) 'Inequality and the Global Economy', in W. Hutton and A. Giddens (eds) *On the Edge – Living with Global Capitalism*. Vintage: London. pp. 93–111.

Featherstone, M. (1991) *Consumer Culture and Postmodernism*. London: Sage.

Ferguson, J. (1999) *Expectations of Modernity: Myths and Meanings in the Zambian Copperbelt*. Berkeley, CA: University of California Press.

Feuer, L. (1962) 'What is Alienation? The Career of a Concept', *New Politics* 1 (3): 116–34.

Fine, R. (2007) *Cosmopolitanism*. London: Routledge.

Forst, R. (2011) *The Rights of Justification: Elements of a Constructivist Theory of Justice*. New York: Columbia University Press.

Forst, R. (2014) *Justice, Democracy, and the Right to Justification: Rainer Forst in Dialogue*. London: Bloomsbury.

Foucault, M. (1970) *The Order of Things: An Archaeology of the Human Sciences*. London: Tavistock Publications.

Foucault, M. (1972) *The Archaeology of Knowledge*. New York: Pantheon Books.

Foucault, M (1973) *The Birth of the Clinic: An Archaeology of Medical Perception*. New York: Pantheon Books.

Foucault, M. (1978) *Discipline and Punish. The Birth of the Prison*. Penguin: Harmondsworth.

Foucault, M. (1979) *The History of Sexuality: Volume One*. London: Allen Lane.

Foucault, M. (1980 *Power / Knowledge: Selected Interviews and other Writings, 1972 –1977*, C. Gordon, (ed.). New York: Harvester Wheatsheaf.

Foucault, M. (1982) 'Afterword: the subject and power', in H. Dreyfus and P. Rabinow, *Michel Foucault: Beyond Structuralism and Hermeneutics*. Brighton: Harvester. pp. 208–26.

Fraser, N. (1981) 'Foucault on modern power: Empirical insights and normative confusions', *Praxis International* 3: 272–87.

Fraser, N. (1995) 'From redistribution to recognition? Dilemmas of justice in a "post-socialist" age', *New Left Review* 212: 68–93.

Fraser, N. (1997) *Justus Interruptus: Critical Reflections on the 'Postsocialist' Condition*. New York: Routledge.

Fraser, N. (2001) 'Recognition without Ethics?', *Theory, Culture, and Society* 18 (2): 21–42.

Fraser, N. (2003a) 'Social justice in the age of identity politics: Redistribution, recognition, and participation', in N. Fraser and A. Honneth, *Redistribution or Recognition? A Political-Philosophical Exchange*. London: Verso. pp. 7–109.

Fraser, N. (2003b) 'Distorted beyond all recognition', in N. Fraser and A. Honneth, *Redistribution or Recognition? A Political-Philosophical Exchange*. London: Verso. pp. 198–236.

Fraser, N. (2009) *Scales of Justice*. London: Verso.

Fraser, N. (2011) 'Marketization, social protection, emancipation: Toward a neo-Polanyian conception of capitalist crisis', in C. Calhoun and G. Derluguian (eds) *Business as Usual: The Roots of the Global Financial Meltdown*. New York: New York University Press. pp. 137–57.

Fraser, N. (2013a) 'A triple movement? Parsing the politics of crisis after Polanyi', *New Left Review* May–June: 119–32.

Fraser, N. (2013b) *Fortunes of Feminism: From State-Managed Capitalism to Neoliberal Crisis*. London: Verso.

Fraser, N. et al. (2014) *Transnationalizing the Public Sphere* (K. Nash ed.). Cambridge: Polity Press.

Fraser, N. and Honneth, A. (2003) *Redistribution or Recognition? A Political-Philosophical Exchange*. London: Verso.

Fraser, N. and Nicholson, L. (1990) 'Social criticism without philosophy: An encounter between feminism and postmodernism', in L. Nicholson (ed.) *Feminism/Postmodernism*. New York: Routledge. pp. 19–38.

Fromm, E. (1968) *The Revolution of Hope*. New York: Harper & Row.

Fromm, E. (1971) *The Crisis of Psychoanalysis*. Harmondsworth: Penguin.

Gambetta, D. and Hertog, S. (2009) 'Why are there so many engineers among Islamic Radicals', *European Journal of Sociology* 50 (2): 201–30.

Gauchet, M. (1998) *The Disenchantment of the World*. Princeton: Princeton University Press.

Gautney, H. (2012) *Protest and Organization in The Alternative Globalization Era*. New York: Palgrave Macmillan.

Gehlen, A. (1983) 'Uber die Geburt der Freiheit aus der Entfremdung', in *Philosophische Anthropologie und Handlunglehre Gesamtausgabe*, Vol. 4. Frankfurt/Main: Klostermann. pp. 366–79.

George, S. (2010) *Whose Crisis, Whose Future*. Cambridge: Polity Press.

Giddens, A. (1979) *Central Problems in Social Theory*. London: Macmillan.

Giddens, A. (1981) *A Contemporary Critique of Historical Materialism: Power, Property and the State*. London: Macmillan.

Giddens, A. (1984) *The Constitution of Society: Outline of the Theory of Structuration*. Cambridge: Polity Press.

Giddens, A. (1985) *The Nation-State and Violence*. Cambridge: Polity Press.

Giddens, A. (1990) *Consequences of Modernity*. Cambridge: Polity Press.

Giddens, A. (1991) *Modernity and Self-Identity*. Cambridge: Polity Press.

Giddens, A. (1994a) *Beyond Left and Right: The Future of Radical Politics*. Cambridge: Polity Press.

Giddens, A. (1994b) 'Living in a Post-Traditional Society', in U. Beck, A. Giddens and S. Lash (eds) *Reflexive Modernization*. Cambridge: Polity Press. pp. 56–109.

Giddens, A. (1998) *The Third Way*. Cambridge: Polity Press.

Giddens, A. (1999) *Runaway World*. London: Profile Books.

Giddens, A. (2000) *The Third Way and its Critics*. Cambridge: Polity Press.

Giddens, A. (ed.) (2003) *The Progressive Manifesto*. Cambridge: Polity Press.

Good, M.-J.D.V., Hyde, S.T., Pinto, S. and Good, B.J. (eds) (2008) *Postcolonial Disorders*. Berkeley, CA: University of California Press.

Graeber, D. (2012) 'Occupy Wall Street's Anarchist Roots', in Janet Byrne (ed.) *The Occupy Handbook*. Boston, MA: Back Bay. pp. 141–9.

Gray, A. (2004) *Unsocial Europe – Social Protection or Flexploitation?* London: Pluto Press.

Grumley, J. (1991) 'Marx and the philosophy of the subject: Markus contra Habermas', *Thesis Eleven* 28: 52–69.

Grumley, J. (1992) 'Two views of the paradigm of production', *Praxis International* 12: 181–204.

Grumley, J. (2005) *Agnes Heller – A Moralist in the Vortex of History*. London: Pluto Press.

Haber, S. (2007) *L'alienation: Vie sociale et expérience de la dépossession*. Paris: Presses Universitaires de France.

Habermas, J. (1970a) 'On Systematically Distorted Communication', *Inquiry* 13: 205–18.

Habermas, J. (1970b) 'Toward a Theory of Communicative Competence', in H.P. Dreitzal (ed.) *Recent Sociology.* New York: Macmillan. pp. 114–48.

Habermas, J. (1971) *Toward a Rational Society: Student Protest, Science and Politics.* London: Heinemann.

Habermas, J. (1974) *Theory and Practice.* London: Heinemann.

Habermas, J. (1976) *Legitimation Crisis.* London: Heinemann.

Habermas, J. (1978a) *Knowledge and Human Interests,* 2nd edition. London: Heinemann.

Habermas, J. (1978b) 'Knowledge and human interests: A general perspective', in J. Habermas, *Knowledge and Human Interests.* London: Heinemann. pp. 303–17.

Habermas, J. (1979) *Communication and the Evolution of Society.* Boston: Beacon Press.

Habermas, J. (1982) 'A reply to my critics', in J.B. Thompson and D. Held (eds) *Habermas: Critical Debates.* London: Macmillan. pp. 219–83.

Habermas, J. (1983) *Philosophical-Political Profiles.* Cambridge, MA: MIT Press.

Habermas, J. (1984) *The Theory of Communicative Action: Volume 1: Reason and the Rationalisation of Society.* Boston: Beacon Press.

Habermas, J. (1986) *Autonomy and Solidarity: Interviews,* P. Dews (ed.). London: Verso.

Habermas, J. (1987a) *The Theory of Communicative Action, Volume 2: Lifeworld and System.* Cambridge: Polity Press.

Habermas, J. (1987b) *The Philosophical Discourse of Modernity: Twelve Lectures.* Cambridge, MA: MIT Press.

Habermas, J. (1989a) *The New Conservatism: Cultural Criticism and the Historian's Debate.* Cambridge: Polity Press.

Habermas, J. (1989b) *The Structural Transformation of the Public Sphere: an Inquiry into a Category of Bourgeois Society.* Cambridge, MA: MIT Press.

Habermas, J. (1990) *Moral Consciousness and Communicative Action.* Cambridge, MA: MIT Press.

Habermas, J. (1992a) *Postmetaphysical Thinking.* Cambridge, MA: MIT Press.

Habermas, J. (1992b) 'Further Reflections on the Public Sphere', in C. Calhoun (ed.) *Habermas and the Public Sphere.* Cambridge, MA: MIT Press. pp. 421–61.

Habermas, J. (1996a) *Between Facts and Norms: Contributions to a Discourse Theory of Law and Democracy.* Cambridge, MA: MIT Press.

Habermas, J. (1996b) 'Citizenship and national identity', in J. Habermas, *Between Facts and Norms.* Cambridge, MA: MIT Press. pp. 490–515.

Habermas, J. (1996c) 'Popular sovereignty as procedure', in J. Habermas, *Between Facts and Norms.* Cambridge, MA: MIT Press. pp. 463–90.

Habermas, J. (1998) *The Inclusion of the Other: Studies in Political Theory.* Cambridge, MA: MIT Press.

Habermas, J. (2000) 'Globalism, ideology and traditions – Interview with Jürgen Habermas', *Thesis Eleven* 63: 1–10.

Habermas, J. (2001a) *The Postnational Constellation.* Cambridge: Polity Press.

Habermas, J. (2001b) 'From Kant's "ideas" of pure reason to the "idealizing" presuppositions of communicative action: Reflections on the detranscendentalized "use of reason"', in W. Rehg and J. Bohman (eds) *Pluralism and the Pragmatic Turn*. Cambridge, MA: MIT Press. pp. 11–39.

Habermas, J. (2003) 'Toward a Cosmopolitan Europe', *Journal of Democracy* 14 (4): 86–100.

Habermas, J. (2006) *The Divided West*. Cambridge: Polity Press.

Habermas, J. (2008) *Between Naturalism and Religion*. Cambridge: Polity Press.

Habermas, J. (2009) *Europe – The Faltering Project*. Cambridge: Polity Press.

Habermas, J. (2011) *The Crisis of the European Union*. Cambridge: Polity Press.

Habermas, J. (2015) *The Lure of Technocracy*. Cambridge: Polity Press.

Hage, G. (1998) *White Nation: Fantasies of White Supremacy in a Multicultural Society*. Leichhardt: Pluto Press.

Hage, G. (2003) *Against Paranoid Nationalism: Searching For Hope in a Shrinking Society*. Annandale: Pluto Press.

Hardt, M. and Negri, A. (2000) *Empire*. Cambridge, MA: Harvard University Press.

Hardt, M. and Negri, A. (2004) *Multitude: War and Democracy in the Age of Empire*. London: Penguin.

Harrison, P. (1991) 'Power, culture and the interpretation of democracy', *Praxis International* 11 (3): 340–53.

Harrison, P. (2001) 'Models of Modernity: Capitalism, democracy and the nation-state', in C. Browne, K. Edwards, V. Watson and R. van Krieken (eds) *TASA 2001 Conference*, Sydney.

Harvey, D. (2000) *Spaces of Hope*. Berkeley, CA: University of California Press.

Harvey, D. (2005) *A Brief History of Neoliberalism*. Oxford: Oxford University Press.

Hegel, G.W.F. (1967[1820]) *Philosophy of Right*. Oxford: Oxford University Press.

Hegel, G.W.F. (1977) *Phenomenology of Spirit*. Oxford: Oxford University Press.

Hegel, G.W.F. (1979) *System of Ethical Life (1802/3) and First Philosophy of Spirit (part III of the System of Speculative Philosophy 1803/4)*, H.S. Harris and T.M. Knox (eds). Albany, NY: State University of New York Press.

Hegel, G.W.F. (1986) *The Jena System, 1804–5: Logic and Metaphysics*, G. Di Giovanni, H.S. Harris and J.W. Burbidge (eds). Kingston: McGill-Queen's University Press.

Heidegger, M. (1962) *Being and Time*. Oxford: Blackwell.

Heidegger, M. (1977) *The Question Concerning Technology and Other Essays*. New York: Harper & Row.

Heidegger, M. (1993) *Basic Writings: From Being and Time (1927) to The Task of Thinking (1964)*, D.F. Krell (ed.). San Francisco: Harper & Row.

Held, D. (1980) *Introduction to Critical Theory: Horkheimer to Habermas*. London: Hutchinson.

Held, D., McGrew, A., Goldblatt, D. and Perraton, J. (1999) *Global Transformations*. Cambridge: Polity Press.

Heller, A. (1976) *The Theory of Need in Marx*. London: Allison & Busby.

Heller, A. (1982) 'Habermas and Marxism', in J.B. Thompson and D. Held, (eds) *Habermas: Critical Debates*. London: Macmillan. pp. 21–41.

Heller, A. (1984a) *A Radical Philosophy*. New York: Blackwell.

Heller, A. (1984b) *Everyday Life*. London: Routledge & Kegan Paul.

Heller, A. (1984c) 'Marx and Modernity', *Thesis Eleven* 8: 44–58.

Heller, A. (1985) *The Power of Shame: a Rational Perspective*. London: Routledge & Kegan Paul.

Hirst, P. and Thompson, G. (1996) *Globalization in Question*. Cambridge: Polity Press.

Hochschild, A.R, (1983) *The Managed Heart: Commercialization of Human Feeling*. Berkeley, CA: California University Press.

Hohendahl, P.U. (1991) *Reappraisals, Shifting Alignments in Postwar Critical Theory*. Ithaca, NY: Cornell University Press.

Hollingsworth, J.R. and Boyer, R .(1998) 'Coordination of economic actors and social systems of production', in J.R. Hollingsworth and R. Boyer (eds) *Contemporary Capitalism*. Cambridge: Cambridge University Press. pp. 1–47.

Honneth, A. (1991) *The Critique of Power: Reflective Stages in a Critical Social Theory*. Cambridge, MA: MIT Press.

Honneth, A. (1993) 'Conceptions of "Civil Society"', *Radical Philosophy* 64: 19–22.

Honneth, A. (1994) 'The social dynamics of disrespect: On the location of critical theory today', *Constellations* 1(2): 255–69.

Honneth, A. (1995a) *The Struggle for Recognition: the Moral Grammar of Social Conflicts*. Cambridge: Polity Press.

Honneth, A. (1995b) *The Fragmented World of the Social: Essays in Social and Political Philosophy*, C. W. Wright (ed.). Albany, NY: State University of New York Press.

Honneth, A. (1998) 'Democracy as reflexive cooperation: John Dewey and the theory of democracy today', *Political Theory* 26 (6): 763–83.

Honneth, A. (1999) 'Reply to Andreas Kalyvas, "Critical Theory at the Crossroads: Comments on Axel Honneth's Theory of Recognition"', *European Journal of Social Theory* 2 (2): 249–52.

Honneth, A. (2000) 'The possibility of a disclosing critique of society: The *Dialectic of Enlightenment* in light of current debates in social criticism', *Constellations* 7 (1): 116–27.

Honneth, A. (2001) 'Recognition or Redistribution? Changing Perspectives on the Moral Order of Society', *Theory, Culture and Society* 18 (2–3): 43–55.

Honneth, A. (2002) 'An interview with Axel Honneth: The role of sociology in the theory of recognition', *European Journal of Social Theory* 5 (2): 265–77.

Honneth, A. (2003a) 'Redistribution as recognition: A response to Nancy Fraser', in N. Fraser and A. Honneth, *Redistribution or Recognition? A Political-Philosophical Exchange*. London: Verso. pp. 110–97.

Honneth, A. (2003b) 'The point of recognition: A rejoinder to the rejoinder', in N. Fraser and A. Honneth, *Redistribution or Recognition? A Political-Philosophical Exchange*. London: Verso. pp. 237–68.

Honneth, A, (2004) 'A social pathology of reason: on the intellectual legacy of Critical Theory', in F. Rush (ed.) *The Cambridge Companion to Critical Theory*. Cambridge: Cambridge University Press. pp. 336–60.

Honneth, A. (2007) *Disrespect. The Normative Foundations of Critical Theory*. Cambridge: Polity Press.

Honneth, A. (2008) *Reification: A New Look at an Old Idea*. Oxford: Oxford University Press.

Honneth, A. (2009) *Pathologies of Reason*. New York: Columbia University Press.

Honneth, A. (2012) *The I in We*. Cambridge: Polity Press.

Honneth, A. (2014) *Freedom's Right: The Social Foundations of Democratic Life*. Cambridge: Polity Press.

Honneth, A. and Hartmann, M. (2012) 'Paradoxes of Capitalist modernization: A Research programme', in A. Honneth, *The I in We*. Cambridge: Polity Press. pp.169–90.

Horkheimer, M. (1972) *Critical Theory: Selected Essays*. New York: Herder and Herder.

Horkheimer, M. (1974) *Eclipse of Reason*. New York: Continuum.

Horkheimer, M. (1985) *Critique of Instrumental Reason: Lectures and Essays Since the End of World War II*. New York: Continuum.

Horkheimer, M. (1993) *Between Philosophy and Social Science: Selected Early Writings*. Cambridge, MA: MIT Press.

Horkheimer, M. and Adorno T. (1972) *Dialectic of Enlightenment*. New York: Herder and Herder.

Howard, D. (1988) *The Marxian Legacy*. Basingstoke: Macmillan.

Hudson, W. (1982) *The Marxist Philosophy of Ernst Bloch*. London: Macmillan.

Husserl, E. (1960) *Cartesian Meditations*. The Hague: Nijhof.

Husserl, E. (1964) *The Phenomenology of Internal Time Consciousness*. The Hague: Nijhof.

Hutton, W. and Giddens, A. (eds) (2001) *On the Edge – Living with Global Capitalism*. London: Vintage.

Huysmans, J. (2006) *The Politics of Insecurity – Fear, Asylum and Migration in the European Union*. London: Routledge.

Inglis, D. (2013) 'What is Worth Defending in Sociology Today? Presentism, Historical Vision and the Uses of Sociology', *Cultural Sociology* 8 (1): 99–118.

Jaeggi, R. (2007) *Entfremdung: Zur Aktualität eines sozialphilosophischen Problems*. Frankfurt a.M.: Campus Verlag.

Jaeggi, R. (2014) *Alienation*. New York: Columbia University Press.

Jameson, F. (2004) 'The Politics of Utopia', *New Left Review* 25 (1–2): 35–54.

Jay, M. (1973) *The Dialectical Imagination: A History of the Frankfurt School and the Institute of Social Research, 1923–1950*. London: Heinemann Educational.

Jay, M. (1984) *Marxism and Totality: the Adventures of a Concept from Lukács to Habermas*. Berkeley, CA: University of California Press.

Jay, M. (1992) 'The Debate over performative contradiction: Habermas versus the poststructuralists', in A. Honneth, et al. (eds) *Philosophical Interventions in the Unfinished Project of the Enlightenment*. Cambridge, MA: MIT Press. pp. 261–79.

Jeffreys, S. (2009) *The Industrial Vagina: The Political Economy of the Sex Trade*. London: Routledge.

Joas, H. (1993) *Pragmatism and Social Theory*. Chicago: University of Chicago Press.

Joas, H. (1996) *The Creativity of Action*. Chicago: University of Chicago Press.

Joas, H. (2000) *The Genesis of Values*. Cambridge: Polity Press.

Joas, H. and Honneth, A. (eds) (1991) *Communicative Action*. Cambridge: Polity Press.

Jütten, T. (2015) 'Is the market a sphere of social freedom?', *Critical Horizons* 16 (2): 187–203.

Kant, I. (1964) *Groundwork of the Metaphysics of Morals*. New York: Harper & Row.

Karagiannis, N. and Wagner, P. (2005) 'Towards a Theory of Synagonism', *Journal of Political Philosophy*, 13 (3): 235–62.

Karagiannis, N. and Wagner, P. (2007) *Varieties of World-Making – Beyond Globalization*. Liverpool: Liverpool University Press.

Katznelson, I. (2005) *When Affirmative Action Was White*. New York: W. W. Norton.

Kearney, M. (1998) 'Transnationalism in California and Mexico at the end of empire', in T. Wilson and H. Donnan (eds) *Border Identities: Nation and State at International Frontiers*. Cambridge: Cambridge University Press. pp. 117–41.

Kellner, D. (1989) *Critical Theory, Marxism and Modernity*. Cambridge: Polity Press.

Kepel, G. (2006) *Jihad – The Trail of Political Islam*. London: I. B. Tauris.

Keucheyan, R. (2013) *The Left Hemisphere: Mapping Critical Theory Today*. London: Verso.

Klooger, J. (2012) 'Plurality and Indeterminacy: Revising Castoriadis's overly homogeneous conception of society', *European Journal of Social Theory* 15 (4): 488–504.

Kompridis, N. (2004) 'From Reason to Self-Realization? On the "Ethical Turn" in Critical Theory', *Critical Horizons* 5 (1): 323–60.

Kompridis, N. (2007) 'Struggling over the meaning of recognition – A matter of identity, justice, or freedom?", *European Journal of Political Theory* 6 (3): 277–89.

Koselleck, R. (1988) *Critique and Crisis*. Cambridge, MA: MIT Press.

Kosik, K. (1967) 'The Individual and History', in N. Lobkowicz (ed.) *Marx and the Western World*. Indianapolis: Notre Dame Press. pp. 177–90.

Kosik, K. (1976). *Dialectics of the Concrete*. Dordrecht: D. Reidel.

Kurasawa, F. (2014) 'An alternative transnational public sphere? On anarchist cosmopolitanism in post-Westphalian times', in Nancy Fraser et. al. (K. Nash ed.), *Transnationalizing the Public Sphere*. Cambridge: Polity Press. pp. 79–97.

Kymlicka, W. (1995) *Multicultural Citizenship: A Liberal Theory of Minority Rights*. Oxford: Clarendon Press.

Lacan, J. (1977) *Écrits: A Selection*. New York: W. W. and Norton.

Lacan, J. (1981) *The Four Fundamental Concepts of Psycho-Analysis*. New York: W. W. and Norton.

Lagrange, H. and Oberti, M. (eds) (2006) *Émeutes Urbaines et Protestations. Une Singularité Française*. Paris: Presses de Sciences Po.

Laing, R.D. (1965) *The Divided Self*. Harmondsworth: Pelican Books.

Lake, M. (2008) 'Equality and exclusion: The racial constitution of colonial liberalism', *Thesis Eleven* 95: 20–32.

Lapavitsas, C. et al. (2012) *Crisis in the Eurozone*. London: Verso.

Lasch, C. (1977) *Haven in a Heartless World*. New York: Basic Books.

Lefebvre, H. (1968) *The Sociology of Marx*. Harmondsworth: Penguin.

Lefebvre, H. (1991) *The Production of Space*. Oxford: Blackwell.

Lefebvre, H. (1995) *Introduction to Modernity: Twelve Preludes September 1959–May 1961*. London: Verso.

Lefebvre, H. (2008) *Critique of Everyday Life*. London: Verso.

Lefort, C. (1978) 'From one vision of history to another', *Social Research* 45: 615–66.

Lefort, C. (1986) *The Political Forms of Modern Society: Bureaucracy, Democracy, Totalitarianism*. Cambridge: Polity Press.

Lefort, C. (1988) *Democracy and Political Theory*. Cambridge: Polity Press.

Lentin, A. (2004) *Racism and Anti-Racism in Europe*. London: Pluto Press.

Lévi-Strauss, C. (1966) *The Savage Mind*. Chicago: The University of Chicago Press.

Levitas, R. (ed.) (1986) *The Ideology of the New Right*. Cambridge: Polity Press.

Levitas, R. (1990) *The Concept of Utopia*. London: Phillip Allan.

Levy, J. (1999) *Tocqueville's Revenge. State, Society, and Economy in Contemporary France*. Cambridge, MA: Harvard University Press.

Levy, J. (2005) 'Redeploying the state: Liberalization and social policy in France', in W. Streeck and K. Thelen (eds) *Beyond Continuity – Institutional Change in Advanced Political Economies*. Oxford: Oxford University Press. pp. 103–26.

Lieberman, R. (1998) *Shifting the Color Line: Race and the American Welfare State*. Cambridge, MA: Harvard University Press.

Luhmann, N. (2005) *Risk: A Sociological Analysis*. New Brunswick, NJ: Transaction Publishers.

Lukács, G. (1971) *History and Class Consciousness*. London: Merlin.

Lukács, G. (1975) *The Young Hegel: Studies in the Relations Between Dialectics and Economics*. London: Merlin Press.

Lukács, G. (1978) *The Ontology of Social Being*. London: Merlin.

Lyotard, J.-F. (1984) *The Postmodern Condition: A Report on Knowledge*. Minneapolis: University of Minnesota Press.

MacPherson, C.B. (1977) *The Life and Times of Liberal Democracy*. Oxford: Oxford University Press.

Mann, M. (2003) *The Dark Side of Democracy*. Cambridge: Cambridge University Press.

Mann, M. (2004) *Fascists*. Cambridge: Cambridge University Press.

Mannheim, K. (1949) *Ideology and Utopia*. London: Routledge.

Marcuse, H. (1964) *One-Dimensional Man*. London: Routledge and Kegan Paul.

Marcuse, H. (1966) *Eros and Civilization; a Philosophical Inquiry into Freud*. Boston: Beacon Press.

Marcuse, H. (1967) *Reason and Revolution*. London: Routledge and Kegan Paul.

Marcuse, H. (1968) *Negations: Essays in Critical Theory*. Boston: Beacon Press.

Marcuse, H. (1969a) *An Essay on Liberation*. Boston: Beacon Press.

Marcuse, H. (1969b[1928]) 'Contributions to a Phenomenology of Historical Materialism', *Telos* 4: 3–34.

Marcuse, H. (1970) *Five Lectures: Psychoanalysis, Politics and Utopia*. London: Allen Lane.

Marcuse, H. (1973) 'On the Philosophical Foundations of the Concept of Labour in Economics', *Telos* 16: 9–37.

Marcuse, H. (1976) 'On the Problem of the Dialectic', *Telos* 27: 12–39.

Marcuse, H. (1978) *The Aesthetic Dimension: Toward a Critique of Marxist Aesthetics*. Boston: Beacon Press.

Marcuse, H. (1983) *From Luther to Popper*. London: Verso.

Marcuse, H. (1987) *Hegel's Ontology and the Theory of Historicity*. Cambridge, MA: MIT Press.

Markle, G. (2004) 'From struggles for recognition to a plural concept of justice – an interview with Axel Honneth', *Acta Sociologica* 47 (4): 383–91.

Márkus, G. (1978) *Marxism and Anthropology: The Concept of 'Human Essence' in the Philosophy of Marx*. Assen: Van Gorcum.

Márkus, G. (1980) 'Four Forms of Critical Theory: Some Theses on Marx's Development', *Thesis Eleven* 1: 78–93.

Márkus, G. (1982) 'Alienation and Reification in Marx and Lukács', *Thesis Eleven* 5/6: 139–61.

Márkus, G. (1986a) *Language and Production a Critique of the Paradigms*. Dordrecht: Reidel.

Márkus, G. (1986b) 'Praxis and Poiesis: Beyond the Dichotomy', *Thesis Eleven* 15: 30–47.

Márkus, G. (1993) 'György Márkus interviewed by Anthony Uhlmann', *Active: Reactive* (March): 38–44.

Márkus, G. (1999) 'On freedom: Positive and negative', *Constellations* 6 (3): 273–89.

Marshall, T.H. (1950) *Citizenship and Social Class*. Cambridge: Cambridge University Press.

Marshall, T.H. (1991) *Citizenship and Social Class and Other Essays*. London: Pluto Press.

Marx, K. (1971[1867]) *Capital: A Critique of Political Economy*. Harmondsworth: Penguin.

Marx, K. (1973) *Grundrisse: Foundations of the Critique of Political Economy (Rough Draft)*. Harmondsworth: Penguin Books.

Marx, K. (1977a) *Economic and Philosophical Manuscripts of 1844*. Moscow: Progress Publishers.

Marx, K. (1977b) 'Critique of the Gotha Programme', in D. McLellan (ed.) *Karl Marx: Selected Writings*. Oxford: Oxford University Press. pp. 564–70.

Marx, K. (1977c) 'On the Jewish Question', in D. Mclellan (ed.) *Karl Marx: Selected Writings*. Oxford: Oxford University Press. pp. 39–62.

Marx, K. and Engels, F. (1977) 'The Communist Manifesto', in D. McLellan (ed.) *Karl Marx: Selected Writings*. Oxford: Oxford University Press. pp. 221–47.

McCarthy, T. (2002) 'On Reconciling Cosmopolitan Unity and National Diversity', in P. de Greiff and C. Cronin (eds) *Global Justice and Transnational Politics*. Cambridge, MA: MIT Press. pp. 235–74.

McDonald, K. (2006) *Global Movements: Action and Culture*. Oxford: Blackwell.

McDonald, K. (2012) 'They can't do nothin' to us today', *Thesis Eleven* 109 (1): 17–23.

McGrew, A. (ed.) (1997) *The Transformation of Democracy?* Cambridge: Polity Press.

McNay, L. (2014) *The Misguided Search for the Political*. Cambridge: Polity Press.

Mead, G.H. (1934) *Mind, Self and Society*. Chicago: The University of Chicago Press.

Melucci, A. (1996) *Challenging Codes: Collective Action in the Information Age*. Cambridge: Cambridge University Press.

Merleau-Ponty, M. (1964) *Signs*. Evanston, IL: Northwestern University Press.

Merleau-Ponty, M. (1968) *The Visible and the Invisible: Followed by Working Notes*. C. Lefort (ed.). Evanston, IL: Northwestern University Press.

Merleau-Ponty, M. (1969) *Humanism and Terror: An Essay on the Communist Problem*. John O'Neill (ed. and trans.). Boston: Beacon Press.

Merleau-Ponty, M. (1973) *Adventures of the Dialectic*. Evanston, IL: Northwestern University Press.

Merleau-Ponty, M. (2010) *Institution and Passivity: Course Notes from the Collège de France (1954–1955)*. Evanston, IL: Northwestern University Press.

Misztal, B. (2011) *The Challenges of Vulnerability: In Search for a Less Vulnerable Social Life*. Basingstoke: Palgrave Macmillan.

Mitterauer, M. and Sieder, R. (1982) *The European Family: Patriarchy to Partnership from the Middle Ages to the Present*. Chicago: University of Chicago Press.

Mouffe, C. (ed.) 1999 *The Challenge of Carl Schmitt*. Verso: London.

Murphy, P. (2012) *The Collective Imagination – The Creative Spirit of Free Societies*. Farnham: Ashgate.

Nussbaum, M. and Sen, A. (2004) *The Quality of Life*. London: Routledge.

Offe, C. (1984) *Contradictions of the Welfare State*. Cambridge, MA: MIT Press.

Offe, C. (1996) *Modernity and the State: East, West*. Cambridge: Polity Press.

Ong, A. (2006) *Neoliberalism as Exception*. Durham, NC and London: Duke University Press.

Ozouf, M. (1991) *Festivals and the French Revolution*. Cambridge, MA: Harvard University Press.

Palier, B. (2005) 'Ambiguous agreement, cumulative change: French social policy in the 1990s', in W. Streeck and K. Thelen (eds) *Beyond Continuity – Institutional Change in Advanced Political Economies*. Oxford: Oxford University Press. pp. 127–45.

Parsons, T. (1951) *The Social System*. New York: Free Press.

Pateman, C. (1970) *Participation and Democratic Theory*. Cambridge: Cambridge University Press.

Pels, P. (1997) 'The anthropology of colonialism: Culture, history, and the emergence of Western governmentality', *Annual Review of Anthropology* 26: 163–83.

Petrovic, G. (1967) *Marx in the Mid-Twentieth Century*. New York: Anchor Books.

Pettit, P. (1997) *Republicanism: A Theory of Freedom and Government*. Oxford: Oxford University Press.

Pleyers, G. (2010) *Alter-globalization*. Cambridge: Polity Press.

Pieterse, J.N. (1995) 'Globalization as Hybridization', in M. Featherstone, S. Lash and R. Robertson (eds) *Global Modernities*. London: Sage. pp. 45–68.

Pieterse, J.N. (2004a) *Globalization and Culture – Global Mélange*. New York: Rowan and Littlefield.

Pieterse, J.N. (2004b) *Globalization or Empire?* New York: Routledge.

Piketty, T. (2014) *Capital in the Twenty-First Century*. Cambridge, MA: Belknap.

Pleyers, G. (2010) *Alter-Globalization: Becoming Actors in the Global Age*. Cambridge: Polity.

Polanyi, K. (1957[1944]) *The Great Transformation*. Boston: Beacon Press.

Postone, M. (2012) 'Thinking the Global Crisis', *South Atlantic Quarterly* (Spring): 227–49.

Pusey, M. (1991) *Economic Rationalism in Canberra – A Nation-Building State Changes its Mind*. Melbourne: Cambridge University Press.

Putnam, R. (1993) *Making Democracy Work: Civic Traditions in Italy*. Princeton: Princeton University Press.

Rawls, J. (1971) *A Theory of Justice*. Oxford: Oxford University Press.

Renault, E. (2007) 'From Fordism to post-Fordism: Beyond or back to alienation?', *Critical Horizons* 8 (2): 205–30.

Roberts, D. (2012) 'From the cultural contradictions of capitalism to the creative economy: Reflections on the new spirit of art and capitalism', *Thesis Eleven* 110 (1): 83–97.

Rorty, R. (ed.) (1967) *The Linguistic Turn*. Chicago: University of Chicago.

Rorty, R. (1999) *Philosophy and Social Hope*. London: Penguin Books.

Rosa, H. (2005) 'The speed of global flows and the pace of democratic politics', *New Political Science* 27 (4): 445–59.

Rosa, H. (2009) 'Kritik der Zeitverhältnisse. Beschleugnigung und Entfremdung als Schlüsselbegriffe der Sozialkritik', in R. Jaeggi and T. Wesche (eds) *Was ist Kritik?* Frankfurt am Main: Suhrkamp. pp. 23–54.

Rosa, H. (2010) *Alienation and Acceleration: Towards a Critical Theory Late-Modern Temporality.* Aarhus: Aarhus University Press.

Rosa, H. (2013) *Social Acceleration: A New Theory of Modernity.* New York: Columbia University Press.

Rousseau, J.–J. (2009) *The Social Contract.* London: Penguin.

Sartre, J.P. (1968) *Being and Nothingness.* New York: Washington Square Press.

Sartre, J.P. (1976) *Critique of Dialectical Reason.* London: New Left Books.

Sassen, S. (1988) *The Mobility of Labour and Capital: A Study in International Investment and Labour Flow.* Cambridge: Cambridge University Press.

Sassen, S. (1998) *Globalization and its Discontents.* New York: The New Press.

Sassen, S. (2006) *Cities in a World Economy,* 3rd edition. Princeton: Princeton University Press.

Sassen, S. (2007) *A Sociology of Globalization.* New York: W. W. Norton and Company.

Sassen, S. (2008) *Territory, Authority, Rights.* Princeton: Princeton University Press.

Sassen, S. (2011) 'A Savage Sorting of Winners and Losers', in C. Calhoun and G. Derluguian (eds) *Aftermath – A New Global Economic Order?* New York: New York University Press. pp. 21–38.

Sassen, S. (2014) *Expulsions – Brutality and Complexity in the Global Economy.* Cambridge, MA: Belknap Press.

Sayad, A. (2004) *The Suffering of the Immigrant.* Cambridge: Polity Press.

Schacht, R. (1971) *Alienation.* London: George Allen and Unwin.

Schafer, A. and Streeck, W. (eds) (2013) *Politics in the Age of Austerity.* Cambridge: Polity Press.

Schmidt, V. (1994) 'Bounded justice', *Social Science Information* 33 (2): 305–33.

Schmitt, C. (2007[1932]) *The Concept of the Political: Expanded Edition,* George Schwab (trans.). Chicago: University of Chicago Press.

Schor, I. (1980) *Critical Teaching and Everyday Life.* Boston, MA: South End Press.

Schutz, A. (1967) *The Phenomenology of the Social World.* Evanston, IL: Northwestern University Press.

Schwartz, H. (1998) 'Globalization, social protection and sociology: Old problems in a new world order', in M. Alexander, S. Harding, P. Harrison, G. Kendall, Z. Skrbiš and J. Western (eds) *Refashioning Sociology: Responses to a New World Order.* Brisbane TASA Conference Proceedings 1998. pp. 331–5.

Sennett, R. (1998) *The Corrosion of Character.* New York: W. W. Norton and Company.

Sennett, R. (2004) *Respect – The Formation of Character in an Age of Inequality.* London: Penguin.

Sennett, R. (2006) *The Culture of the New Capitalism.* New Haven, CT: Yale University Press.

Sennett, R. (2008) *The Craftsman.* New Haven, CT: Yale University Press.

Sennett, R. and Cobb, J. (1973) *The Hidden Injuries of Class.* New York: Vintage.

Smith, N.H. (2008) 'Analysing hope', *Critical Horizons* 9 (1): 5–23.

Smith, N.H. and Deranty, J.-P. (eds) (2012) *New Philosophies of Labour: Work and the Social Bond*. Leiden: Brill.

Smith, T.B. (2004) *France in Crisis*. Cambridge: Cambridge University Press.

Somers, M (2008) *Genealogies of Citizenship. Markets, Statelessness, and the Right to Have Rights*. Cambridge: Cambridge University Press.

Sousa Santos, B. de. (ed.) (2005) *Democratizing Democracy – Beyond the Liberal Democratic Canon*. London: Verso.

Sousa Santos, B. de (ed.) (2006) *Another Production is Possible: Beyond the Capitalist Canon*. London: Verso.

Sousa Santos, B. de (2008) 'The world social forum and the global left', *Politics and Society* 36 (2): 247–70.

Standing, G. (2011) *The Precariat: The New Dangerous Class*. London: Bloomsbury.

Stones, R. (2005) *Structuration Theory*. London: Palgrave Macmillan.

Streeck, W. (2011) 'The Crises of Democratic Capitalism', *New Left Review* 71 (9/10): 5–29.

Streeck, W. (2014) *Buying Time*. London: Verso.

Susen, S. (2007) *The Foundations of the Social – Between Critical Theory and Reflexive Sociology*. Oxford: Bardwell Press.

Susen, S. and Turner, B. (eds) (2014) *Spirits of Boltanski: Critical Perspectives*. London: Anthem Press.

Taylor, C. (1975) *Hegel*. Cambridge: Cambridge University Press.

Taylor, C. (1985a) *Philosophical Papers Vol. 2: Philosophy and the Human Sciences*. Oxford: Oxford University Press.

Taylor, C. (1985b) 'What's wrong with negative liberty', in C. Taylor *Philosophical Papers Vol. 2: Philosophy and the Human Sciences*. Oxford: Oxford University Press. pp. 211–29.

Taylor, C. (1989) *Sources of the Self: The Making of Modern Identity*. Cambridge: Cambridge University Press.

Taylor, C. (1991) *The Ethics of Authenticity*. Cambridge, MA: Harvard University Press.

Taylor, C. (1994) 'The Politics of Recognition', in A. Gutman (ed.) *Multiculturalism and the Politics of Recognition*. Princeton: Princeton University Press. pp. 25–73.

Taylor, C. (2004) *Modern Social Imaginaries*. Durham, NC: Duke University Press.

Taylor, C. (2007) *A Secular Age*. Cambridge, MA: Harvard University Press.

Therborn, G. (1995) *European Modernity and Beyond*. London: Sage.

Therborn, G. (2011) 'The Return of Class', *Global Dialogue: ISA-Newsletter* 2 (1): 3–5.

Tormey, S. (2001) *Agnes Heller – Socialism, Autonomy and the Postmodern*. Manchester: Manchester University Press.

Touraine, A. (1971) *The Post-industrial Society: Tomorrow's Social History: Classes, Conflicts and Culture in the Programmed Society*. New York: Random House.

Touraine, A. (1977) *The Self-Production of Society*. Chicago: University of Chicago Press.

Touraine, A. (1995) *Critique of Modernity.* Oxford: Blackwell.

Touraine, A. (2000) *Can We Live Together? Equality and Difference.* Cambridge: Polity Press.

Urry, J. (2000) *Sociology Beyond Societies.* London: Routledge.

Urry, J. (2007) *Mobilities.* Cambridge: Polity Press.

Wacquant, L. (2008) *Urban Outcasts.* Cambridge: Polity Press.

Wacquant, L. (2012) 'The Wedding of Workfare and Prisonfare in the 21st Century', *Journal of Poverty* 16 (3): 236–49.

Wagner, P. (1994) *Sociology of Modernity.* London: Routledge.

Wagner, P. (2001a) *Theorizing Modernity.* London: Sage.

Wagner, P. (2001b) *A History and Theory of the Social Sciences: Not All That is Solid Melts Into Air.* London: Sage.

Wagner, P. (2001c) 'Modernity, capitalism and critique', *Thesis Eleven* 66: 1–31.

Wagner, P. (2005) 'The *problematique* of economic modernity: Critical Theory, political philosophy and the analysis of capitalism', in C. Joerges, B. Sträth and P. Wagner (eds) *The Economy as a Polity – The Political Constitution of Contemporary Capitalism.* London: UCL Press. pp. 37–56.

Wagner, P. (2008) *Modernity as Experience and Interpretation.* Cambridge: Polity Press.

Wagner, P. (2012) *Modernity – Understanding the Present.* Cambridge: Polity Press.

Walby, S. (2009) *Globalization and Inequalities: Complexity and Contested Modernities.* London: Sage.

Wallerstein, I. (1974) *The Modern World System.* New York: Academic Press.

Wallerstein, I. (1979) *The Capitalist World Economy.* Cambridge: Cambridge University Press.

Wallerstein, I. (1983) *Historical Capitalism.* London: Verso.

Wallerstein, I. (1996) 'The Global Possibilities, 1990–2025', in T. Hopkins and I. Wallerstein (eds) *The Age of Transition – Trajectory of the World System, 1945–2025.* Leichhardt: Pluto Press. pp. 226–43.

Walzer, M. (1987) *Interpretation and Social Criticism.* Cambridge, MA: Harvard University Press.

Waterman, P. (1998) *Globalization, Social Movements, and the New Internationalisms.* London: Mansell.

Webb, D. (2007) 'Modes of Hoping', *History of the Human Sciences* 20 (3): 65–83.

Weber, M. (1930) *The Protestant Ethic and the Spirit of Capitalism.* London: George Allen and Unwin.

Weber, M. (1958) 'Science as a Vocation', in C. Wright Mills and H. Gerth (eds) *From Max Weber.* London: Routledge. pp. 129–56.

Weber, M. (1994) *Weber: Political Writings*, P. Lassman and R. Spiers (eds). Cambridge: Cambridge University Press.

Weichman, J.C. (ed.) (2006) *Institutional Critique and After.* Zürich: JRP Ringier.

Weiss, L. (1997) 'Globalization and the myth of the powerless state', *New Left Review* 125 (Sept/Oct): 3–27.

Wellmer, A. (1985) 'Reason, utopia and the dialectic of enlightenment', in R.J. Bernstein (ed.) *Habermas and Modernity*. Cambridge, MA: MIT Press. pp. 35–66.

Wellmer, A. (1998) *Endgames: the Irreconcilable Nature of Modernity. Essays and Lectures*. Cambridge, MA: MIT Press.

Whitebook, J. (1995) *Perversion and Utopia*. Cambridge, MA: MIT Press.

Wieviorka, M. (2005) 'Violence in France', Social Science Research Council [online]. Available: riotsfrance.ssrc.org/Wieviorka/ [Accessed December 2005].

Wiggershaus, R. (1994) *The Frankfurt School: Its History, Theories, and Political Significance*. Cambridge: Polity Press.

Winnicott, D.W. (1964) *The Child, the Family and the Outside World*. Harmondsworth: Penguin.

Wittrock, B. (2000) 'Modernity: One, none, or many? European origins and modernity as a global condition', *Daedalus* 129 (1): 31–60.

Wrong, D. (1961) 'The over-socialised conception of man in modern sociology', *American Sociological Review* 26: 183–93.

Young, I.M. (1996) 'Communication and the other: beyond deliberative democracy', in S. Benhabib (ed.) *Democracy and Difference: Contesting the Boundaries of the Political*. Princeton: Princeton University Press. pp. 120–35.

Young, I.M. (2008) 'Unruly categories: A critique of Nancy Fraser's dual systems theory', in N. Fraser, *Adding Insult to Injury: Nancy Fraser Debates her Critics*, K. Olson (ed.). London: Verso. pp. 89–106.

Zurn, C. (2003) 'Identity or Status? Struggles over "Recognition" in Fraser, Honneth and Taylor', *Constellations* 10 (4): 519–37.

INDEX